THE HISTORY OF BRAZIL

Robert M. Levine

palgrave
macmillan

To the people of Brazil, for their warmth, hospitality, and humanity.

First published 2003 by PALGRAVE MACMILLAN™
175 Fifth Avenue, New York, N.Y. 10010 and
Houndmills, Basingstoke, Hampshire, England RG21 6XS.
Companies and representatives throughout the world.

PALGRAVE MACMILLAN is the global academic imprint of the Palgrave Macmillan division of St. Martin's Press, LLC and of Palgrave Macmillan Ltd. Macmillan® is a registered trademark in the United States, United Kingdom and other countries. Palgrave is a registered trademark in the European Union and other countries.

ISBN 1-4039-6255-3

Library of Congress Cataloguing-in-Publication Data is available from the Library of Congress.

First published in 1999 by Greenwood Press.

First PALGRAVE MACMILLAN edition: October 2003.

10 9 8 7 6 5 4 3 2

Printed in the United States of America.

Contents

Series Foreword

The Greenwood Histories of the Modern Nations series is intended to provide students and interested laypeople with up-to-date, concise, and analytical histories of many of the nations of the contemporary world. Not since the 1960s has there been a systematic attempt to publish a series of national histories, and, as series editors, we believe that this series will prove to be a valuable contribution to our understanding of other countries in our increasingly interdependent world.

Over thirty years ago, at the end of the 1960s, the Cold War was an accepted reality of global politics, the process of decolonization was still in progress, the idea of a unified Europe with a single currency was unheard of, the United States was mired in a war in Vietnam, and the economic boom of Asia was still years in the future. Richard Nixon was president of the United States, Mao Tse-tung (not yet Mao Zedong) ruled China, Leonid Brezhnev guided the Soviet Union, and Harold Wilson was prime minister of the United Kingdom. Authoritarian dictators still ruled most of Latin America, the Middle East was reeling in the wake of the Six-Day War, and Shah Reza Pahlavi was at the height of his power in Iran. Clearly, the past thirty years have been witness to a great deal of historical change, and it is to this change that this series is primarily addressed.

With the help of a distinguished advisory board, we have selected nations whose political, economic, and social affairs mark them as among the most important in the waning years of the twentieth century, and for each nation we have found an author who is recognized as specialist in the history of that nation. These authors have worked most cooperatively with us and with Greenwood Press to produce volumes that reflect current research on their nations and that are interesting and informative to their prospective readers.

The importance of a series such as this cannot be underestimated. As a superpower whose influence is felt all over the world, the United States can claim a "special" relationship with almost every other nation. Yet many Americans know very little about the histories of the nations with which the United States relates. How did they get to be the way they are? What kind of political systems have evolved there? What kind of influence do they have in their own region? What are the dominant political, religious, and cultural forces that move their leaders? These and many other questions are answered in the volumes of this series.

The authors who have contributed to this series have written comprehensive histories of their nations, dating back to prehistoric time in some cases. Each of them, however, has devoted a significant portion of the book to events of the past thirty years, because the modern era has contributed the most to contemporary issues that have an impact on U.S. policy. Authors have made an effort to be as up-to-date as possible so that readers can benefit from the most recent scholarship and a narrative that includes very recent events.

In addition to the historical narrative, each volume in this series contains an introductory overview of the country's geography, political institutions, economic structure, and cultural attributes. This is designed to give readers a picture of the nation as it exists in the contemporary world. Each volume also contains additional chapters that add interesting and useful detail to the historical narrative. One chapter is a thorough chronology of important historical events, making it easy for readers to follow the flow of a particular nation's history. Another chapter features biographical sketches of the nation's most important figures, in order to humanize some of the individuals who have contributed to the historical development of their nation. Each volume also contains a comprehensive bibliography, so that those readers whose interest has been sparked may find out more about the nation and its history. Finally, there is a carefully prepared topic and person index.

Readers of these volumes will find them fascinating to read and useful in understanding the contemporary world and the nations that comprise it. As series editors, it is our hope that this series will contribute to a heightened sense of global understanding as we enter a new century.

Frank W. Thackeray and John E. Findling
Indiana University Southeast

Preface

When I was a college student traveling through Great Britain, I fell in love with the bookstores found in every town and in every neighborhood of large cities. Among the most popular series of books published in the United Kingdom in the 1960s were books about topics that in the academic world would be considered too large: "The Eighteenth Century," "The Late Middle Ages," "Russia." This book aims to follow in these footsteps. Its aim is to introduce Brazil to readers who neither are specialists nor are seeking exhaustive detail. It has not been written as a research monograph, nor is it intended to discuss all of the standard themes in Brazilian history. It is up to date, and it synthesizes much of the current social literature on Brazil. This should give readers a notion of how Brazil is viewed by specialists today, as the country faces the new century.

The book begins by examining some of that vast country's basic attributes: its geography, its economic and social systems, its politics, its people, and its culture. The first chapter identifies the major points of similarity and difference between Brazil and its Spanish-American hemispheric neighbors. The second looks for singularity in Brazil's nineteenth-century experience, when it not only retained a monarchical form of government while every other independent country in Latin

America became a republic, but declared independence while keeping the Portuguese royal family on the throne. Each successive chapter treats a shorter period of time, and the book concludes with two chapters on Brazil today. A biographical list of representative Brazilians in history completes the volume.

The Portuguese language is related to the other Latin-derived "Romance" languages of Western Europe: Spanish, Catalán, French, Italian, and Rumanian. Brazilian Portuguese differs from the language of Portugal, its mother country, mostly in pronunciation. Over the years, Brazilian officials have modified some of the basic rules governing spelling and accents, so that over a person's lifetime one's name may have been spelled differently (Mello, then Melo; Gonzalves, then Gonçalves). This is further complicated by the fact that some insist on using the traditional spelling of their surname: hence Gilberto Freyre, not Freire, as the modern spelling requires.

Portuguese uses not only the Spanish *tilde* (~), the é accent, and ç (as in the word *laço*) but the è used in French, the circumflex (ê), and occasionally the German umlaut (ö). Writing in Portuguese on an old-fashioned manual keyboard requires a Western Europe or "international" keyboard, and on computers one needs all the macros listed above, as well as the symbol Rs., for today's Brazilian currency unit, the *real* (pl. *reais*). Earlier currency units included the *milréis*, the *cruzado*, and the *cruzeiro*. These monetary units used to be written using the U.S. dollar sign, but in this way: 5$000, indicating five *milréis* or *cruzeiros*.

I am indebted to the staff of the libraries of the University of Wisconsin, Madison, and of the University of Miami, Coral Gables, for their assistance. Thanks also to Robin Bachin, John J. Crocitti, Nikolas Kozloff, Ethel Kosminsky, and Juliano Spyer.

Timeline of Historical Events

1415	Portuguese capture North African port of Ceuta
1494	Papal treaty of Tordesillas divides world between Portugal and Spain
1500	Landfall of Pedro Álvares Cabral in Brazil en route to India
1511	First Amerindians brought from Brazil to Portugal for display
1530	First colonists arrive
1534	King divides Brazil into thirteen territories
1539–1542	Exploration of Amazonia by Francisco de Orellana
1549	Arrival of first Jesuit missionaries; Portugal establishes central government
1555–1560	French Huguenot settlement near Rio de Janeiro
1562–1563	Epidemic wipes out as many as half of the surviving native population
1580–1640	Spanish and Portuguese royal dynasties merge
1607–1695	Palmares *quilombo* of fugitive slaves holds out

1630–1654	Dutch invasion of Northeast Brazil
1695	First discoveries of gold in Minas Gerais
1727	Coffee introduced into Brazil
1750	Treaty of Madrid ends the Treaty of Tordesillas
1763	Capital moved from Salvador to Rio de Janeiro
1777	Treaty of San Ildefonso resets Portuguese-Spanish boundaries
1808	Transmigration: arrival of Bragança royal family
1810	Commercial treaty gives Britain control of Brazilian trade
1817	Republican uprising in Pernambuco
1822	Brazil gains its independence from Portugal under Pedro I
1824	First Brazilian constitution
1831	Pedro I abdicates
1835	Outbreak of regionalist revolt in Rio Grande do Sul
1840	Pedro II ascends to the throne
1845	Rio Grande do Sul revolt suppressed by Caixias
1848–1849	Revolt of Confederation of the Equator
1850	Slave trade ends
1858	Coffee becomes primary export
1865–1870	War with Paraguay
1870	Manifesto of Republican Party
1871	Law of the Free Womb
1873–1875	Church-state conflict over royal privilege of naming bishops
1885	Saraiva-Cotegipe Law frees slaves at age sixty
1888	Princess Isabel frees remaining slaves (Golden Law)
1889	Military coup overthrows the Empire and exiles Dom Pedro II

1890	Economic crisis cripples the country
1891	President Deodoro da Fonseca dissolves Congress and is deposed
1893	Naval revolt threatens Republic
1897	Massacre at Canudos
1904	Vaccination riots in Rio de Janeiro
1906	Price supports given to coffee industry
1910	Contested presidential election
1922	Copacabana Fort cadet uprising launches nationalistic *tenente* movement
1924–1926	*Tenente* rebellion continues
1930	Vargas takes power after coup d'etat
1932	Revolt in the state of São Paulo against the provisional government
1934	New constitution promulgated; Vargas given four year term
1935	Revolts in three cities in name of a soviet republic
1937	Declaration of Estado Novo
1938	Fascist Integralist putsch against the presidential palace
1942	Brazil declares war on Axis
1945	Ouster of Getúlio Vargas
1946	Inauguration of Volta Redonda; first national steel mill
1954	Vargas commits suicide in office
1957	Start of construction of new national capital, Brasília
1964	Armed forces oust civilian government
1968	Additional Act #5 closes Congress tightens dictatorship
1969	Outbreaks of urban and rural guerrilla action against the regime

1985   Civilian government restored

1990–1992   Collor administration ends in resignation under threat
              of impeachment

1994   Hyperinflation reaches 2,500 percent, introduction of
              Real Plan

1998   Fernando Henrique Cardoso completes his term in of-
              fice, only the second president since 1930 to do so,
              and is reelected

1999   Brazilian economy withstands shock of Asian fiscal
              crisis

1

An Earthly Paradise

In primeval times, South America was locked together with Africa, Australia, Antarctica, and India in a "supercontinent" that for 300 million years circled the South Pole in perpetual cold. Geologists tell us that about 100 million years ago, a fissure opened between Brazil and Africa, forming the South Atlantic Ocean and shifting the whole landmass north toward the Equator. South America separated from Antarctica. Humidity and the northward drift formed an environment suitable for the rise of vast rain forests. Two to four million years ago, collisions of vast tectonic plates formed the Andes Mountains in western South America, and the inland sea tilted to the east, where it formed the vast Amazon River basin. When the last glacial period ended, about twelve thousand years ago, the Atlantic Forest reached across 3,500 kilometers of Brazil's seacoast.

Humans arrived, possibly from the Baikal region of Siberia via the Bering Strait and North America, or from Polynesia, Borneo, or Australasia. The long-standing belief among Paleo-Indian anthropologists that the first inhabitants of the New World arrived about twelve thousand years ago has been challenged recently; new estimates suggest that the first Brazilians came as long as forty thousand years ago. Remains of settlements have been discovered in Brazil that may be fifty thousand

Map of Brazil Showing State Capitals

years old. The last glaciers retreated twelve thousand years ago, forming the modern basis for human life. We have evidence that hunter-gatherers lived in the region of the Atlantic Forest about ten thousand years ago, and some inhabited caves north of present-day Belo Horizonte at roughly that time. There were so many game animals in the forests that prey did not need to be stalked. The rivers teemed with fish; oysters clung to the mangrove hammocks along the shore. For the next four hundred generations hunting depleted this source of food, and the hunters penetrated more deeply into the forests in search of sustenance.

Brazil's area of 3,286,426 square miles, nearly half the area of South America, makes it the fifth-largest nation in the world, after Russia, Canada, China, and the United States. Four times the size of Mexico, Brazil borders on every country in South America except Chile and Ecuador. Brazil was a huge territory during its colonial period, and diplomatic efforts in the nineteenth century added to its territory in the southwest and in the region of the Amazon. Its climate is subtropical; only its far south lies in the temperate zone. Its shore stretches for 4,600 miles, and is as near to Africa as it is to the United States. Brazil is prone to neither earthquakes nor hurricanes, but there have been devastating droughts, their effects worsened by poor land use over the centuries. Few rivers run east to west; the central plateau and its hinterland are cut off from the coastal region by a wall-like slope known as the Great Escarpment. Oceangoing ships cannot reach the interior, although by entering the Amazon River at Belém in the far north they can journey inland almost a thousand miles, to the steamy jungle city of Manaos. These physical barriers have over the centuries hindered access to the interior. Only recently has Brazil's frontier opened to settlements of any size.

Portuguese colonists took possession of the land five hundred years ago but developed only a small portion of the whole, preferring to remain near the seacoast. Charles Darwin, visiting the enormous and diverse Atlantic Forest (covering more than a million square kilometers) in 1832, found it "nearly impossible to give an adequate idea" of his emotional reaction. The tattered forested areas that have survived are regrowths; their primal ancestors were felled long ago to clear land for plantations and for cooking fuel. The name for this region—the *zona da mata* (the forest zone)—makes no sense today, but it reminds us that once the humid coastal borders of the Brazilian subcontinent were covered by trees.

To outsiders, Brazil has seemed an earthly paradise ripe for the picking, and its natural wealth has produced immense wealth. Although there is only a small amount of coal, most of it low grade, mining has yielded immense amounts of iron ore, manganese, bauxite, nickel, tungsten, tin, uranium, rubber, semiprecious stones, and industrial diamonds. Brazilian forests provide pulp (for paper), hardwoods, waxes, firewood, and charcoal. Formerly energy dependent, by the 1990s the country drew more than two-thirds of its electricity from offshore petroleum and its enormous hydroelectric plants—the largest, at Itaipu, being one of the major hydroelectric projects in the world, shared by Argentina, Brazil, and Paraguay. In the 1970s scientists converted most of the nation's trucks and official vehicles to the use of alcohol produced from sugar cane stalks. However, consumers resisted the alcohol-burning engines, to the point that two decades later Brazil continues to be dependent on imported petroleum, since domestic oil provides only half of the nation's needs.

Brazil's vastness has given rise to significant regional variations, much like Russia's. The twenty six states and the Federal District are only precariously linked, mostly by airplane. Roads and railroads are seriously inadequate for a country of Brazil's size and importance. The country's five major regions—the North, the Northeast, the Southeast (or Center-South), the South, and the Center-West—have been likened to islands in a huge archipelago, floating in a sea of geographical diversity. Although Portuguese is universally spoken, regional differences in pronunciation are as pronounced as the differences between English spoken in Mississippi and New England.

Both the North and Northeast are equatorial. Days are always hot, although the temperature dips a bit in the winter months during which rain falls along the coastal *zona da mata*. Further inland, especially at higher elevations, the sun shines brilliantly, and there is virtually no shade, because the forest was long ago felled; what tall plants remain, mostly in scattered oases, are cactuses and other spiny vegetation. Further inland lies the *sertão*, a mostly flat hinterland stretching far into the interior. The *sertão*, whose name means "large desert" in Portuguese, is watered by a small handful of streams, many of which dry up seasonally. Although the region's climate is not unlike that of California's Imperial Valley, which ample irrigation has made into one of the world's most productive food gardens, the northeastern *sertão* lies barren, its stunted vegetation scorched by the torrid sun, unable during periodic droughts to sustain its miserable population of people and livestock.

The North, which contains the states of Acre, Amazonas, Rondônia, Roraíma, Amapá, Pará, and Tocantins, comprises nearly half of the national territory. The Amazon basin contains more than 2.4 million square miles of rain forest, under assault for centuries by settlers (mostly landless claim jumpers), rubber tappers, and, only in the last few years, contracted developers. Its climate is tropical—humid, with sweltering temperatures and frequent, heavy rains. The tree canopy provides welcome protection from the sun, but more than 12 percent of the original rain forest has been cut down, and nearly ten thousand square miles are destroyed each year. In the last decade the Amazon region has been integrated into the international economy, for better or worse. New towns have sprung up out of the jungle, and the construction and agro-industry sectors are booming. The impact on the formerly desultory way of life has yet to be understood.

A VAST RANGE OF DIFFERENCES

Nowhere in Brazil is the gulf separating rich and poor more pronounced than in the northern part of the country. There one finds a landscape scarred by human striving, its gashes carved by centuries of improvident mining, farming, and grazing. In the hinterland one passes mile after mile of fertile but uncultivated land. Some caretaker families live in shacks or lean-tos, but mostly the land lies empty, dotted by tiny squatments in which rural workers have been permitted to erect wooden shacks, nearly as close to one another as in the crowded *favelas* of the cities. Fewer than 1 percent of the landowners, with a thousand or more hectares, own 44 percent of the land. The hinterland is dotted with sleepy hamlets, although the advent of nationwide television networks has reduced substantially the historical isolation of such places.

The coast from Maranhão to Espírito Santo, very rainy during the winter "wet" months, used to be covered by nearly seven hundred thousand square miles of lush trees, the *zona da mata*, but it is now mostly stripped. Only 8 percent remains of the original forest, which once provided erosion control and other ecological benefits for the 70 percent of Brazil's population who live along the coast. The northern states—Pará, Maranhão, Piauí, and Ceará—have long suffered from overpopulation, lack of industry, and fierce domination by the landed oligarchy, although Ceará in recent years has made economic strides under a dynamic state government. The Northeast, from Rio Grande do Norte to Bahia, has been plagued by centuries of periodic drought and lack of economic opportunity. Pernambuco was during the early colonial period one of the most profitable agricultural colonies in the world, but decline had set in by the seventeenth century, exacerbated in the late nineteenth century by the failure of efforts to modernize sugar production. The decline further lowered the quality of life for the region's wretched inhabitants.

The São Francisco River forms in the mountains of Minas Gerais, six to nine thousand feet in altitude, and flows east and north through the dusty backlands of Bahia and Pernambuco until it ends at the coast in the state of Sergipe. The weather along the river is hot during the day but cool after dusk, and during part of the year light showers fall almost daily. For generations—until the arrival of the airplane—the river, though filled with sandbars and treacherous for navigators, was the easiest way to the interior and therefore the route of immigrants, settlers, and migrants. The vast and ruggedly beautiful central plateau is still largely unpopulated, despite the creation of the new national capital, Brasília, in the late 1950s. Its northern end, the Pantanal region, is a large but shrinking environment of pristine natural flora and fauna, and Indian reservations. It is the world's largest wetland, home to legions of rare and endangered species, including hyacinth macaws and jabiru storks. The lands on either side of riverbanks are covered by thornwood and scrub brush and, where fresh water is available, cattle ranches. Clusters of small farms have produced subsistence crops, maize, and manioc. Developers are planning to make the Pantanal wetlands one of the links of the *hidrovia*, a 2,150-mile navigation project connecting Brazil, Bolivia, Paraguay, Argentina, and Uruguay. It threatens, unfortunately, to destroy the Pantanal.

Brasília, the new capital, rose out of the bare earth of the Central Plateau as a symbol of the country's confidence in its future and also as an effort to shift the political center away from the dominating cities of São Paulo and Rio de Janeiro. As early as 1810, members of the Portuguese court in Rio de Janeiro advocated building a new capital in the interior, to preserve Brazil's territorial integrity. The name Brasília, in fact, was suggested in 1823 by independence leader José Bonifácio. The idea stayed alive: Article 3 of the 1891 republican constitution called for the construction of a new national capital on fourteen thousand square kilometers in Goiâs. The 1946 constitution did the same, authorizing the selection of a specific site; nine years later, in 1955, the federal government created a fifty-thousand square-kilometer zone and designated it the Federal District.

In April 1958, President Juscelino Kubitschek approved a massive plan to construct the capital. Formal dedication ceremonies took place on April 21, 1960. Brasília's architecture, considered futuristic in the late

1950s when it was built, has become weathered and in places dilapidated, and the utopian goals of its visionary architect, Oscar Niemeyer, were never achieved. Still, Brasília did attract thousands of urban pioneers from all over the country, and by the 1990s it had achieved at least in part its objective of stimulating national integration. In 1987 Brasília was designated by UNESCO as a "Historic and Cultural Patrimony of Humanity."

The Center-South is so densely populated in comparison with the rest of Brazil that geographers use the term "hyperconcentrated" to describe it. Mountainous Minas Gerais balances agricultural productivity with mining and industry; it is linked commercially with Rio de Janeiro, the steadily declining former capital and tourist mecca, to the east, and vigorous São Paulo to its south and west. São Paulo, sprawling over a series of hills and valleys, holds pollution in the same way Los Angeles does but it is vibrant, a city of neighborhoods and massive skyscrapers surrounded by industrial zones stretching for dozens of miles. São Paulo's population is heavily influenced by generations of arrivals from other Brazilian regions—especially from the rural Northeast—and from Europe and Asia. The city of São Paulo has more persons of Japanese descent outside of Japan, more of Arab origin outside of the Middle East, and more Italians than any city in Latin America except Buenos Aires.

Rio de Janeiro's residents cope with an alarmingly high frequency of crime, centered in the drug-ridden hillside *favelas*, shanty towns and slums, which look down on the elegant, beautiful city. Rio and its surrounding area is subtropical, hot in summer (temperatures can rise to 106°F or more during February and March), but milder on the coast than in interior sections, because of the cooling effects of the sea. Once the nation's major port of entry, it has lost that distinction to Santos, in the state of São Paulo along the old coastal road that once linked the sixteenth-century settlement of São Vicente to the *paulista* plateau. Rio's five and a half million inhabitants reside in some of the wealthiest (and heavily guarded) residential districts anywhere, but there are more than five hundred *favelas*. The city's natural setting is breathtaking. It is surrounded by rounded mountains, covered with vegetation and jutting into the sky. A handsome statue of Christ the Redeemer sits atop the Corcovado, overlooking the wealthy and congested Zona Sul (South Zone), the site of beachfront Copacabana, Leme, Ipanema, and Leblón. In and beyond the city's North Zone for at least twenty miles sprawl *favelas* and industrial districts mired in poverty. These include the violent Baixada Fluminense, with the highest murder rate in the world. The high rate of muggings and holdups on Rio's streets caused tourism to drop by 62 percent during the 1990s. Rio remains Brazil's most unequal city, with almost half of its residents living below the poverty line. Atmospheric pollution is ruining Rio's beaches and threatening the water supply. In many of Brazil's industrial cities, pollution is so bad that, according to political scientist Ronald M. Schneider, it may pose a more serious environmental peril for Brazilians than the depredation of the tropical Amazonian rain forest.[1]

The southeastern plateau between the cities of Rio de Janeiro and São Paulo is the site of the once-prosperous coffee plantations of the Paraíba Valley, recently abandoned in favor of more productive coffee lands north and west of Campinas as well as further south. Recently, the Paraíba Valley has blossomed as a region of heavy and light manufacturing, favored by multinational investors for its proximity to Brazil's two major cities. The state of São Paulo is also dotted with cities surrounded by farms, many of them providing the prodigious amounts of food needed to feed the more than twenty million in the São Paulo metropolitan area. Cotton is also cultivated here, and coffee, and tobacco.

In the South are the states of Paraná, Santa Catarina, and Rio Grande do Sul. Temperate in climate—even to the point of receiving some light snowfall at higher elevations during the winter months of July and August—this agricultural and ranching region has received hundreds of thousands of immigrants since the middle 1800s; many communities in this region are populated today by descendants of Japanese, Poles, Germans, Ukrainians, and Italians. Of all of the cities of this region, Curitiba, the capital of Paraná, enjoys the reputation for best dealing with growth, by carefully applied urban planning. Curitiba's mayor (later state governor) Jaime Lerner, an architect, created the highest percentage of green space of any Brazilian city; he created pedestrian precincts downtown, reached by efficient and cheap public transportation; he initiated a plan whereby *favela* residents receive bags of food in exchange for their garbage. In the center of the city is the Rua 24 Horas (Twenty-Four Hours Street), an architecturally restored district covered by a cast-iron and glass arcade in which strollers can walk at any hour of day or night and feel safe.

The entire southern region's European flavor remains distinct. Although dictator Getúlio Vargas banned foreign-language newspapers and instruction in 1938, the languages of the immigrants are still spoken today in many small towns. *Gaúchos*, the twentieth-century term for the residents of Rio Grande do Sul but also used loosely for southerners in general, have not only played a major role in national politics since the late nineteenth century but in recent decades have contributed to an outmigration to other parts of Brazil seeking cheaper land. This "gaúcho diaspora" started within the region, in the 1930s and 1940s when settlers moved father south and west in the forested parts of Santa Catarina and Paraná; it crossed regional boundaries in the 1950s and 1960s, when southerners began to migrate to Mato Grosso, and in the 1970s to the Amazon. Just as northeastern migration to the South was not always well received, "gaúcho" settlers in other parts of Brazil were criticized for their aggressiveness and the perception that they felt superior to the populations in whose midst they settled. The term gaúcho refers to the rural cowhand, whose traditional clothing, according to one riograndense sociologist, is mostly of Berber origin. These customs were brought to the La Plata region by maragatos, immigrants from southern Spain during the time that Spain occupied the region. The word gaúcho itself is derived from the Arabic word chaoucho, a packhorse or mule driver.

North of Rio and east of Minas Gerais is the large state of Bahia, the heart of Brazil's Afro-Brazilian civilization. It is the home of community and cultural groups organized during the last decade to preserve and celebrate the African heritage. Southern Brazil is a region of agriculture and ranching, more prosperous than most of the rest of the country, and marked by a high percentage of residents of immigrant stock. The resource-rich state of Mato Grosso on the border with Bolivia was divided into two states during the 1980s, as was the state of Goiás in central Brazil. The new state carved out of Goiás—Tocantins—has virtually no cities or viable sources of income.

To the far west are the underpopulated and backward former territories of Acre, Rondônia, and Amapá, elevated to statehood by cynical politics (new states send senators to the national legislature and create patronage jobs in their new state bureaucracies). The result is that deputies from the state of São Paulo represent more than 450,000 citizens, whereas the population bases for Acre and its sister former territories are below thirty thousand. Lacking resources or infrastructure, these states are especially dependent on the central government, which makes patronage even more critical than in the older states. This is a region where daily temperatures rarely dip below 90°F and can rise much higher, and where industry is almost completely extractive. In Acre, thousands of men and women work to produce charcoal from felled trees and stumps. This incredibly hot activity—working among smoldering wood under the torrid tropical sun—exacts an incalculable price from the human body.

Brazil is so internally diverse that a social geographer once dubbed it "Belindia," a country where the fortunate enjoy a quality of life not unlike that of Belgium, whereas residents of the vast hinterland share lives characteristic of India. Few real cities flourish in rural Brazil. Urban places in the interior are mostly dusty hamlets, rarely with more than one main street, usually unpaved. Except for television, carried by satellite to all parts of Brazil, rural residents live in isolation. Intracity trains are nonexistent except along the coast, and even there people more often travel by bus or on the backs of open trucks. Better houses in rural Brazil are of cement block; many more are made of mud-and-straw bricks, covered by thatch, exactly the same way as they were built a century ago. Most rural structures lack running water, and only rarely do they have glass windows. Pigs roam the dusty streets foraging for garbage; emaciated dogs lie in the hot sun.

Cities, in contrast, pulse with noise and traffic. Modern high-rise building dwarf the old mansions and churches built before 1900. Except in cities like Curitiba and the baroque colonial towns of Minas Gerais, which value historic preservation, urban renewal is constant. Bus and truck diesel fumes blacken the air in São Paulo and Rio de Janeiro, competing with clean, modern subways, whose fares are usually too high for most commuters. Affluent families live in the heart of cities. Elegant neighborhoods of single-family houses have high walls and often concrete guardhouses on the sidewalk; most well-to-do families live in luxurious condominium apartments in tall buildings, always with elaborate security.

Poor people live in *favelas* or in the *subúrbios* (suburbs). The word "suburb," however, holds a unique connotation in Brazil. *Subúrbios* extend well beyond city limits. This means that men and women who work in the city as construction workers or maids or in commerce have commutes of from one to three hours each way, with train and bus fares often costing a sizable proportion of their daily wage. *Favelas* are rife with crime, drugs, and violence. The poorest Brazilians live precariously in daily makeshift squatments, sometimes along highways or under concrete bridges. Housing is expensive—even *favela* shacks—and in recent years most employed Brazilians earned the official minimum wage, which varies from region to region but never exceeds a hundred dollars a month, in an economy where consumer goods often cost more than in the United States.

Of all of the countries in the New World, Brazil is the largest in which people of mixed racial origin are represented in the overall population. Brazilians include more blacks and browns than any country on Earth except for Nigeria. There is prejudice against nonwhites, but it is usually expressed as a feeling against poor people. The prevailing explanation has been that prejudice in Brazil is a matter of class, not of race, but there is ample de facto discrimination against nonwhites. Despite Brazil's long history of race mixing, race remains the leading indicator of privilege in society.

The complex realm of race relations, more than any other cultural characteristic, gives Brazil its appearance of distinctiveness. In many ways, Brazil is a model for the world: a country where taboos against interracial interaction long have been considered a matter of economic class, not of racial prejudice. In 1993, the population was classified as 54 percent "white," 40 percent "persons of mixed race," 5 percent "blacks," and 0.6 percent natives and Asians. Given this, and the relaxed day-to-day attitudes about intermingling, established wisdom holds that Brazilians are more color-blind than most other peoples. There have never been demonstrations by angry blacks demanding redress of grievances as blacks, for example, and when riots and other manifestations of anti-establishment hostility do occur, the participants are invariably described by their economic or social characteristics (prison inmates, for example, or enraged bus riders, or hungry peasants)—even if they happen to be almost all nonwhite.

Brazilians span the racial and ethnic spectrum, from descendants of black African slaves to children of immigrants from all over the world. Many Brazilians are descended from peoples from Japan and Korea, Jamaica and the Guyanas, the Muslim lands of Middle East, and Europe, from the Baltic to Wales. There are trace elements of gypsies. Families from the former Confederate States of America came after the U.S. Civil War so they could continue to live in a place where slavery was sanctioned. Millions descended from the main immigrant groups, southern Europeans from Portugal, Spain, and Italy. In contrast to the United States but as in Canada, Brazilian immigrants (and the immigrantlike rural migrants from the impoverished hinterland) stayed long in their groups of origin, although their children learned Portuguese and blended into the behavior of their social classes.

Widespread race mixing—or miscegenation, in the now-obsolete term used for so many years—made it possible for intellectuals to label Brazil a racial democracy, in spite of the fact that nonwhites, and especially blacks, lived in poverty. The state, unlike the United States and South Africa, for example, imposed no categories of segregation or legal discrimination. Despite the commonness of early racism and continued inequality, Anthony W. Marx observes, Brazil did not enact anything equivalent to apartheid or Jim Crow.[2] Indeed, during the 1930s Brazilian intellectuals embraced the interpretation of sociologist Gilberto Freyre, that slavery in Brazil had been relatively benign and that Brazil had evolved into a "racial democracy." This was historically inaccurate, an "ideological project of a state anxious to unify popular support without formal exclusion," and in fact the pervasive acceptance of this myth made it more difficult for black identity groups that emerged after World War II, and especially during the 1970s and 1980s, to gain public sympathy or support.[3] Although surveys demonstrated that on economic grounds nonwhites in Brazil earned half or less the wages of whites, it was easy to sidestep the problem by appealing to the racial democracy myth and to Brazil's live-and-let-live social tradition. As a result, a paradox remained. On one hand Brazil by the late twentieth century had become the most open and least racially neurotic society in the world; yet on the other, nonwhites, and especially Brazilians of black skin tone and African features, faced de facto prejudice and lack of opportunity for advancement.

The descendants of the slaves always fared worst. Associations formed by blacks in Brazil to defend their rights and foster social acceptance started in 1931, with the establishment of the Brazilian Negro Front, but the Front attracted only a handful of members. In 1936 it reorganized as a political party, only to be closed down two years later when the government outlawed all political parties. It was not until 1978 that a new group emerged, the Movement for Black Unification. In 1995 President Fernando Henrique Cardoso created a cabinet-level task force to look into ways to assist the nonwhite population. This was the first such official effort in all of Brazilian history; at the outset its work was more to gather data and conduct studies than to propose a specific plan of action.

The election in late 1996 of Celso Pitta to the mayor's office in São Paulo marked the first time in 442 years that a Brazilian city of any significance had elected a leader who in the United States of the early 1950s would have been barred, at least in the South, from drinking fountains or lavatories marked "for whites." Pitta, a social and economic conservative linked to the powerful right-wing politician Paulo Maluf, would be considered in the United States "black"; in Brazil he is a medium-skinned mulatto, a *pardo* (but not a *preto*, a term for blacks of darker skin). Brazil, in fact, has never had any regulations or legal proscriptions discriminating on the basis of race. When the African American dancer Katherine Dunham was barred from a chic hotel in São Paulo in 1951, the government enacted an antidiscrimination statute, the Afonso Arinos Law, but it has almost never been applied. Discrimination exists, but unofficially; no Brazilian legislature would ever sanction laws reminiscent of the Jim Crow laws of the American South. The 1988 constitution made discrimination punishable by prison; in 1993, the governor of São Paulo, Luiz Antonio Fleury Filho, established a private bureau to investigate alleged cases of racial discrimination, but in practice little or nothing changed.

Today, nonetheless, Brazil's racial climate is one of the most tolerant in the world. Its tolerance is rooted in the fact that after the abolition of slavery in the late nineteenth-century, the low-caste status of nonwhites was not accompanied by either belligerence or by rancor. Although there are some 120 million Brazilians of African descent today, from 1890 until 1940 race was not enumerated regularly in the Brazilian federal census. Brazil is a multiracial society, sharing a spectrum of racial distinctions. At the least, Thomas E. Skidmore notes, Brazilian social practice has recognized white, black, and mulatto. Brazilians not only have not practiced formal segregation, but they lack the Negrophobia that has categorized society in the United States. It is telling that in the United States, where since the Civil Rights movement government officials have attempted to show sensitivity to the issue of race, the category of mixed-race (mulatto), included in national censuses from 1850, was dropped in 1920, forcing Americans to be considered either white or black, with nothing in between.

The official Brazilian position, based on the hypotheses of the sociologist Gilberto Freyre (1900–1980), argues that Brazil is a racial democracy in which even during slavery whites treated blacks better than was the case elsewhere, because of relaxed attitudes about interracial sexual activity. Few take this seriously any more, although many Brazilians insist that the poor just happen to be overwhelmingly black. Everyday life in Brazil, on the other hand, is filled with examples of discriminatory social behavior, based on unwritten understanding that nonwhites, and especially blacks, hold lower status. Few Brazilians of color enjoy membership in the economic and social elite, which lives in luxury while most

Brazilians live far below in terms of privilege, access to education, and opportunity. Brazil, then, is multiracial but socially stratified by race. Yet although darker skin has generally meant lower status, racial lines remained fluid and in some ways blurred. In recent years there has been a movement, especially in the cities of Salvador and Rio de Janeiro, to mobilize nonwhites in black-consciousness associations celebrating the African heritage—and to include mulatto, on the grounds that all nonwhites in Brazil face discrimination. Members of this movement have revived the bipolar term "negro" to refer to all Brazilian nonwhites; they feel that the gap between themselves and whites is so great that they can make progress only by uniting.

THE POLITICAL SYSTEM

Brazil's government is based on the Aristotelian ideal that hierarchy leads to order. Unlike the other Latin American nations, which declared themselves republics after winning independence, in Brazil seven decades of monarchy followed colonialism before giving way to a federal republic, which itself was only nominally democratic. The Empire period reinforced the paternalistic and elitist values of colonial life. The republican movement, starting in the early 1870s and ultimately victorious in 1889, saw life in terms that were even more hierarchical, borrowing from the French philosopher August Comte's positivist notion of a state based on technological advances (progress) and rooted in social stability (order). This preserved Aristotle's notions about government (aristocratic) and voting rights (dominated by the landowning class).

Brazil's peaceful transition to independence contrasted with the Spanish-American tradition of armed insurrection. Except for Cuba and Puerto Rico, every part of Spain's New World empire either won its independence as a republic or was "liberated" by troops from the creole armies of its newly independent neighbors. Brazil eased into independence as a constitutional monarchy. The monarchy fell in 1889. In 1891 Brazil adopted a constitution patterned after that of the United States. The United States of Brazil, as the nation now called itself, actually was closer to the United States as it had been under the late-eighteenth-century Articles of Confederation. Individual states retained almost all powers; they could raise revenue, set their own laws, and maintain powerful militias. Under this reign of extreme federalism, a few states in the Center-South, notably São Paulo, prospered, while most of the rest of the states languished and declined economically.

The monarchy and the republic that succeeded it were dominated by Brazil's tightly knit landed elite, heir to the system of legal slavery that remained in force until 1888 and benignly unconcerned with the condition of the lower classes, most members of which were men, women, and children of mixed race or descendants of former slaves transported from Africa. Neither the imperial aristocracy (which included men granted the titles of duke, viscount, and baron) nor the modernizing republicans, whose movement was organized in 1870, favored democracy. Many of the republicans were positivists, who advocated education for the masses but did little to put a public school system in place. They put the phrase "order and progress" on the new Brazilian flag, symbolizing positivism's dual creed. In practice, "progress" meant industrial growth and economic development sustained by "order," which meant the preservation of a docile polity through the use of policy brutality when needed. It also tolerated fraudulent voting dominated by rural bosses, the *coronéis*.

In 1930, the republic was toppled by a military coup in support of a civilian, Getúlio Vargas, who assumed power. Vargas had run in opposition to the establishment's candidate in an election that year, but the economic impact of the worldwide Depression had shattered coffee prices and bolstered the sense of protective nationalism in the armed forces that had first surfaced in 1922, when cadets disgusted with elite politics had raised the banner of insurrection. In 1937, Vargas and the military overthrew his own government and imposed the Estado Novo (New State) dictatorship, based loosely on the Portuguese fascist regime of the same name and kept in power by repression. During the Estado Novo, Brazil allied with the United States; Vargas pressed Washington for as many economic concessions as possible. At the end of World War II, Vargas's worst fears were realized. Brazil's fascist constitution had to be discarded, Vargas himself was ousted by the military (in 1945) and the country found itself more dependent on foreign investment and more influenced by American popular culture than the nationalists had wanted.

Brazilians under the Estado Novo were subject to the cancellation of the protection of habeas corpus (protection against arbitrary arrest) and to the imposition of government censorship, which extended to newspapers, magazines, radio programs, theater, and films. Educated Brazilians accommodated themselves to the loss of free speech, because they had little choice and also because restrictions were only selectively applied. The country then entered a two-decade period in which representative democracy prevailed, starting in 1950, when Vargas was elected president, and continuing through the terms of three elected successors. A free press blossomed, although in the general euphoria many newspapers launched fierce and unsubstantiated political attacks that demoralized Vargas and in part led to his suicide in 1954. Unrestrained press partisanship continued after Vargas and polarized the political arena. The early 1960s saw continued instability, yielding to a military coup in March 1964.

The new military regime vowed to rid Brazil of corruption and communist influence, and it applied censorship to the media and to public expression. It banned opposition to the regime; persons hostile to the dictatorship were arrested and often tortured or exiled, and censorship was imposed. In 1972, a statement denying that censorship existed in Brazil, issued by the majority leader of the Senate, ex–Nazi sympathizer Felinto Müller, was prohibited from appearing in Rio de Janeiro's leading newspaper, the *Journal do Brasil*, by secret order. For years, the Federal Police subjected the press to daily censorship, "encouraging" editors to do what the censors demanded. Because compliance was technically voluntary, the system was known as "self-censorship." Any publication that reached newspaper kiosks without having been vetted by censors could see its entire press run seized and destroyed. Individual police or army officials, acting capriciously and on their own, would confiscate and destroy periodicals that they disliked even when the offending material had been passed by higher-level censors. These occurrences put added pressure on publishers, who were all the more cautious about printing anything controversial lest they suffer stinging financial losses. The censorship system, then, banal and mundane, nonetheless operated effectively, although on the fringes individuals, journalists, and editors managed to challenge the government, mostly through the use of irony and subtly disguised humor. Brazil's military never produced the equivalent of Chile's Augusto Pinochet, the general whose brutal and arrogant reign led in 1998, at the age of eighty-three, to his arrest in London on charges of genocide.

The military remained in power until 1985, when its leaders voluntarily stepped down and returned the country to civilian rule. Lacking any real balance of powers, however, the national government continued to struggle. The judiciary had historically played no role in government, and the legislature, dominated by politicians from rural areas connected closely to local political machines, debated endlessly, while the executive governed by decree. Popular democracy stirred briefly in the mid-1980s, when a nationwide campaign demanded direct elections. It took root firmly during the volatile 1980s and early 1990s, when one elected president, Tancredo Neves, died before being able to take office, and another, Fernando Collor, a political outsider who won election on the strength of a powerful media campaign, was removed from office after impeachment for massive corruption (although he and his partisans denied any misdeeds). By this time, every Brazilian over the age of sixteen had not only been granted the vote but was required by law to exercise the franchise, under a system adapted by the 1946 constitution from Australia and the "socialist republics" of the former Soviet Union.

The Collor episode disgusted observers, who found ample evidence of support for the allegations of corruption, but in the end it confirmed the resilience of Brazil's democratic institutions. Three years later, Fernando Henrique Cardoso was elected, a moderate reformer and brilliant social scientist who as an exiled academic had diagnosed many of the ills that had hindered Brazil's independent development. He was buoyed by his success in dealing with economic problems, but his successes in the political and social spheres were less compelling, likely because the political system was still based on patronage and undue influence of entrenched interests.

Plebiscites in the early 1990s considered changing Brazil's government to a monarchy or parliamentary regime, but the existing presidential system prevailed. There are eighty-one members of the Senate and 513 representatives in the Chamber of Deputies. Senators serve eight-year terms, and deputies, four. Members of Congress are overwhelmingly male and Caucasian although in recent years women, blacks, and persons of indigenous background have been elected. Seventy-six percent of electors live in rural areas, although Brazil is predominately urban. This gives significant weight to rural politicians, who tend to be ultra-conservative and dedicated to slowing change and controlling patronage. In the recent past, Congress divided two large but underpopulated states—Mato Grosso and Goiás—into two parts. The new states, Mato Grosso do Sul and Tocantins, had little reason to exist except to create additional rural senators and new state bureaucracies. Similar motives promoted the Congress to convert into states the outlying frontier territories of Acre, Amapá, Roraíma, and Rio Branco. The judiciary is weak and dominated by conservatives from the traditional landowning elites.

For decades, the accepted self-view of Brazilian political history has held that unlike in most other countries, conciliation, not conflict, has characterized national life. This interpretation is only superficially persuasive, because that conciliation was limited by a framework of social and political control. Individuals and groups challenging the system have often been repressed, sometimes brutally.

THE ECONOMIC SYSTEM

From 1500 to 1822, Brazil's economy was run by, and for the benefit of, the crown of Portugal. The only entrepreneurs permitted to make profits were the handful of nobles—fourteen in all—granted contracts by the crown allowing them to finance colonial settlements in Brazil, which they would finance themselves. Unlike Spain, whose crown embarked on a massive crusade to conquer, baptize, and control the lands and peoples of the Western Hemisphere under its control, Portugal's priorities always lay in the Far East, where it had established lucrative trading posts, and in Africa, where it dominated the slave trade. Smaller than Spain in population, it lacked the surplus population that Spain sent to the New World, and its Roman Catholic hierarchy, less powerful and less zealous than that of the Spanish church, did not give nearly the same emphasis to forced religious conversion (although its Inquisition in Brazil was cruel and extensive).

By the middle sixteenth century, Portugal's colonization experiment had largely failed. Only two of the captaincies had been settled at all, and only one of them, in Pernambuco on the northeastern coast, had been successful. The French, who had established a colony at Rio de Janeiro in 1560, were driven away. The Portuguese cane plantations failed, however; the native slaves resisted, ran away, and even while captive, were too troublesome to be efficient. In São Vicente, in the south, the Portuguese had conducted sweeping raids into the hinterland to capture Indians to work as slaves, but the natives fought back, and by 1580 plans for permanent settlements in the colony had been given up, although incursions beyond the coast continued.

Only in the Northeast were initial efforts to grow crops profitable enough to permit the purchase of African slaves, whose price was high, because slave owners had to bid against planters in the Caribbean, where sugar and other crops were also being introduced. Pernambuco was set up on the plantation model, with vast acreage under sugar cane cultivation and worked by slaves. This ultimately became the economic model for most of Brazil, especially along the coast, where the cleared land yielded not only sugar but cacao, beans, cotton, and products of pasturage (cattle, goats, pigs). The crown collected 10 percent of all production, including wealth from the gold mines discovered in the 1690s, and most of the population (slaves, their masters, and natives) lived under poor conditions, in collective poverty if not semistarvation. Sugar, for several centuries, remained the most profitable crop. The construction of sugar-grinding mills on lands where cane could be cut year after year without replanting meant that sugar production could become a nearly nonstop enterprise, avoiding the need to import free settlers. Brazil remained, in the most literal sense of the term, a "king's plantation" long after the neighboring Spanish-American colonies had built great cities fully integrated into the economic and political world of Spain's overseas empire.

The native population quickly dwindled, decimated by disease and by being forced to work as slaves. Roman Catholic missionaries, who arrived by 1550, also contributed to the destruction of the native population. The natives, after all, were promiscuous and practiced cannibalism. To subdue them—less to save souls than to acquire slaves—the colonists used flogging, torture, and imprisonment. The Jesuits commanded expeditions to the interior and brought back captured natives, as many as one or two thousand at a time, who were set up in villages (*aldeias*) under Jesuit control. These natives were stripped of their indigenous culture. Those not captured retreated deeper, away from the coast and the rivers from which the whites launched their raids. Those forced to live on the coast were devastated by infectious microparasites, which subjected native populations throughout the New World, completely lacking built-up resistance, to death rates higher than those caused by the worst epidemics of Europe or Asia.

Over the next three hundred years, the Portuguese plantation model was borrowed in the New World by the Dutch, the English, and the French, all seeking an intensely exploitative cultivation worked by slaves. In Brazil, moreover, the system remained so wholly dominant that the total population in 1600 probably did not exceed sixty-five thousand people, fewer than ten thousand of them Europeans. Even including the town populations, density was about four per square kilometer. A hundred years later, with the indigenous populations driven into the wilderness and the captives listless and disease ridden, sugar profits in the Northeast had declined substantially, the victim of competition from the Caribbean. Only the discovery of riches in the mountains of Minas Gerais in 1690 and thereafter jolted Brazil's colonial lethargy. Precious minerals extracted from the central Mantiquera range by slave labor during the seventeenth century amounted to a million kilograms of gold and 2.4 million carats of diamonds, with untold more in riches smuggled away in contraband. The mining region and its outlet to the sea—the port city of Rio de Janeiro—became the dynamic center of the colony, and the royal capital was moved from Salvador to Rio in 1763. Brazil became more important within the Portuguese overseas empire; in 1720 Lisbon elevated Brazil to the status of a viceroyalty. The Portuguese moved to challenge the Spanish on the left bank of the River Plate, the route of clandestine trading in silver smuggled from Spanish Potosí. These new objectives led to massive numbers of new settlers from Portugal and to the belated growth of what in another century, under an independent monarchy, would become a nationally based economy.

The cycle of sugar profitability gave way to the gold boom of the eighteenth century; when gold reserves dwindled, Brazil's economic fortunes turned to coffee. By the 1820s, coffee had become Brazil's major export crop; by the last decade of the nineteenth century, exports had grown by more than fifteen times. Most coffee was raised in the region north and west of the imperial capital of Rio de Janeiro, although it was also grown in hilly parts of the Northeast and on the frontier westward from São Paulo in to Paraná. Through the 1860s, plantation labor was performed by slaves; later free workers, including ex-slaves, did the work. They were paid so poorly that they barely subsisted, forced to live outside the market economy.

The Portuguese treated their Brazilian colony as an appendage, largely outside of the market economy. With the establishment of the Council of the Indies in 1642 and a royal decree in 1785 prohibiting all industry, they imposed one of the "legally most complete mercantilist trading systems in the world," relieved, an economic historian has noted, "only by official corruption and inability to prevent smuggling, which reached such proportions that in the 18th century roadbuilding was prohibited in mining regions as a control measure."[4] The great imbalance in Brazilian trade was made up with gold shipments to Portugal, although gold remained undervalued in Brazil to encourage exports. Once the mines began to run low, fifty years after the gold boom began, contraband silver, smuggled from ships, began to take its place as a form of currency.

The need for food in the growing towns and cities made room for independent farmers. Some used slave labor; others hired laborers or simply used family members. Extensive trade networks using mule trails, river and coastal shipping, and, in the nineteenth century, trains, permitted producers to ship meat products to the cities in exchange for cash (or cloth, or kerosene). Planters in Recôncavo, at the gateway to the interior of the province of Bahia, grew cassava root—*mandoica*—a starchy tuber imported from Africa that in dried and powdered form became the mainstay of the Brazilian diet.

Local markets, then, kept pace with the expansion of export markets. The growth of British-owned railroads linked agricultural areas to ports. Of great importance were the lines linking the city of São Paulo to the port of Santos as well as to the new coffee zone in the west; as the soil was depleted, the bulk of coffee production shifted westward as well. Still, Brazilian coffee was in great demand around the world. Arabica varieties known as Rio "Number 7" and, later, "Santos Number 4" became the standards by which coffee beans were measured. In 1906, 82 percent of the world's coffee harvest came from Brazil; in most other years, the figure topped 60 percent. Coffee was not the only boom product: the Amazon's rubber production captured 90 percent of the world market, although the bubble had burst by 1910. Coffee prosperity, on the other hand, continued until prices fell precipitously after the Wall Street crash of 1929. Coffee profits bolstered São Paulo's emergence as Brazil's major economic power and fueled the political machinery of the Old Republic (1889–1930), dominated by São Paulo and its client states.

The Great Depression had a jarring impact on Brazil. Between 1929 and 1932 the value of Brazilian exports, mainly coffee beans, fell by 75 percent. The currency depreciated by roughly the same amount, wiping out local investment and reducing wages to virtually nothing. The standard of living for all but the very rich fell abruptly by 25–30 percent, a harsh condition given that millions of Brazilians had lived on the margin of starvation even before 1929. Policy makers long remembered the vulnerability brought about by export-based development, and during the 1930s they followed Vargas's lead in advocating nationalistic programs that would speed industrialization and make Brazil less reliant on imported goods. The impact of World War II, further cutting off manufactured imports, reinforced these feelings and influenced the intention, shared by civilian and military leaders, to replace imports of capital goods by domestic production after the war. What they did not advocate, however were measures to increase the purchasing power of consumers, for this would mean raising wages. Instead, they counted on Brazil's new steel plant at Volta Redonda and increased development of basic goods (cement, electric power, industrial chemicals) to pave the way for industrialization based on a controlled labor market, an influx of modern technology to replace archaic production methods, and strong state incentives (and controls).

Import substitution spurred growth, but it also encouraged xenophobia. It did not absorb the burgeoning new labor pool created by the extremely high birth rate and the steady flow of migrants to the cities. These economic refugees, arriving in open trucks (dubbed *pau de arara*, or parrot's perch) came forty to sixty at a time, jostling over unpaved roads for thousands of miles. Between 1950 and 1960, the number of industrial jobs grew by 29 percent, in the face of a jump in the urban population of 70 percent. Urban growth, then, was not keeping pace with the urban population increase. At best this forced hundreds of thousands into the underground economy; at worst, it sowed the seeds of a permanent underclass, beyond the reach of limited social services and kept from real jobs by their lack of marketable skills. In frustration, labor leaders and intellectuals lashed out at foreign imperialists, in part because they believed that foreign greed was fueling inflation and depressing the standard of living, and in part because it was safer to attack foreigners than the entrenched Brazilian elite, which maintained tight social control and punished dissent.

Brazil's gross domestic product in 1998 stood eighth in the world, behind the United States, China, Japan, Germany, France, Britain, and Italy. In terms of per capita income, of the ten world economic leaders, only China's was lower than Brazil's. Brazil is also a member today of the "trillion-dollar-economy country club," which makes the extreme contrast between rich and poor especially startling: the upper 20 percent of the population owns 60 percent of the nation's wealth.

The national Geography and Statistics Institute (IBGE) has estimated that thirty-five million Brazilians earned their living in the underground economy, half of the entire work force, a percentage equal to those for Bangladesh and Somalia. Off-the-books workers earn less than the minimum wage and receive none of the protections of Brazilian labor law, including pensions, workman's compensation, health benefits, and safety rules in the workplace. In some ways, this represents a step backward to the years of the Estado Novo (1937–1945), when only members of government-sanctioned unions were protected. Informal-economy workers, excluded from labor unions of any kind, must fare for themselves. The greatest obstacle to economic development remains the structural barriers to enlargement of the domestic market. With per capita income stuck at $3,500 per year, most Brazilians have little or no discretionary income.

THE SOCIAL SYSTEM

Although voices attacking the institution of slavery—including those of some of the very few *mulatos* who had risen to prominence—helped bring emancipation in 1889, virtually no one spoke out against the plight of the ex-slaves or the de facto social and economic segregation thereafter. Brazil lived under the banner of laissez-faire, rejecting the notion that government should interfere with the "natural" course of things, and establishing effective social discrimination against the masses of the population lacking in privilege. Brazil was slow to develop institutions that might have championed the cause of have-nots. Only a tiny group of women fought for women's suffrage—for upper-class women. The Brazilian Roman Catholic Church opted to follow a conservative path, isolated from currents of European Catholic social conscience. There were no comprehensive universities until the 1930s, and even then Brazilian universities rarely produced effective critics of the status quo. Philanthropy, in the absence of tax incentives, languished. The Santa Casa de Misericordia, which for centuries had provided help for orphans and medical care to the indigent, saw its funds slowly reduced and ultimately became a poorly funded agency of the state. Newspapers played important roles in towns and cities, but virtually all of them were mouthpieces for their owners. Not until the late 1950s did some newspapers and news magazines promote investigative journalism, an activity abruptly curtailed by the 1964 military dictatorship. Television and print journalists courageously resumed their vigilance as the country returned to civilian rule in the mid-1980s, and today they retain an important watchdog role in a society essentially lacking effective nongovernmental organizations pursuing reform and social change.

Brazil's lower class falls into two groups, rural and urban. Before 1930 most Brazilians were rural poor, dependent almost entirely on the elite for sustenance. They were illiterate and were kept in misery by the general system of land tenure, which kept most land out of cultivation. The standard of living of this class has always been miserably low. They lived as squatters on the land, or as renters, or in rural towns, where they hired out as day laborers when they were needed, for pitiful wages. Denied all but the most meager of food, they were often flogged or beaten for fishing in streams or for picking fruit on land owned by others. The rural lower-class diet was mostly manioc flour flavored by beans, dried beef, or salt fish. Rice was a luxury, as well as bread, fresh meat, or vegetables. Chronic hunger and the cyclical devastation of periodic droughts in the northeastern "drought polygon" (all or parts of eight northeastern states) historically have driven families of drought refugees and other migrants to the coast and to the slums of the industrializing cities of the Center-South. But the urban poor have fared badly as well. Lacking skills, men and women work as manual laborers and maids and live in substandard housing: either tenements or shanty towns.

Two factors make the plight of the very poor—more than half of Brazil's population—especially difficult to improve. One is the survival of the rigid social structure. Hierarchy and inherited status is taken for granted; public values do not extol opportunities for upward mobility. The second is the country's embrace of industrialization and free market economics. This has meant that economic development has not provided new jobs; in fact, modernization in agriculture and in industry has actually cost jobs. Privatization has led to the dismissal of tens of thousands of bureaucrats and others whose jobs—in many cases sinecures—had been the source of their families' incomes. There is no safety net, no welfare system or protection for persons thrown out of work. Only since very recently have poor people had access to health care, and even today the waits at government clinics are long and the quality of treatment uneven. The number of stillbirths registered with the state is astonishingly high—although many of these likely are abortions. The rich, of course, can afford clinical abortions if they want them; the poor resort to clandestine, unsanitary methods. Brazil has become more than ever a country of vast economic inequalities, where the small affluent elite lives in luxury in the midst of an ocean of the hard pressed and destitute.

The plight of some groups, notably Indians and urban street children, has received world attention. In recent decades it has been disclosed that the government's National Indian Foundation, the successor to the Indian Protection Service (SPI) founded in 1910, was for years complicit in widespread actions against the interests of the Indian population, including violence. The problem of nationwide poverty remains unsolved, and in some ways it is worsening under Brazil's embrace of the free market economy.

CULTURAL CHARACTERISTICS AND RELIGION

Since the nineteenth century, Brazilians have considered their language culturally superior to Portugal's, which Brazilians consider provincial and old-fashioned. The foundation in 1897 of the Brazilian Academy of Letters provided the means to validate Brazilian Portuguese, with its rich regional variations and flexible willingness to absorb words and phrases from a wide range of sources, including indigenous peoples and immigrants.

The colonial era witnessed artistic expression at all levels of society. Members of the elite enjoyed Baroque music as sophisticated as in Europe. Some plantations and mines had slave orchestras. Craftsmen constructed sidewalks of inlaid stone; carpenters turned out handsome furniture, using native mahogany and *jacarandá*. Colonial architecture followed the Portuguese style of simple exteriors of whitewashed stone. Brazil lacked the monumental cathedrals of Spanish America, but in the royal captaincy of Bahia and in the small towns of the mining region in Minas Gerais, the high point of colonial-era culture was reached in the beautiful interiors of churches, many of them decorated with expressive statues and icons, all heavily gilded. Most memorable was the sculpture of the gifted *mineiro* artist Aleijadinho (Antonio Francisco Lisboa 1730–1814), the mulatto son of a Portuguese father and an African slave mother. Though crippled by leprosy, he carved magnificent statues of religious figures in wood and soft soapstone in and around Baroque churches in Conhongas, Sabará, and Ouro Preto. Since Aleijadinho was illegitimate he could not receive commissions in his own name, but his fame quickly spread. His works were marked by remarkable detail and expression, as memorable as that of any eighteenth-century art anywhere in the world.

Toward the end of the nineteenth century, many Brazilian intellectuals began to turn away from imported culture and to probe local cultural expression for its unique properties. In the Northeast, the critic Sílvio Romero lamented that the elite had too long focused on itself and its European roots; in 1885 and 1888 he published anthologies of folk songs and poems he had collected among the lower classes. He argued that true Brazilian culture represented an amalgam of European, African, and native expression, a remarkable assertion in the face of conventional attitudes of the day, which held non-Europeans to be racially inferior. Romero praised the results of miscegenation and predicted that Brazil would some day emerge as the source of a hybrid civilization. He advocated a Brazilian literature with roots in the common people.

Brazilians have long pondered their nation's character. Fernando de Azevedo, a journalist and educator whose 1943 book on the subject was received as a classic, barely hid his disdain for the unwashed masses. "Brazilians," he wrote, "are subject to an irregular and offbeat rhythm, to depressions and recoveries, and to indolence and impetuosity. Despite the appearance of laziness, lassitude, and indifference, an explosive will and an ability to maintain reserves of energy—to be released when needed or when Brazilians are shocked emotionally—clearly show a marked preponderance of sensibility over intelligence."[5] Azevedo also called Brazilians "resigned and docile," as if a willingness to avoid conflict was regrettable. Others have constructed more charitable interpretations. Overall, however, they trivialize the complex coping mechanisms that have permitted Brazilians to survive. In a society that has valued hierarchy for half a millennium, only those on the periphery of elite life have questioned the persistence of misery and society's reluctance to face hard issues about income maldistribution, wage repression, and lack of avenues for upward mobility.

Brazilians nominally constitute the largest Roman Catholic population on earth, but the number of practicing Catholics has always been relatively small. Protestantism, brought to Brazil by settlers in the mid-nineteenth century as well as by English and German engineers and businessmen who stayed, played a minor role until the second half of the twentieth century. At that point, sizeable numbers of lower and middle-class Brazilians began to flock to fundamentalist sects, which, through the power of television, have since attained significant influence. Indian tribes usually have retained their animist practices, as have many descendants of African slaves.

More than a hundred Protestant denominations, most of them evangelical or Pentecostal, won converts during the 1980s, at a rate three times higher than the growth of population. By 1997, sixteen million Brazilians *crentes* (believers) followed daily practices—austerity in dress, abstention from alcohol, a fierce puritanism—that represented the antithesis of Brazil's historical popular culture, characterized by exuberance, relaxed sexual and interpersonal relations, and the pulsating rhythms of Carnival. The Pentecostal explosion has deeply affected its followers, instilling a disciplined work ethic that has produced astonishing gains in earning power for its members, most of them from the poorest social groups. Pentecostal churches encourage birth control, run hundreds of clinics for rehabilitation from drug and alcohol abuse, and exert what critics term a chilling effect on the climate of artistic expression, extolling followers to read only the Bible and to be vigilant against immorality. Evangelical radio and television stations, schools, and even banks employ more than six hundred thousand persons. The Universal Reign of God Church, with 321,000 members, runs a network of forty-seven television and twenty-six radio stations and in 1997 elected six members to the federal legislature. The Assembly of God Church, with three million adherents, has a rival television network and operates newspapers, schools, bookstores, and health clinics.

Still, Afro-Brazilian *candomblé*, with its percussive music, white and black magic, and sessions where believers enter trancelike states, has remained the predominant religion of millions more. Slaves masked their religious faith, twinning their spiritist deities with Roman Catholic saints to give the outward appearance of Catholic piety. Africanized Roman Catholicism then, as in much of Africa today, shed more and more of Christian practice. Brazilians of European background embraced spiritism as well, but generally the French version—emphasizing healing through spiritual energies and communing with the departed through seances—popularized in the nineteenth century by Alain Kardec. *Umbanda*, a hybrid mixture of Afro-Brazilian and European spiritist practices, is said to have nearly thirty million followers in Brazil today, most of them middle-class whites. In today's Brazil, practitioners are more open about revealing their feelings. "I'd like to thank God," a Bahian-born mezzo soprano told her Rio de Janeiro audience at a tri umphal 1997 performance, "and the gods."[6] Affirming membership in two or more religious faiths is not unusual in Brazil. Some visit both Protestant and Roman Catholic churches regularly; more, like the Afro-Brazilian singer Virginia Rodrigues and the late black writer Carolina Maria de Jesus, have garnered strength from both Catholicism and *candomblé*.

Social values have changed slowly. Brazil's school system provides free education through the university level, but in practice most Brazilians never pass the lower primary grades. Public schools are handicapped by astonishingly low salaries for teachers, inadequate budgetary resources, and insistence on learning by rote. The vast majority of university students in Brazil graduate from private primary and secondary schools as well as from intensive *cursinhos*, preparatory cram courses for the difficult national entrance examinations, the *vestibuláres*. As a result of this system, elite students, whose families could easily afford college tuition, fill all of the places in the schools of engineering, law, arts and letters, architecture, and medicine, tuition free.

One element that has made Brazil healthily singular is its rich popular culture. Brazilians over the years have learned the art of emotional release. Pre-Lenten Carnival, an annual festivity lasting several days and nights, interrupts everyday life with brilliant color, percussive sound, and revelry. Carnival in the large cities has become a tourist attraction, removing some of its spontaneity, but in smaller cities, towns, and hamlets the celebration has lost none of its magic. Brazilians celebrate exuberantly on many other occasions as well. There are the frequent World Cup soccer victories—Brazil has won four world championships and almost won in 1998, in France; Roman Catholic festivals (especially São João day in June, accompanied by fireworks and flaming paper balloons launched into the skies). Northeasterners play at *bumba meu boi*, a costumed, ritualistic dance; youths in Salvador deftly practice *capoeira*, a choreographed martial art. On New Year's Eve, black Afro-Brazilian women in white *candomblé* dresses toss bouquets of flowers into the sea. In the south, people hold enormous *churrascos*, or barbecues. Brazilians from all parts of the country enjoy parades, circuses, rock concerts; they play not only soccer but volleyball, basketball, judo, tennis, and, in the Japanese neighborhoods of São Paulo, baseball. Brazil has produced champions in automobile racing and sailing. Aerobics is very popular. Brazilian popular music is one of the most sophisticated and rich forms of expression in the world. Brazil has a centuries-old tradition of poetry, which in the rural hinterland has become a form of folk art. The emotional geography of Brazil varies from place to place, but above all it embraces life.

Brazil differs from its Spanish American neighbors significantly and in many ways. It not only preserved Portuguese as its sole language but maintained its territorial integrity despite its vast size. Brazil did not split up, like Bolívar's Gran Colombia, nor was it torn apart by civil war, as was the United States. It did not lose national territory, as did Mexico, half of which was taken by the United States, or like Bolivia and Peru, in regional wars. Conservatism, not the anticlerical liberalism of mid-nineteenth-century Mexico, characterized Brazil's political life under the Empire, but reformism was tolerated. Under the republic, proclaimed in 1889 after a nonviolent political coup, Brazil moved tentatively forward in the direction of elections and rule of law to an extent not seen in half of its neighbors in the region.

Another Brazilian cultural characteristic is the *jeito*, a "knack" or "fix," the way in which citizens cope with the often-unyielding formal legal system. Some use personal connections relatives or other members of their *panelinhas* (networks)—to see that a rule is bent or not applied. Others, mostly less well placed in the power structure, hire professional expediters (*despachantes*) to cut through red tape to obtain permits, passports, official documents, and the like. The unwitting foreigner who does not understand the *jeito* system may spend hours or days waiting in line, mired in a bureaucracy that seems to have been created simply to provide sinecures.

Often, moreover, the Brazilian "way" requires tips or small gifts, whether or not a *despachante* has been used. Doing business in Brazil often requires these payments, although this rule is unwritten. When the United States consulate prior to President Bill Clinton's visit in October 1997 issued a pamphlet describing the country's business climate as "generally corrupt," Brazilians yelled in protest and the Americans apologized—although both sides knew that the description was not incorrect, at least from the American perspective.

The fact that local and state bureaucracies frequently lack mechanisms for enforcement has resulted in a kind of *jeito* mentality that rewards insiders. After Congress passed the Eloy Chaves Law in 1923 for railroad workers—the first to provide benefits and pensions for skilled workers—records show that many retired railroad men married on their deathbeds, so that their "widows" could continue to collect their pensions. Another example of official laxity occurred during the 1980s and 1990s, when tens of thousands of public employees opted for retirement at full pay only to take new jobs as soon as the paperwork was completed.

NOTES

1. Ronald M. Schneider, *Brazil: Culture and Politics in a New Industrial Powerhouse* (Boulder, CO: Westview, 1996), 4.
2. Anthony W. Marx, "Race-Making and the Nation State," *World Politics* 48 (January 1996), 181.
3. For quotation, ibid., 182.
4. Norman A. Bailey, "Brazil as a Monetary Model," paper published by the Committee for Monetary Research and Education, New York, 1975, 2.
5. Fernando de Azevedo, *A Cultura Brasileira*, 5th ed. (São Paulo: Mel-

horamentos, 1943), translated and cited by G. Harvey Summ, ed., *Brazilian Mosaic* (Wilmington, DE: SR Books, 1995), 6.

  6. Diana Jean Shemo, "A Debut in Rio," *New York Times*, June 25, 1997, B3.

2

Early Brazil (1500–1822)

In 1500, the year that the Portuguese sea captain Pedro Álvares Cabral landed on the Brazilian coast, nearly seven million native people dwelled in the lowland rain forest of greater Amazonia. The rain forest teemed with life. The Amazon and its tributaries contained more than 1,800 varieties of fish, as well as caimans, manatees, and turtles. Humans had inhabited this region for at least ten thousand years, divided into hundreds of tribes representing four major language groups: Tupi (or Tupi-Guaraní), Gê, Carib, and Aruak (Arawak). The largest group, the Tupi-Guaraní, along the Atlantic coast, was the most belligerent, engaging in warfare against other tribes. Other Tupi groups resided on the south bank of the Amazon River and upstream almost to Peru. The Gê lived on the vast central plateau; they may have been descended from peoples who are known to have lived in Minas Gerais more than ten thousand years earlier. It is speculated that they may have been remnants of peoples dispersed by the invading Tupi. The peoples of the Amazon basin, the Tupi, Carib, and Aruak, lived in communities that were in some ways more advanced—they made elaborate pottery, for example—than the societies encountered by the Europeans at the outset of the sixteenth century. The cultural patterns of the Aruaks, whose language family extended as far north as Florida and the circum-Caribbean, may have originated on the Amazon River. The Aruaks plied the rivers of the rain forest but left few artifacts.

Nomadic native tribal groups inhabited the land that became Brazil after 1500. The Europeans did not know what to make of the peoples they encountered. They stood in awe of the virgin forests, which seemed to be as old as the world. Some of the trees in fact topped thirty-five meters in height and were more than a thousand years in age. The Europeans were shocked at the primitive existence of the natives and puzzled by the fact that they did not covet wealth. Some of the tribes were warlike and therefore dangerous. Some practiced cannibalism. They did not plant crops but hunted and gathered fruits and berries. Their lack of prior exposure to European germs made them terribly vulnerable to the diseases that swept the New World in the first centuries of European conquest.

Maize (corn) cultivation started about 3,900 years ago, well after farming began in Mesoamerica and in the Andes. Farming came late to Brazil because earlier it had not been needed; the population was modest and freely growing food plentiful. Eventually native Brazilians started to grow manioc, burning the brush to yield nutrients. This technique was wasteful—sometimes the fires would spread and burn for weeks—but the forests seemed limitless.

Brazil's clusters of autonomous tribes lived in the forest and had neither gold nor silver. They were skilled craftsmen, but they used materials that were entirely perishable. They had no cities, no calendar, no knowledge of metallurgy or architecture or scientific farming, as did their counterparts in the Andes and Mesoamerica. Because of their presence, Portuguese officials could not put domesticated animals ashore to multiply, as they had done in the Azores and on Madeira. Nor was Brazil safe for newcomers: some of the Amerindians were cannibals, a fact not lost on the first Portuguese who came to explore. Further, the apparent simplicity of the Indian villages was deceptive. Complex rules governed behavior, and trade was highly developed. But the Portuguese undermined and ultimately destroyed Indian society. Missionaries threw Indian tribes together in their settlements without regard to linguistic and cultural differences.

About 400 C.E., tribal invaders came to the coast and drove the agriculturalists away, taking over their plots of manioc cultivation. These were the Tupi, aggressive warriors who lived in semipermanent settlements and traveled stealthily in canoes. They used bows' and arrows as their principal weapons; the French Huguenot explorer Jean de Léry reported that the Tupis' bows were longer than the bows used in Europe and that they could fire twelve arrows at once. The bows' tension, he added, was so tight that no European could bend them. They also used spears and clubs, as well as blowpipes, from which darts tipped with curare could strike targets fifty feet away.

The Tupi fiercely resisted incursions of outsiders. Their villages numbered about six hundred persons, controlling a population of more than nine persons per square kilometer. They resided in *malocas*, long, palm-thatched dwellings housing as many as thirty families. Their slash-and-burn farming methods caused the forests to shrink further (but nothing like the assault that developed when the Europeans came with their African slaves, clearing the land for plantations and cattle ranches). In addition to the Tupis there were nearly 1,400 other tribes, supporting forty major linguistic families and dominated by the Tupi-Guaranis on the coast, the nomadic Macro-Jê in the central interior, and the Aruak in the equatorial rain forest. One tribe in the Jê (or Gé) group, the Goayanazes, original inhabitants of the São Paulo region, lived in caves and fished and hunted, but they lacked any knowledge of cultivation. All of the Tupi and the Aruak practiced cleanliness—they were much cleaner than the Portuguese, for example, who marveled at the fact that the Indians bathed frequently—but the Caribs, in the far north, lived in filth. The Tupis practiced cannibalism, although they ate only prisoners taken in war. Not only the Tupis fought back against the Europeans; other groups achieved some degree of success, if only for a while. These included the Guaranis, who fought against Luso [Portuguese]-Spanish troops in the Jesuit mission regions of Rio Grande do Sul and Paraguay during the period of the consolidation of the Portuguese and Spanish thrones (1580–1640), and the Potiguars and Carirís, who resisted in the North between 1683 and 1713.

THE PORTUGUESE BACKGROUND

Portugal was one of the oldest nations in Europe. In the twelfth century, King Afonso Henriques contacted the English and worked out a commercial treaty that became the basis for the longest-standing alliance in the West. Muslims were expelled from the Algarve in 1250, leaving Portugal intact and without foreign occupiers. Modern Portugal was consolidated during the early thirteenth century as a mercantile state. Merchants as well as landowners came to play major roles in economic life.

The Roman Catholic Church was not nearly as strong as it was in Spain. Portuguese, not Latin, was the language used by the clergy.

Portugal had long been linked with Asia through tenuous land routes but the Portuguese were known for their seafaring prowess. Arabic tradition remembers the *Mogharriun*, Portuguese sailors from Lisbon. From 1450 to 1500 the Portuguese had their age of maritime glory. Prior to the fifteenth century, no maritime traffic plied south of Cape Bojador in Africa, because of ocean currents that made it difficult to sail north, even along the African coast. Once the Portuguese built ships large enough and acquired sufficient seagoing experience, their expeditions explored all the world's oceans except for the Antarctic. In 1415, they captured Ceuta, a great Muslim trading center and the key to North Africa. Four years later, in 1419, Prince Dom Henrique (Henry the Navigator) sponsored a colony of mapmakers and navigators at Sagres, on the rocky southwestern tip of Portugal. Generations of historians portrayed Henry as a mystic visionary, alone in his quest; more recent scholars portray him as an opportunity seeker who was but one of several principals in the inception of the maritime expansion of Europe. Beginning in 1420, Henry sent ship after ship to explore the western coast of Africa, places that had been known previously by Europeans but forgotten. Colonial officials built fortified outposts, typically within sight of the sea, emphasizing commerce, not colonization. The Portuguese occupied the islands of the Atlantic—the Canaries, Madeira, the Azores, Cape Verde—and explored the West African coast. On the islands they introduced agricultural colonies, whose output went to Portugal, where merchants sold it after first paying a tithe to the crown.

INDIGENOUS PEOPLES

When they landed in Brazil, the Portuguese did not know what to make of the peoples they encountered there. They stood in awe of virgin forests. Northern and eastern South America is not plagued by earthquakes or other natural disasters, save for flooding on the banks of rivers, so some of the life forms were indeed ancient. The newcomers were plagued by sweltering humidity, vast reaches of mud, and swarming ticks, mosquitos, flies, and spiders. The natives seemed physically perfect—since any infant with a deformity was killed at birth. Amerigo Vespucci (the Italian cartographer, 1454–1512, for whom America is named), writing to his Medici patron about the tribes he observed, claimed that the Indians lived to great old age (an assertion that had no basis in fact) and that the *caá-etê*—Tupi for "undisturbed forest"—provided all that they needed. The tropical climate made clothing unnecessary. Vespucci believed that the Indians lived in an earthly paradise. His observations, published as *Mundus Novus* in 1504, started a decades-long debate in Europe about the New World's "noble savages." "They live together without king, without government, and each is his own master. They marry as many wives as they please. . . . They live according to nature." Pero Vaz de Caminha wrote to the king that the Indians were "bestial people, of very little knowledge," but "well cared for and very clean." The French philosopher Montaigne took up the debate. Quoting the Roman philosopher Seneca, he called the Indians "men fresh from the gods," writing that "their world surpasses the pictures with which the poets have adorned the golden age."

The Caribs, warlike hunters and gatherers, were driving south when the foreigners arrived, attacking tribes deeper and deeper in the lower Amazon. Some of the Caribs practiced cannibalism and shrank the heads of their victims, using the same method as the Dyaks of Borneo. They were preliterate, and they used perishable materials, mostly wood, vines, and grasses, to build their settlements. Since lowland South America had no native animals that could be domesticated (like the llamas and guinea pigs of the Incas), they were constantly on the move. For that reason they acquired few possessions, and in consequence the Europeans thought them to be indigent.

It was a harsh environment: the soil on the forest floor was porous, riddled with parasites; when cleared, it was seared by a burning sun and washed away by seasonal floods. Agriculture such as that practiced in the Andes and in Central America was impossible, and there was no evidence of the precious metals so coveted by the Europeans. Indians who lived beyond the forest, in the Brazilian *sertão* (outback), knew how to cope with the parched landscape but were easily driven from their lands by the Portuguese settlers.

The Suruí peoples of remote Rondônia, who had their first peaceful contact with modern Brazilians only in 1969, believe that the world was created by a spirit named Palop. When he came to Earth to visit their Suruí's ancestors, however, he arrived covered with dirt, and they were not hospitable to him. Palop was hungry and asked for a corn pancake, but they gave him only food that was scattered on the ground. They told him to eat from the broken pot that contained scraps for the dogs. As a result, he punished men and took away their immortality.[1]

Brazil's indigenous population, like others elsewhere, was brutalized by encroaching settlement and modernization. The number of Indians residing in Brazilian territory has shrunk from an estimated 7 million in 1500 to a tiny remnant today. Reputable historians and anthropologists—most of them foreigners, because only recently have Brazilians become concerned with this issue—have spoken out angrily against the actions taken by Europeans against Brazil's indigenous population, whether intentional or unintentional. The conquerors—including the Jesuit missionaries, who placed Indians under a life of regimentation and coerced labor in fortified villages (*aldeias*)—ignored the complexity of Indian culture, ignoring cultural and linguistic differences among tribal groups and generally treating all Indians as children in need of discipline and instruction. Still, the missionaries were protecting their charges from worse treatment by landowners and settlers. When in 1661 Father Antônio Vieira, a Jesuit, pressed efforts to shield Indians in Maranhão from the colonists of the province, the colonists rose up in revolt; authorities arrested Vieira and his aides and deported them to Portugal. Legalized slavery for Indians went unchallenged. In 1693 the entire Amazon basin was divided up among missionary groups—the Franciscans, Capuchins, the Fathers of Piedade and Conceição, the Carmelites, and the Jesuits on the upstream south bank of the Amazon—who placed the Indians under their care to shield them from further depredations. Not all of the tribes submitted willingly; rebellions, some of them extensive, flared throughout the region. One of the fiercest was the uprising in 1723 of the Manau on the river Negro, under their leader Ajuricaba. Five years later, the Carmelites sent a massive force to subdue the uprising, capturing Ajuricaba. He committed suicide rather than be taken.

Resistance from landowners and colonists to the missionaries, especially against the Jesuits, led to their expulsion from Brazil in 1759. The Jesuits, on their arrival in 1549, had established missions as far south as Paraná and throughout the Northeast to the Amazon. They had been excluded from Minas Gerais—religious work there was performed by secular clergy—but elsewhere throughout Brazil had established schools, seminaries, churches, and plantations. They had sent fleets of canoes filled with the products of the rain forest to the coast, and they had dominated retail trade. Their zeal, in Dauril Alden's words, had made them Brazil's largest landowner and greatest slave master, as well as "the premier missionary order in the colony."[2] In 1750 these villages, with their stable populations, were the basis for the award of most of the

Amazon basin to Brazil by the Treaty of Madrid, signed in Madrid and Lisbon.

Father Vieira was one of the lone voices raised against the treatment of Indians, although he did not speak out against enslavement of Africans. His warnings were forceful and ominous. In 1653, on the first day of Lent, he addressed his congregation in São Luis de Maranhão:

> Christians, nobles, and people of Maranhão, do you know what God wants of you this Lenten season? That you break the chains of injustice and let free those whom you have made captive and oppressed. These are the sins of Maranhão; these are what God commanded me to denounce to you. Christians, God commanded me to make these matters clear to you and so I do it. All of you are in mortal sin; all of you live in a state of condemnation; and all of you are going directly to Hell. Indeed, many are there now and you will soon join them if you do not change your ways.

Portugal's rulers, however, were only mildly concerned with the welfare of indigenous people. Under the dynastic house of Aviz, Portugal established a far-flung sea empire stretching from the Atlantic islands to Africa, India, China, and elsewhere in the Far East. The tiny Western European nation emphasized shipbuilding and navigational technology, establishing trading posts on the coasts of the places it explored rather than seeking to occupy and settle large tracts of territory. Unlike the Spanish, the Portuguese had no crusading or proselytizing mission, and although they sought gold and precious minerals, they more pragmatically established commercial monopolies, including in African slaves. They permitted the Jesuits to settle in Brazil in 1549, ceding to that order the task of establishing the institutional presence of the Catholic Church in the colony.

DISCOVERY, EXPLORATION, AND SETTLEMENT

One of the first acts of the Portuguese when they landed on the Brazilian coast in 1500 was to cut down a tree to erect a cross and celebrate Mass beneath it. Some history books say that the discovery was accidental—that Cabral, taking the advice of the explorer Vasco da Gama (who had reached India three years earlier), looking for southward-blowing winds to carry him around the West African coast, where the currents were languid, had ventured much farther into the Atlantic than he had planned. It is a fact, however, that some Portuguese sea charts had shown a huge island, the "Land of the True Cross," and this was the name Cabral gave to Brazil. The Portuguese claim to the territory was based on the 1494 papal Treaty of Tordesillas, which had demarcated control of the non-Christian world by a north-south line about 1,700 miles west of the Cape Verde Islands; Brazil fell in the Portuguese sphere. Unlike the Spanish, with their dreams of gold and fountains of youth, the Portuguese imagination, influenced by years of exploration of the African coast was sober and businesslike. They sought good locations for trading posts; the Spanish quested for Eden.

To register his territorial claim, Cabral dispatched a ship back to Lisbon with samples of a rich dye-producing wood that the Tupi called *ibirapitanga* and the Portuguese *pau* [wood]-*brasil* (from *brasa*, a red, glowing ember). Wood from similar trees had been brought from the East and was in enormous demand. Cabral dropped off in Brazil a number of *degregados*—convicted criminals who had been sentenced to banishment; officials hoped that they would learn native languages and serve as interpreters for later expeditions. One of the results was the beginning of the process of miscegenation. The convicts' mixed-race offspring served as brokers between Indians and Europeans. One of the castaways, Diogo Álvares, fathered a large family and acted as intermediary between the Tupinambas and Portugal's King Dom João III.

The third Portuguese voyage, whose pilot was Amerigo Vespucci, took the first steps toward the establishment of the brazilwood trade. The Europeans were impressed by the sight of the native tribesmen who met their ship. "They walk on the shore, burned by the sun and naked, using no clothing to cover their shame. They have reddish skin, close cropped hair, well-formed faces." The scribe added, "We do not have knowledge of whether there is gold or silver here, or any other metal."[3] The Tupi bartered with the Portuguese and did not make war, even though Portuguese ships, as early as 1511, began taking natives back as curiosities to nobles, and soon thereafter as slaves. Descriptions of Brazil as a "tropical paradise," taking a phrase from Vespucci, circulated widely within Europe.

Overextended in the face of competition from other European powers, Portuguese overseas officials took few steps to consolidate their foothold in the New World. Many believed that Brazil was simply a large, unpromising tropical island—a belief that held out the hope that a sea route could still be found to Asia. Asia was the goal of a Portuguese expedition in 1511–12 that found the La Plata estuary. Spain countered, however, with an expedition headed by Juan de Solís in 1515, and the Portuguese never pressed their claim. Ferdinand de Magellan, sailing from Spain in search of a westward passage in 1519, stopped in Brazil before going on to the Spice Islands, which were ceded to Portugal in 1529 by the Treaty of Zaragoza.

By this treaty, Spain and Portugal put aside their territorial rivalry for the time being, but the French had by then entered Brazilian waters to poach on the dyewood trade. In 1503–1504, the French captain Gonneville of Honfleur traded goods with natives on the coast from his ship, the l'Espoir. The French crown had denounced Tordesillas, considering Brazil open for anyone. Not only did the French incursions threaten to deprive Lisbon of revenue, but it lowered the price of brazilwood in European markets. The French traded from their ships and sent agents ashore to make contacts with the Indians, whom the Portuguese largely ignored except to seize as slaves. French naval expeditions made incursions north and south of the Portuguese zone of influence. The French, and the English as well, made territorial gains in the Caribbean and Guiana; even the Danes and the Dutch established New World colonies. The French settled near Rio de Janeiro in 1555 before being expelled by Portuguese troops. Their most important settlement in present-day Brazil was in "Equinoctial France," at St. Louis (São Luis) in Maranhão, which remained French until 1615.

The first European to travel down the Amazon River was the Spaniard Francisco de Orellana, a relative of the Pizarro family from Trujillo, in Estremadura. His first trip to the New World had been in 1527, when he was sixteen. He had participated in the invasion of Peru, losing an eye in one of the battles between the Spanish and Incas. His ten-thousand-man expedition started out in 1541 from Quito in present-day Ecuador and after eight months reached the Atlantic Ocean in present-day Pará, which Orellana named Nueva Andalucia. The expedition was not unlike the Louis and Clark journey to Oregon, although the purpose of Orellana's adventure was to find gold, not to explore. His men were aided in their travels by peaceful Indians, including "a girl of great intelligence." They encountered one tribe ruled by women; they named them "Amazons," perhaps after the Greek story of warrior women in Scythia. In August 1542 they returned to Quito, retracing the 270 leagues they had traveled. When Orellana sailed to Europe to report on his findings, he first landed in Portugal, where the king offered hospitality, hosting him for several weeks. The information extracted from

Orellana whetted the desire of the Portuguese to explore the northern reaches of the Amazon themselves, a plan they justified because the area fell partially within the limits of the territory ceded to them by the Tordesillas treaty (although by the Tordesillas map most of the Amazon should have been Spanish). Spain remained in nominal control of the Amazon through the seventeenth century, but because there was no visible wealth there they did not attempt settlement. The Portuguese established Belém in 1616, and twenty-one years later, in 1637, Captain Pedro Teixeira sailed up and down the Amazon to solidify Portugal's claim.

The patterns of settlement and colonization of the Atlantic islands established many of the bases of Portugal's New World colony. There were differences, of course. The islands had been largely uninhabited. Officials had had to set ashore goats and sheep in the Azores, to multiply as a future source of food. To Madeira settlers brought livestock, including cows. They burned down the island's forests and planted wheat, although in time the soil became depleted and production fell. Along the coast of Africa, the Portuguese followed a different pattern. They established fortified trading centers, because they did not intend to found settlements. From their coastal outposts they traded in African slaves in collaboration with Arab merchants, wresting control of slaving from the Genoese. Bartolomeu Dias rounded the Cape of Good Hope in 1488. The consolidation of Portugal's empire was accomplished by King Manoel (1495–1521), who took the title "Lord of the Conquest, Navigation, and Commerce of Ethiopia, Arabia, Persia, and India." Manoel, who was a cousin of Ferdinand and Isabella of Spain, pressed on with Henry's work, though other European powers disparaged his mercantile emphasis. A rival, King François I of France, reputedly called Manoel the "grocer king," ignoring the reality that the Portuguese had few products to sell. But Manoel's efforts made Portugal the world's first overseas power.

Christopher Columbus himself sailed with the Portuguese to the Fortress of El Mina, on the Gold Coast of Africa. The Portuguese captain Vasco da Gama reached Goa in India in 1498. He was not the first foreigner to land in Asia seeking trade—Muslim merchants from as far away as Mecca regularly visited India—but he was the first European, and his voyage inaugurated the age of European imperialism in Asia. Unlike the Spanish in the New World, the Portuguese built their empire not through seizure of land and warfare but through negotiations with indigenous native rulers. What da Gama and his contemporary explorers did was little more than locate the key nodes of preexisting, sophisticated commercial networks, chart coastal and oceanic waters, and carve out small niches in those trade systems. The visitors did not make much of an impression on the rulers of the lands they visited, because they did not bring many goods with them that the Asians wanted. This would change only much later, after the advent in Europe of the Industrial Revolution, and the change would benefit neither Portugal nor Spain.

Portuguese ship captains had worried about the impact of Columbus's 1492 landfall, but they knew the size of the circumference of the earth and believed that the eastern route would be better for them, given their priorities. Voyages between Brazil and Lisbon took a month and a half or more, and the Portuguese did not have many ships they could divert from their main destination, the Far East. The New World was an afterthought; their first priorities were Africa, India, Japan, and the East Indies. During the 1540s, when the Spaniards were beginning to develop the rich silver mines of Potosí, in modern Bolivia, the Portuguese thought they would become Midases in their own right, with the discovery of gold in Portuguese Mozambique. Time proved them wrong, although vast amounts of gold were found in Brazil a century and a half later.

THE COLONIAL ERA

Portugal's thrust seaward emerged from a society in contraction. It had, like most of the rest of Europe, suffered intense population decline, especially because of the Black (bubonic) Plague, which began in 1347 (although by the fifteenth century the population of both Spain and Portugal was growing again). Still, fewer than two million people inhabited Portugal—a tiny base from which to launch an overseas empire. The country's aristocracy had become wealthy—although not on the scale of some Spanish aristocrats—but because it was convenient to buy manufactured goods from abroad, the nation never industrialized. Portugal's expulsion of all unbaptized Jews in 1497, under pressure from the Spanish crown, deprived it of part of its merchant class upon which it depended to take advantage of the investment opportunities offered by the Portuguese successes in the Far East. The strain of defending its far-flung empire proved too great; soon expenses began to outrun revenues, and Portugal retreated from the status of a great power. Portugal had been overwhelmed by its early success. By the sixteenth century, the Portuguese had been forced to become skillful manipulators and tightrope walkers.

Spanish and Portuguese government and society abruptly came together in 1580, when the Portuguese crown, previously held by the Braganças, passed by marriage to the Spanish royal family, the Hapsburgs. Spain's Philip II, the nephew of the former Portuguese king, became Philip I of Portugal. During this period of dual monarchy, which lasted sixty years, the two empires remained separate, and Spain permitted Portugal broad autonomy. Yet there were important consequences of the dynastic merger. Portugal received a new legal code, named after Philip and promulgated in 1603. Crown policy toward Brazil had changed abruptly in 1558, when authorities, realizing that the *donatário* (or captaincy) system would not work, sent a royal governor, Mem de Sá, to make coastal areas safe for sugar cane plantations and to enforce colonial regulations. Sá led a number of expeditions that drove back indigenous tribes, who were further decimated by European disease. Epidemics killed as many as one half of Brazil's native population in 1562–1563. Even a French colony of Huguenots near Rio de Janeiro in the 1560s failed in part because of the sickness of the colonists.

Officials in Lisbon, however, increased recruitment of Portuguese peasant emigrants to Brazil, and by the 1580s half of the estimated twenty-five thousand inhabitants of Portuguese Brazil were of European origin. The need for labor to work the coastal plantations led to increased raids on Indians in the interior—and to Jesuit efforts mentioned above to protect tribes by housing them in remote, fortified missions, where they would be instructed in Christian ritual and taught how to plant the land. Beginning in the 1570s, Brazilian agricultural producers stopped relying on raiding parties to capture Indians for forced labor; they began instead to import shiploads of Africans from their African trading posts. By 1600 Brazil had become dependent on slave labor; the most successful of the small, scattered colonies became vast plantations.

Only two of the crown's captaincies—Pernambuco in the northeast and São Vicente (later São Paulo) in the Central South—survived initially. Due mostly to lack of interest from the proprietors faced with the daunting task of paying for settlement, the others languished. One after another, they were returned to the crown. It was actions by residents of Brazil, not by Portugal, that made possible the exploration of the interior—even if for less than idealistic reasons. These explorers were the mixed-race *bandeirantes* (so named for their quasimilitary flags, or *bandeiras*), who, starting at the end of the sixteenth century, forged deep into the interior beyond São Vicente in search of indigenous slaves.

Overseas colonial administration was reorganized on the Spanish model. Spain's Roman Catholic Church pressured its less-aggressive

Portuguese counterpart to increase its missionary activities overseas. In 1580, the Inquisition was introduced to Brazil—with brutal conse-quences. The Portuguese navy was incorporated into the Spanish Ar-mada of 1588, and many of the Portuguese vessels were lost. Brazil remained a vast territory of undeveloped land, undistinguished cities that were more like towns, no schools or universities, and considerable miscegenation among natives, Africans, and the Portuguese officials and slaveowners. Overseas policy changed dramatically during the seven-teenth century, when gold was found in Brazil. Exports from the Brazil-ian colony fueled economic recovery in Portugal and encouraged reform of the colonial administration.

The union of the Iberian crowns had the effect of forming a new mili-tary alliance between Madrid and Lisbon but also exposing Portugal to new enmities, specifically from the Protestant Dutch, long enemies of Spain. The Dutch invasion of 1630, financed by the Dutch West India Company, proved to be the most extensive and longest-lasting incursion into colonial Brazil. It left various legacies, including the port of Recife and a revitalization of sugar cane production by technological innova-tion. The key to the Dutch success was the arrival in 1637 of Governor Johan Mauritz of Nassau-Siegen, Count Maurice of Nassau. Thirty-three years old when he came to Pernambuco, he had served in the Thirty Years' War (1618–1648) as a colonel, and he was related to the royal House of Orange. He came not only to be military commander but to construct what he called New Holland. He put Portuguese troops on the defensive, sending a force to drive them out of Pernambuco, and also organized a successful attack on the Portuguese slaveholding fortress of El Mina in West Africa. This gave the Dutch access to slaves, whom they imported to their New World colonies.

Portugal reacted angrily, sending a fleet of forty-six ships from Lisbon, along with eighteen Spanish galleons. The assault on Dutch Brazil was led by Dom Fernão de Mascarenhas, the Count of Torre, who, as Bailey W. Diffie has remarked, "was unfitted for the task but who was forced to assume it because of his high title and because nobody [else] wanted it."[4] Torre's troops went out of control once they landed in Salvador, raping and looting, and although Maurice's own forces were depleted, the Dutch prevailed. The Portuguese regrouped, however, and pressed their attack, aided by *moradores* (landless rural renters) nominally subject to the Dutch in southern Pernambuco and by the arrival of reinforce-ments. In this year a revolt in Lisbon had placed the Bragança dynasty back in power, spurring anti-Spanish (and pro-Portuguese) feeling in Brazil. War between Spain and Portugal from 1640 to 1668 furthered the development of Brazilian nationalism.

The Dutch revitalized Pernambuco. They built their capital city, Recife, on the European model, paving streets and public squares with stone. Nassau established orchards and a zoological garden, and he inaugurated a museum for Brazilian artifacts, especially carvings in regional hardwoods. He invited to Brazil several scientists (including George Marcgrave and Willem Piso) and the distinguished painters Frans Post and Albert Eckhout, who painted dozens of scenes showing Brazilian life, not only its people but its flora and fauna. Until the nineteenth century, there were no scientific or naturalistic observations of Brazil superior to those done under Count Maurice's direction. Dutch engineers improved the water supply and made other improvements in urban facilities. Cartographers made maps of Recife and the Bahian coast, including its fortifications. Sugar was now shipped directly to the United Provinces. Recife, under Nassau, became one of the most important, and most cosmopolitan, cities in the Western Hemisphere.

Englishmen and some Protestant Frenchmen were permitted to reside in Dutch Pernambuco, and in some cases they married into prominent Brazilian families. A large number of Germans and some Poles served as mercenary soldiers. Danes and Swedes also served in the Dutch forces. Still, relations between the different groups were anxious at best. At least a thousand Dutch Jews, whose ancestors had gone in the 1490s from Spain and Portugal to Holland, migrated to the colony after it was secured by Dutch forces. They were Sephardic (Western European) Jews, and because their language, Ladino, was derived from classical Spanish (though written in Hebrew letters), they adapted easily to Brazil. Since they learned Portuguese and also spoke Dutch, the Sephardim proved invaluable as intermediaries between Dutch officials and the Luso-Brazilians. The Jews were permitted freedom of worship, although both Catholic and Calvinist clergy angrily protested. "The Israelites," a Catholic group protested, have "open synagogues, which even the Moors and Turks find scandalous."[5] Jews who accepted baptism (known as New Christians) faced prejudice even greater than that directed at practicing Jews. When the Portuguese regained control, the Jews were expelled from Brazil. Part of the exiled community were to take refuge in British-owned Jamaica and the remainder in Peter Stuyvesant's New Amsterdam, an enterprise like Recife, of the Dutch West India Company.

Nassau seized sugar plantations abandoned by their Portuguese owners and put them up for auction. Dutch merchants provided credit to the new *senhores de engenho* and helped them rebuild and purchase new slaves. Nassau appointed a municipal council to handle local administration and to oversee links with the outlying captured territories of Alagoas, Paraíba, Rio Grande do Norte, and Itamaracá. He established a court system and collected taxes. He also punished Dutch soldiers who stole from or injured members of the local population and he set limits on interest rates for loans. Nassau ordered planters to cultivate manioc to allay food shortages, and on his own estate he planted citrus trees, coconut palms, figs, and pomegranates. Nassau permitted religious freedom in Pernambuco, although when his troops captured Maranhão in 1641 he prohibited freedom of worship there after protests from Calvinist ministers in Holland and in Recife. He earned a high degree of popularity, and when rumors surfaced in 1642 that he would be returning to Europe, many local leading residents asked him to stay.

The occupation of Pernambuco drove up the price of African slaves, although within a decade (and especially by 1654, when Caribbean sugar began to cut sharply into Brazilian sugar profits) the *bandeirantes* gave up slave hunting. Instead, they began searching for precious minerals, not only gold nuggets but emeralds, diamonds, and silver, which had been rumored to exist in the deep interior. Officials in Lisbon, anxious to gain new sources of revenue, encouraged immigration and offered bounties to successful prospectors. *Bandeirante* expeditions, accompanied by slaves and soldiers of fortune, traveled north and west into Mato Grosso, the Amazon, and in the north, the arid *sertão*. *Bandeirante* groups reached Peru and explored much of the Amazon basin. Now known as *paulistas* (residents of São Paulo the successor colony to São Vicente), by the end of the seventeenth century, expeditions searched and pillaged the interior on an almost continual basis. They attacked religious missions whenever convenient, and they plundered from one another. Because of a shortage of European women race mixture was very high, and the *paulistas* learned to speak Tupi-Guaraní. Poverty fueled many of the expeditions: sugar cane did not flourish in the temperate climate, and there were few other ways of making a living. Some *paulistas*—especially Fernão Dias Pais, who led a seven-year trek through south-central Brazil beginning in 1674, were wealthy, having profited from selling Indian slaves. Dias Pais's expedition however was a failure. Many of his men died from hunger, fighting, or disease, and he hanged one of his own sons for attempted mutiny. Later, after gold and diamonds were discovered in the 1690s in the territory that would become known as Minas Gerais, the knowledge gathered by Dias Pais and others made it much easier to open up the region.

The shortage of indigenous laborers in Brazil and the expansion of exports (sugar, cacao—which grew wild throughout the interior—tobacco, and gold and diamonds in the eighteenth century) led colonial officials in Brazil, unconcerned with the legal status of its underclass, to rely increasingly on the captive Africans imported from their overseas trading centers. The Jesuit theologian Luis de Molina argued in 1592 that in the context of natural (and Roman) law, men had the right to "enslave themselves." Blacks, whom Molina called "Aethopians," could legitimately be taken as captives in warfare, and their children could be enslaved to punish their parents. Molina deplored the fact that the slave trade often was conducted violently, but this, he suggested, was also true of war and "other undertakings." Francisco Suárez, drawing on Molina in a book published in 1614 at Coimbra, took his argument further, reconciling it with the orthodoxy of St. Thomas Aquinas and arguing that both "human" and "natural" law permitted slavery. These attitudes were shared by Brazilian *senhores de engenhos* and other landowners, who believed that their slaves were varieties of dumb animals, "to be inventoried and named like horses, oxen or cattle."

Although they did not challenge the right of Europeans to possess slaves, the Jesuits who came to the New World considered Africans and Indians worthy of salvation and therefore acted to protect them from mistreatment. The Jesuits as well as other religious orders forged a chain of missions across the continent until they were expelled in the eighteenth century. Native peoples of the New World did not always easily acquiesce to foreign domination: they played off European rivalries to further their ends against traditional enemies, and they proved inconstant allies to Europeans.

Both Spanish America and Brazil developed economies based on extractive wealth from the land; neither colonial system encouraged or even permitted the growth of industry, a legacy that each of the new Latin American countries would feel heavily after independence. During Brazil's first hundred years as a Portuguese territory, it remained crown policy to send criminals and other undesirables there, and as a result Brazil—like Australia two centuries later—became popularly known as a place inhabited by malefactors. Spanish America, which strictly excluded anyone not meeting narrow definitions of worthiness, did not suffer the same reputation.

Plantation life was "hell," wrote Father Andrés de Gouveia in 1627, but it was from land worked by slaves that the economy and society of Brazil unfolded.[6] Tobacco was the main product exchanged for slave cargoes. Foreigners continued to covet Brazil's wealth and considered its setting a kind of Eden, so much so that in his first edition of *Robinson Crusoe*, the seventeenth-century English writer Daniel Defoe cast his main character as an English owner of a Brazilian plantation ship-wrecked en route to Africa to bring back slaves.

Slave vessels transported men and women under conditions so appalling that the ships were called *tumbeiros* (hearses). Slavers considered it so desirable to pack their ships that up to half of the slaves died before landing, although the decision seems to have made little economic sense. In Brazil, slavery lasted until late in the nineteenth century, by which time millions of mixed-race lower-class Brazilians had formed an underclass who would inherit manual labor as the bondsmen grew older but could no longer be replaced because traffic in slaves had been forcibly halted by pressure from foreign governments, principally Great Britain. In Spanish America, the colonial labor system, based on exploitation of village-centered Indian labor, evolved over time into the system of debt peonage, which still survives.

In the closing decades of the sixteenth century and into the seventeenth, Brazilian colonial expansion proceeded well beyond the line drawn by the Tordesillas treaty. Brazilian port cities, especially Salvador, became emporiums for silks from the Orient, spices, African ivory, and manufactured goods from western Europe. Peripheral regions were sparsely peopled except by their indigenous populations, and thus they were ripe for picking, as sources not only of natives to enslave but of land that was virtually free. In the North, the Portuguese displaced the French and their Indian allies, and they asserted control over the lower Amazon basin. Expansion in the South came a century later, although most of the *Banda Oriental*, as the territory north of the La Plata estuary is known, became Spanish. Expansion in the North led in 1621 to the formation of a separate administrative entity—the state of Maranhão—formed from the consolidation of several crown captaincies, including Ceará, Pará, and Maranhão. There was little direct contact between São Luis, the administrative center of the new northern territory, and the rest of the colony, which received the name "State of Brazil." A century later, the two parts of the colony were reunited, following decades of internal competition among the diverse captaincies of the south, especially between Pernambuco, the crown captaincy of Bahia, and Rio de Janeiro. In

1720, the governor-general in Salvador became a viceroy, although his office was never given the same all-encompassing powers as his counterparts in the Spanish New World empire. A generation later, in 1750, Spain and Portugal signed the Treaty of Madrid. The agreement abandoned the Treaty of Tordesillas, endorsing instead the principle of *uti possidetis*, recognition of territorial rights on the basis of what had been settled and occupied to that date. The treaty gave Portugal control over more than half of South America and set the boundaries, with only minor later modifications, of Brazil as they are today.[7] This foundation of administrative stability was followed in 1755 by economic decrees that integrated the outlying regions, especially the northern captaincies, into the transatlantic trading system.

GOLD, SMUGGLING, AND FUGITIVE SLAVES

The new century saw modest growth in urban settlements that would pave the way for a gradual shift in population from the countryside to cities, a shift that would accelerate for centuries. Between 1532 and 1650 six cities and thirty-one towns, or *vilas*, were established, mostly along the coast between Olinda and Santos. To the north, Natal (1599), São Luis (1615) and Belém (1616) were also established. Later, after the discovery of gold in Minas Gerais, urban development began to occur in the interior as well. Stuart B. Schwartz calls the result of the peculiar process of Brazilian urban growth not a network of cities but an "archipelago of ports, each surrounded by its own agricultural hinterland and in closer contact with Lisbon than with each other."[8] Had Brazil been part of the Spanish American colonial system, it would have been subdivided into viceroyalties and captaincies-general, which would likely have led in the nineteenth century to the creation of several independent nations. Instead, the loose but flexible ties between Brazil's diverse colonial units and the mother country served as a strong factor in the remarkable ability of Brazil to remain unified after the withdrawal of the Portuguese and the collapse of the colonial system.

Although slaveowners paid bounties for the return of escaped slaves (and sometimes beat the runaways to death as an example to the others), many slaves continued to flee the hellish life of the plantations. When they could, small groups of fugitive slaves banded together in runaway communities called *quilombos* (or *mocambos*). The longest-lived one was in Palmares, in present-day Alagaos; it was so well defended that neither the Dutch nor the Luso-Brazilians could dislodge them for nearly eighty years, from 1607 to 1695. The Palmares *quilombo* represented a safe haven and a remarkable experiment in outlaw communal living, but it was the only one of its scale known to have existed. The reason was that land-owners and officials, in response to the military failures to subdue and destroy the community, trained a new kind of professional slave hunter—the *capitães do mato*, or bush captains, ruthless men who knew the hinterland intimately.

The escaped *quilombo* slaves had to defend themselves against pursuit. They maintained surreptitious contact with slaves still in captivity, as well as with *forros* (free blacks) and merchants willing to supply them. Nor were the *quilombos* populated only by Africans: their communities included natives, people of mixed race, and whites. More than 160 such *quilombos* are known to have existed in Minas Gerais; in Goiás, fugitive slaves panned for gold and used it to buy their freedom. In Mato Grosso, the process of establishing *quilombos* in the far reaches of that wild and underdeveloped territory helped expand Brazil's frontier in the far west. In Rio Grande do Sul, *quilombos* ringed towns and cities throughout the southern province. In Bahia, cassava planters actually hired residents of nearby *quilombos* as laborers. In the city of Salvador, fugitive slaves plotted with others to rebel against colonial authorities. *Quilombos* survived into the nineteenth century in Pernambuco, where divisions among the elites hindered attempts to subdue them. Throughout the twentieth century, descendants in still-surviving Amazonian communities remember in oral histories stories of the flights of their slave ancestors.

More common were the cases of slave men and women who were freed by their owners. Although the annual rates of manumission were very low—in many cases, the slaves freed were those not considered likely to be good workers, such as slaves who had been badly injured or simply frail with age—by 1805, two-thirds of the free population of the province of Minas Gerais were nonwhite.

Brazil's coastal towns and cities were often attacked by pirates, who plied the shores looking for merchant ships. The most successful was Bartholomew Roberts ("Black Bart"), a British naval officer who turned pirate in 1719 after being captured off West Africa, and who successfully attacked Portuguese ships in the harbor of Bahia de Todos os Santos.

Invariably, economic interest determined Portuguese policy on slavery, labor, and commerce. Colonial officials attempted to increase output in Minas Gerais and counter smuggling out of gold, and therefore to raise revenues. Officials dispatched troops and hired *capitães do mato* and bands of *mulatos* and free blacks to pursue smugglers and to seal off the

mining region from the rest of the colony. In 1720, when rioting broke
out in Vila Rica do Ouro Preto against the annual royal gold tax, the tax
was reduced from 20 to 12 percent; as a result, more gold was handed
in through official channels. This worked for a while, but gold smuggling
became more highly organized, and in 1733 the tax was raised back to
20 percent. The new governor of Minas Gerais announced a tax on slaves
and closed smelting houses where contrabanders melted down their nuggets, dust, and other forms of the mineral. The new tax hit struggling
prospectors harder than the rich, and farmers complained that they had
to pay whether their slaves were good workers or infirm. Efforts to increase crown revenue, then, backfired in the mining area.

The lure of instant wealth not only increased smuggling and extralegal
activity in the mining region but led to harsher efforts to suppress outbreaks of rebelliousness among slaves. In 1719, the governor of the province of Minas Gerais, Count Pedro de Almeida, wrote to the Chief
Magistrate of Sabará, near Ouro Preto, encouraging further restrictions
on slaves who were being put to work as miners under frontier conditions which were considerably different from those on plantations:

> Without severe punishment against the blacks it could happen one
> day that this captaincy shall become a pitiable stage for their evil
> deeds and that which occurred at Palmares in Pernambuco will be
> repeated: or even worse[,] for the freedom which the blacks of this
> captaincy have [is] unlike that in the other parts of America, cer-
> tainly it is not true slavery the manner in which they live today as
> it more appropriately can be called licentious liberty.

The gold rush had a profound impact on the Brazilian colony and its
administration. It also altered the quality of life. The need to provide
food and services to the burgeoning population provided economic opportunities and rewarded those successful in entrepreneurship. Life in
cities and even small towns centered around the town square, where
weekly outdoor markets were held and the church or chapel was constructed. (In many small towns there were no priests except for those
who traveled in circuits, visiting a given town every year or so to perform, sometimes after the fact, weddings, baptisms, and other sacraments.)

When the gold began to be depleted, other social changes resulted.
People who were restless picked up and journeyed into the further
reaches of the interior, looking for wealth and the chance to strike it rich.

Manumissions of slaves increased after the decline in gold mining, in part because slaveowners no longer wanted the burden of caring for slaves who were unproductive. Women were more likely to free their slaves than were men, even though married women had more limited control over their property; Portuguese law made men heads of their households and the managers of joint property, the *bens do casal*. Slave women as well as men could purchase their freedom. Since their tasks were on the whole less arduous than those of men, many of whom died toiling in the mines after only a few years of work, some women were able to accumulate enough capital to buy their freedom.

Portugal restricted trade to its own nationals, although unlike Spain it permitted Portuguese merchants to grant licenses to ships of other nations, and to a certain extent it allowed foreign investment in commercial ventures. Portugal lacked a large merchant fleet and had always relied on the English for shipping. A Dutch invasion fleet of twenty-six ships in 1623 under Admiral Pieter Pieterszoon Heyn attacked and secured control of Bahia, although in 1624 the province was recaptured by a combined Spanish-Portuguese fleet. Heyn moved on to the West Indies, and thereafter the Dutch presence was limited to Pernambuco.

In some ways, Brazil had caught up administratively with its Spanish American neighbors by the end of the colonial era. Both imperial systems underwent, in the name of efficiency, reform that benefited not only peninsular elites but the native-born upper class. But in comparison, Spanish America seemed glittering, and Brazil a backwater. Its cities were small, undistinguished architecturally (except for the gilded churches constructed in the wake of the eighteenth-century gold boom), and devoid of high culture.

NATIONAL IDENTITY

Expeditions into the interior from the Portuguese settlements on the coast led to the eventual occupation of over half of South America's land area and forged the basis of Brazil's national identity. It is telling that in contrast to the colonial experiences of the other European powers in the hemisphere, much of the exploration of Brazil was led by mixed-blood Americans (*mamelucos*), operating more on their own than as agents of peninsular authorities. Some became Indian hunters, navigating by canoe over the winding rivers inland from the south-central colony of São Vicente to capture indigenous peoples as slaves, and also to search for nuggets of gold, which had been found in sporadic locations. São Vicente had been founded in 1532 when the Portuguese, led by Martim Afonso de Sousa, drove French settlers from the coast. The crown sought to consolidate further its hold on the land and to spur settlement by granting its use to Portuguese entrepreneurs (*donatários*), but most of the economic ventures failed except for the sugar plantations established in northeastern Pernambuco. In the rest of Brazil, the frontier was too remote for Lisbon to control, and as a result it became a cauldron of people—prospectors, fortune hunters, runaway communities of escaped African slaves, gypsies, New Christians, and other fugitives. As late as 1790, even those in the ruling administrative class who were not Portuguese born still considered themselves primarily Portuguese. The inhabitants of Brazil were seen as members of separate ethnic and economic groups—Indians, black slaves, free blacks, mulattos, *caboclos* (mixtures of Indians, Africans, and Caucasians), newcomers (mostly Portuguese peasants), and members of "good families," as they were called, the upper-class elite. Men and women of high birth but born in Brazil held lower status than the Portuguese-born officials sent by the crown, but the angry *creole-peninsular* division that existed in the Spanish American colonies was less strongly felt in Brazil. Still, some residents of Brazil, merchants as well as intellectuals aware of the American and French revolutions, began to think about separation from Portugal. This did not mean that a Brazilian national identity had yet developed. Still, when events in Europe during the first decade of the nineteenth century forced colonial elites to decide on their loyalties, the sense of being Brazilian developed quite quickly.

NOTES

1. Betty Mindlin and Suruí narrators, *Unwritten Stories of the Suruí Indians of Rondônia* (Austin: Institute of Latin American Studies), 65.

2. Dauril Alden, "Late Colonial Brazil," in Leslie Bethell, ed., *Cambridge History of Latin America*, Vol. II. (Cambridge: Cambridge University Press, 1984), 612.

3. Pero Vaz de Caminha, account to King Manoel, quoted by Francisco Maria Pires Teixeira, *História Concisa do Brasil* (São Paulo: Global, 1993), 24.

4. Bailey W. Diffie, *A History of Colonial Brazil, 1500–1792* (Malabar, FL: Robert E. Krieger, 1987), 230–31.

5. Anonymous source cited by Diffie, 242.

6. Father Gouveia, 1627 letter in the Arquivo Nacional Torre do

Tombo (Lisbon), cited by Stuart B. Schwartz, "Plantations and Peripheries, c. 1580 c. 1750," in Bethell, ed., 67.

7. Frédéric Mauro, "Political and Economic Structures of Empire, 1580–1750," in Bethell, ed.,

8. Schwartz, 127–28.

3

Independence and Empire (1822–1889)

Nothing like the insurrections and civil wars in the name of independence that convulsed Spanish America occurred in Brazil. When Portuguese rebels in 1820 ousted the regency in Lisbon and convoked a liberal parliament, the new government attempted to tighten the colonial ties with Brazil, which had weakened now that the royal family lived in Rio de Janeiro. The British, fearing loss of their own influence over Portugal and Brazil, advised João VI to return to Europe. In April 1821 he did so, taking three thousand members of his court but leaving his twenty-three-year-old son Pedro behind, reputedly advising him to accept the local throne if the Brazilians demanded independence.

When the Lisbon parliament demanded that Pedro return as well, he refused. On September 7, 1822, at Ypiranga, in São Paulo, Pedro, after seeking counsel from members of the Brazilian elite, dramatically threw his sword to the ground and shouted "Independence or death!" Bloodshed occurred only in Bahia, where Portuguese troops resisted, but they were driven off by a small fleet lead by British admiral Lord Cochrane. On December 1, 1822, Pedro was crowned emperor of Brazil.

Most Brazilians remained unaware of who governed Brazil. Elites amounted to a tiny proportion of the overall population, which was made up of African and Brazilian-born blacks and persons of intermediate race—*pardos, mulatos,* and *cabras,* individuals with one black parent and one mulatto parent. These people worked from the time they could walk until they were old and infirm. There were virtually no schools for them; they had no way of learning about the world except through tales told by outsiders. These were few and far between; most Brazilians grew and died without ever traveling more than a few kilometers from their places of birth.

Even for members of the elite, the changes in the eighteenth century— which were significant—did little to impart a strong sense of nationhood. All Portuguese subjects, even those who enjoyed high social standing and personal affluence, were limited and circumscribed by colonial restrictions. When a printing press was brought to Rio de Janeiro in 1749, with the approval of the local governor, word reached Lisbon, and the press was immediately ordered confiscated. Nor had there been a sense of colonial unity. Under the Portuguese system, there had been at least two Brazils, cut off from one another and only loosely governed from Portugal. The most practical way to send a letter from northern Maranhão to the royal city of Salvador or to towns farther south was via ship to Portugal, then another ship to its final destination. Other places in Portuguese America were almost as completely cut off from the royal capital, which in 1763 was moved to Rio de Janeiro because the Minas gold rush had made it necessary to fortify the port and the roads leading to it lest the riches from the interior be entirely smuggled away without payment of the crown's share.

Brazilians lower down the social ladder had more reasons to object to the preeminent position of the *reinóis,* the Portuguese-born residents who dominated commerce and government. Placards placed on walls in Salvador in 1798 implored city residents to rise up against Portugal and impose "social and racial equality." This movement, dubbed the "Conspiracy of the Tailors," led to the arrest and punishment of its leaders, most of whom were men of mixed race. The conspiracy was thus not only a plot against Portugal but a challenge to the privileged minority. One of the conspirators was Lucas Dantas. Responding to news about events in revolutionary France, he had defended the idea of declaring Brazil a republic: "It is so that we can breathe free, since we live oppressed, and because we are mulattoes we are not admitted to any Posts; with a Republic there will be equality for all." Another confederate, João de Deus do Nascimento, argued that once Brazilians embraced the principles of the French Revolution, "all would be rich, released from the misery in which they were living[,] . . . [and] discrimination between white, black, and mulatto [would be] abolished."

THE END OF THE COLONIAL ERA

On the whole, plots against the crown were few and far between. Without exception they sought at most regional autonomy, not national independence. This was even true for the *Inconfidencia Mineira* (1788–1789), a failed conspiracy that led to the execution of its leader, Tiradentes. There was the Revolt of the Tailors, and in Pernambuco the Suassuna Revolt, but neither sought independence for Brazil. In the circum-Caribbean, sixty-two known slave rebellions and conspiracies occurred between August 1789 and December 1815, in contrast to Brazil, where except for a few small insurrections in the province of Bahia there were virtually none. Still, the years between 1808, when the Portuguese royal court unexpectedly arrived in person at Rio de Janeiro, and 1820, when there occurred a rising in Porto in the mother country, led to profound changes in the psychology of the elite residents of the Brazilian colony. They realized that their status would always be secondary to the Portuguese, even when the guests, who had overstayed their welcome, finally departed. "The appeal of the nation-state." writes Roderick J. Barman, "was the appeal of power."[1]

An external event set into motion the steps that over the course of nearly two decades would lead to independence: Napoleon Bonaparte's invasion of the Iberian peninsula in 1807. Protected by a British naval escort, King João VI Alcântara de Bragança e Bourbon and his son Pedro fled to Brazil to escape capture, the fate of Spanish king Ferdinand VII. Once the royal family landed in Brazil, the clock could not be turned back. Rio de Janeiro emerged as a major port, and as a result of a treaty signed in 1810 with London was opened to foreign trade. British policy, which preferred to trade with the Portuguese New World as a single bloc, more than anything else gave would-be regional dissidents pause, in strong contradistinction to the Spanish viceroyalties. Central America split off from Mexico, Paraguay and Uruguay from Argentina, Bolivia and Chile from Peru, and Bolívar's Gran Colombia, despite the Liberator's passionate desire for unity, split up into Venezuela, Colombia, and Ecuador.

The "transmigration," as it became known, irrevocably changed relations between Portugal and its Brazilian colony. The Napoleonic invasion undermined the stability of Portugal and bankrupted its treasury. Brazil, safe under the protection of the British navy, suddenly became the favored site within the empire. As a result, a wave of Portuguese merchants and farmers emigrated to the New World—not from the elite, as in the past, but from groups that would form the basis for the Brazilian "middle sectors," the forerunners of the middle class that would emerge decades later. When the Portuguese Court delayed its return from Brazil, officials in Lisbon became hostile to Brazil, speaking with scorn of its backwardness and its multiracial population, and refusing to ship tax receipts to Brazil. This, in turn, helped create in the colony a sense of Brazilian nationalism, paving the way for feelings of cultural pride, a psychological requirement if any political break was to be countenanced. The polarization of attitudes was fueled by hostility to the new arrivals from Portugal, especially *mascates* (peddlers), as the immigrant merchant class came to be derisively called.

Mercantilist controls were lifted, in deference to the English; the first printing press was brought to Brazil, and imported goods flooded the country, dooming efforts to stimulate manufacturing. Meanwhile, the rest of Brazil chafed under domination from Rio de Janeiro. The royal government there taxed merchants and attempted to collect revenues from the outlying provinces, actions that provoked discontent. Beginning in 1817 this situation provoked a series of abortive rebellions against the crown, all of which sought regional autonomy, not national independence for Brazil. In addition, Argentina, newly independent, annexed the southernmost Brazilian territory, formerly part of Rio Grande do Sul but now known as the Cisplatine Province. In 1828, this territory became independent Uruguay, created with British approval as a buffer between Argentina and Brazil.

Wise leadership exercised by João VI led initially to economic stability. When he came to Brazil, he had brought with him the royal treasury, valued at twenty-two million pounds. Within months of his arrival he established a central bank, replacing gold and silver with printed banknotes, which he used to finance military actions against the Spanish in the south. When he returned to Portugal, the bank was liquidated, and its deficit became Brazil's national debt.

The price Portugal paid to the British for taking the royal family out of harm's way was the 1810 trade treaty opening Brazilian ports. Britain received the exclusive right to build and repair ships in Brazil and to purchase timber. The island of Santa Catarina was made a free port, to facilitate trade with the La Plata region, and a monthly shipping service between Falmouth and Rio de Janeiro was established. João, the prince regent, still in need of British protection, had no option but to agree. Portugal now faced sharply declining revenues from the Brazil trade and could not afford to renew its merchant fleet. New trade duties discriminated against Portugal in favor of Britain—a moot point, because the Portuguese had few manufactured goods to supply its colony. In 1815, Dom João VI (who governed in the name of his mentally incapacitated mother, Queen Maria) elevated Brazil from the colonial status of *estado* (state) to *reino*, or kingdom. The court sought to impose a national culture that would preserve the traditions of Portuguese tutelage while stirring feelings of pride in being Brazilian. This effort was rooted in the Romantic nationalism of early nineteenth-century Europe. One of João's first acts was to construct professional schools, patterned after French models. In 1816, he invited a delegation of French artists to Rio de Janeiro to help found a school of fine arts. What Brazil's elites wanted, of course, was to transplant French culture while maintaining the social distinctions that had prevailed before the great French Revolution.

In 1816, two-thirds of the transatlantic vessels that anchored at Rio de Janeiro were foreign, 113 of them British. More Portuguese ships than foreign came to Salvador, but within five years foreign ships greatly outnumbered Portuguese vessels in all Brazilian ports. Brazil remained politically a part of the Portuguese empire, but economically it had been granted independence whether it liked it or not. Moreover, Britain was in effective control of Portugal. British troops were stationed there, the commander of the Portuguese armed forces was Marshal W. C. Beresford, and a British minister, Charles Stuart, presided over the Council of Regency in Lisbon.

INDEPENDENCE

Brazil's population a year following its unilateral declaration of independence in 1822 was less than three million, including 1.2 million African slaves. Given the country's tiny population for its size and the strength of regional separatism in neighboring Spanish America, it is remarkable that Brazil did not go the way of Bolívar's Gran Colombia or the United Provinces of Central America (which broke away from Mexico only to divide into five tiny nations in the 1820s). There were strong pressures for regional autonomy in Brazil and even for republicanism and independence, but the country held together under the imperial monarchy.

Following the Duke of Wellington's victory over Napoleon at Waterloo, the city of Rio de Janeiro was designated the capital of the Kingdom of Portugal, Brazil, and the Algarve, while Portugal's nobility implored the Bragança royal family to return home, presumably to revoke the formal equality for Brazil that had grudgingly been established. Maria I, known as the "mad queen," died in 1816; two years later her son, João VI, was crowned monarch of Portugal and its empire before returning to Lisbon on April 25, 1821. The coronation had far-reaching effects on Brazil. Six months later, the Portuguese *côrtes* (parliament) voted to abolish the Kingdom of Brazil and to restore the former colonial system. In January 1822, João's son and heir, Prince Regent Pedro I, declared himself emperor of Brazil rather than obey the *côrtes* and sail to Portugal to continue his education. José Bonifácio de Andrada e Silva, a Brazilian-born member of the elite, was named head of the new government. By preserving the royal dynasty, Brazil achieved independence without the legacy of revolution suffered by every Spanish colony in the hemisphere save Cuba and Puerto Rico.

The political autonomy that resulted from the emperor's decision to remain in Brazil did not amount to independence, although it did produce a new flag, and in 1824 a national constitution and formal recognition by the United States and by a year later, Portugal and Great Britain. Moreover, the failure in Europe in the 1820s of the principles of the French Revolution, and the victory in many European countries of the forces of reaction against the notion of popular sovereignty, helped dampen the spirit of the Enlightenment among the tiny number of members of the Brazilian elite who had been sympathetic to its ideas. Still, Brazil's new leaders put their faith in moderate constitutional monarchy, with Great Britain being the model, not the reactionary post-1820 Hapsburg regimes on the continent.

The 1824 constitution created a centralized government and divided the country into provinces governed by officials (called "presidents") named by the emperor. The constitution also gave the emperor the *poder moderador*, the right to veto legislation and even dissolve the parliament when he saw fit. Senators were named for life, the emperor received the right to create titles of nobility, only the lower house was elected, and only males holding property could vote.

The events of 1822 led to sixty-seven years of stable government under a monarchy headed by the heirs of the Portuguese Bragança dynasty. Brazil, in contrast to the new Spanish American republics, developed effective bureaucratic institutions, backed by a cohesive elite and by military commanders who until late in the nineteenth century were content to permit civilians to govern. The imperial government ruled in centralized fashion while forging ties of clientage to regional and local interests. Brazil's empire was in fact an unusually successful experiment in government by which a constitutional monarchy developed political institutions not much different from those of Great Britain, except for the lack of emphasis or personal rights or common law.

The small Brazilian elite that embraced independence under these conditions held the same notions about monarchy as did the elites of Spain, Austria, Italy, most of the German states, and even England during the first part of the nineteenth century. They rejected republicanism as too radical; they clung instead to the divine right of kings. They enjoyed the trappings of royalty, including the creation of Brazilian titles of nobility, given by the monarch to subjects he personally deemed worthy. This attitude represented both an accommodation to the new spirit of national modernization and continuity with the *ancien regime* of colonialism. The men who set up Brazil's constitutional monarchy were economic, not political, liberals; they considered the democratic ideas of the French and American revolutions irrelevant to Brazil or worse. They saw their emperor as a caring father figure, and they likely looked askance at the civil wars and near anarchy that afflicted many of their newly independent Spanish-American republican neighbors.

For the members of the affluent upper class—outnumbered ten to one by Brazilians of color—life during the Empire was comfortable and elegant, in a very European fashion. "Scarcely an English brig had docked since 1808 at any major Brazilian port—Rio de Janeiro, Bahia or Pernambuco—without its cargoes of English china, glassware, fabric, copper, iron and hardware, mostly for household and kitchen use. Black, grey, white articles—vivid colors were rare. The carboniferously industrial West was driving Oriental archaism out of the Brazilian market, along with its glowing colors, its reds, yellows and bright blues. These steadily became plebeian, rustic or unfashionable."[2] Wealthy Brazilians imported not only furniture from Europe but paintings, usually somber landscapes. They darkened rooms with heavy brocaded drapery, arranged piano and embroidery lessons for their daughters, and as much as possible ignored the gaudy, loud (and dirty) world of the street.

Upper-class women ran their households and received little formal education. The overwhelming majority of women in Brazil were poor, working alongside men in the fields or spending day after day weaving or spinning or grinding manioc or working as domestics or prostitutes.

Life for poor women was harsh and unrelenting. It was the usual pattern to bear children continually, and many women died in childbirth. Upper-class women, because they were banned from participation in public life, used their influence on men to pursue change. This encouraged a culture of gossip and intrigue among the leading families, although it appears that a sexual double standard prevailed: elite men kept mistresses and caroused with *mulatas*, whereas their wives generally did not have op-portunities for sexual liaisons.

Historians have traditionally claimed that by the first part of the nine-teenth century, arable land had become so scarce in parts of Brazil, es-pecially the Northeast, that members of the rural aristocracy enjoyed near-monopolistic control over land use. New research, however, has shown that even in agricultural districts as densely settled as Bahia's Recôncavo, abundant room for agricultural expansion existed. Beyond the Recôncavo, moreover, and beyond most established agricultural zones in Brazil, vast stretches of land were only sparsely populated, and homesteading by squatters became increasingly prevalent as the need for food staples in towns and cities grew. During the Minas gold boom, both sides of the long São Francisco River became sites for small and large livestock ranches; in the nineteenth century, farms and ranches sprouted up along the dusty trails plied by muleteers, alongside the new railroads, and on the outskirts of urban areas. Plantations continued to grow sugar, coffee, cotton, and cacao for export—indeed, profits from these exports contributed to the growth of railroads, port improvements, and even-tually utility systems and roads. Small producers of dairy products, cas-sava, black beans, rice, and cattle by-products also expanded their output, their trade linking the countryside with the cities and providing economic opportunity for many.

Political change proceeded with some bumps but on the whole in a smooth fashion. As a constitutional monarch, Pedro I outlived his wel-come. He launched a war against Argentina to regain the Cisplatine province, only to lose it when Uruguay became independent in 1828. He became unpopular for a host of reasons, not the least was his unfaith-fulness to his wife, the Empress Leopoldinha. In 1831, anti-Portuguese sentiment directed at merchants led to a bottle-throwing riot known as the *garrafada*. Incidents such as these helped define a nascent sense of Brazilian identity. The emperor's growing ambivalence toward Brazil, and his desire to return to Portugal to assume its throne led in April 1831 to his abdication in favor of his five-year-old son, the future Pedro II. Control of the government shifted to a regency of three members of the elite. Its members (Padre Diogo Feijó, Aureliano Coutinho, and the journalist Evaristo da Veiga) managed the affairs of state until the boy was crowned, at the age of fifteen, as emperor on July 18, 1841.

Political life under the regency was dominated by two rival elite factions, the moderates (dubbed *chimangos*) and their rivals, the *exaltados*. They disagreed over the powers of the central government but, as members of the same small elite, otherwise had much in common with one another. One reason was that leading members of both groups were given titles of nobility, including Honório Hermeto Carneiro Leão, who became the Marquis of Paraná, and Antônio Francisco de Paula e Holanda Cavalcanti de Albuquerque, later Viscount Albuquerque.

Not all was peaceful. In northeast Brazil, a fierce civil war between 1835 and 1841 known as the *Cabanagem* (or War of the Cabanas) leaving thirty thousand dead, was the bloodiest uprising in Brazilian history. It involved a slave insurrection and, before it ended, had turned into a race war. Because the rebellion was considered by the imperial government as a rising of people of color, the repression was particularly brutal. For a generation after the *Cabanagem*'s end, Indians in the region were pressed into forced labor gangs and deprived of their tribal independence. This would sow the seeds for still more repression of the Indian way of life as time passed.

THE AGE OF PEDRO II

By mid-century, the Empire of Brazil achieved a stable organization that would survive for another four decades. Pedro II, declared to be of age to govern when he turned fifteen, started a long and seemingly untroubled reign that would stretch to 1889. The defeat of regionalist uprisings in 1842 ushered in political calm and a tacit agreement among elites that the nation-state was paramount. The expiration of Brazil's commercial treaty with Great Britain ended the extraterritorial rights and commercial privileges held by foreign states, although Britain continued to dominate Brazilian commerce for another two generations. In 1849 a major new regional insurrection would break out, the Praieira revolt in Pernambuco, in some ways linked to the outbreak of revolutions across Europe a year before. But the Praieira was subdued, the national government enforced the ban on the slave trade demanded by London, and Brazil's success against dictator Juan Manuel de Rosas in Argentina consolidated its southern borders and gave it the status of a hemispheric power. Brazil now set out on its own, independent course of national development.

By the 1860s, Brazil had achieved a maturity in self-understanding that permitted it, for the first time, to step back and admire its achievements as a nation. The British, formerly patrolling Brazilian waters to intercept slave cargos, now took a purely commercial role. Foreign investment poured into Brazil at a steady pace, financing railroad systems, port facilities, and such urban improvements as water-supply systems and paved streets. In December 1861, on Emperor Pedro II's birthday, the government proudly invited foreign dignitaries and members of the Brazilian "better classes," as they were called, to the country's first National Exposition. It was held at Rio de Janeiro's Largo de São Francisco, a square not far from the royal palace, and was modeled after the Great London Exhibition in the Crystal Palace a decade earlier. It was the first of its kind in Latin America. The exposition presented maps and displays and handsome books published for the occasion, all celebrating Brazil's vast size, its unity, and its natural resources.

The national event that precipitated the most far-reaching, if subtle, changes in nineteenth-century Brazilian political life was the War of the Triple Alliance (1865–1870), known in Brazil as the Paraguayan War. The conflict had its origin in events during November 1864, when a Paraguayan warship in the Paraná River intercepted a Brazilian steamer caught in Paraguayan waters and forced it back to Ascunción, the capital of the Paraguayan dictatorship of Francisco Solano Lopez. The passengers and crew of the Brazilian vessel, including the governor-elect of the frontier province of Mato Grosso, were arrested and held in a prison camp. Solano Lopez had provoked the incident; it was claimed later that he used the Brazilian ship's flag as a rug in his presidential office. The act was not entirely capricious, however. Paraguay blamed Brazil for upsetting the balance of power in the region by invading Uruguay months earlier, and it considered Brazil an aggressive imperial power. Brazil, for its part, despised the Paraguayan ruler and read his act as a challenge to the integrity of its own frontier. Overland travel to and from Mato Grosso was then almost impossible, and the Brazilians felt that their use of the water route, up the River Plate and through the Paraná, was necessary.

Three nations—Argentina, Brazil, and Uruguay, at that time a client state of its Portuguese-speaking neighbor—waged war against Paraguay for the next six years. Paraguayan resistance was tenacious, however, and complete victory was never achieved. Although Brazil had emerged as a powerful South American nation, its armed forces were relatively weak, whereas a succession of Paraguayan dictators had built a powerful army made up almost entirely of Guaraní Indians. Argentina was relatively weak in the aftermath of the fall of the Rosas dictatorship, and Uruguay was little more than a frontier province. Brazil's economy still depended on slavery and on foreign prices for its agricultural exports. Still, Emperor Pedro II had reputedly welcomed the war, saying that it would bring "a nice electrical shock to our nationality." Propagandists presented the war as pitting Brazilian civility and moderation against "barbarism" and "despotism." That Brazil was the last country in South America to retain slavery was omitted from the triumphal prose.

When the war dragged on without a quick allied victory, Pedro's popularity began to wane. The Argentines and Uruguayans largely withdrew, leaving much of the war effort to Brazilian troops, who were not accustomed to jungle fighting in guerrilla style and were indifferently trained and equipped. Pedro refused an offer in early 1867 from the United States to mediate a settlement, leading to three more years of conflict. When the Brazilians finally prevailed, it was their commander in Paraguay, the Duke of Caxias, Luís Alves de Lima e Silva (1808–1880), who became the popular hero, not the emperor. The tension between the two men led to a political conflict between the emperor and his cabinet, leading to the removal of Liberal ministers in 1868 and their replacement with a hard-line cabinet loyal to Caxias. This proved to be one the first times in Brazil that military interests would force the government's hand.

IMPERIAL DECLINE

The Empire was highly centralized, but the far-flung provinces were too distant and too difficult to control. At best, imperial policies issued in Rio de Janeiro were followed there if they suited the recipient. While the monarch presided over an ornate court, complete with a titled nobility and a European-style vacation residence in Petrópolis in the mountains, the outer provinces in the north and far south chafed and on several occasions broke out in open revolt. Monetary instability induced an economic crisis in 1875, and the monarchy was preparing to return to the gold standard when it was overthrown in 1889.

More than anything else, the domestic consequences of the Paraguayan War, in upsetting national equilibrium, were responsible for the shift of support away from the monarchy. Unemployed war veterans joined *capoeira* street gangs, so named because of their use of a legally proscribed martial art, and became involved in violent postwar electoral politics. Former slaves who had won their freedom by serving as soldiers were warned after the war to display the deference and gratitude expected of freedmen or they would suffer the consequences. An urban underclass, mostly blacks and persons of mixed race, inhabited Brazil's imperial capital and gave its streets a reputation for sordidness and danger to be avoided by persons of good social standing. Among the poor, the death rate exceeded the birth rate as late as the last decade of the nineteenth century. Epidemics—smallpox, cholera, yellow fever, plague—swept cities and the countryside. The large portion of the adult population could neither read nor write. A quarter of the city's population lived in tuberculosis-ridden tenements, or cortiços. Immigrant Portuguese controlled retail selling, and they were despised.

SLAVERY

It is estimated that more than a third of all Africans shipped to the New World as slaves (60 percent of those shipped in the nineteenth century) came to Brazil. The Portuguese dominated the Atlantic slave trade, and the successive economic cycles in which cheap labor fueled prosperity—sugar, then cacao, then mining, then coffee—encouraged Brazil's elites to hold on to the system as long as possible. The plantation owners took their crops for granted, and did nothing to preserve the fertility of the land. Many did not even keep accounts of costs and returns. As attributed to Sérgio Buarque de Holanda, they were miners of the rich soil, not farmers, speculators rather than cultivators. They treated their slaves as if they were beasts of burden, as replaceable as oxen.

In 1822, the year Brazil won its freedom from Portugal, slaves constituted as much as half the nation's population. The slave trade had been banned in 1817, but it only stopped after 1850, when the British, motivated by a newfound morality in foreign policy, threatened Brazil with a naval blockade. Slaves lived under miserable conditions because owners felt it was more efficient to buy newly arrived Africans than to take care of ones they already owned.

Slaves, mixed-race landless farmers, and floating bands of cowboy drifters—valentões—populated most of the country's hinterland. Coastal cities grew, although the mainstay of their economies was commercial, not industrial; the backlands however, remained impoverished. With the price of slaves rising steadily after mid-century, when the British forced the imperial Brazilian government to stop the slave trade, in vast stretches of the Northeast landowners shut down their agricultural properties and moved to the cities of the coast, turning over their lands—frequently lacking regular sources of potable water—to sharecroppers, who raised subsistence crops under the watchful eyes of overseers. Large numbers of men lacking work congregated in the rural towns. The unemployed, especially free men of color, were often conscripted forcibly into the army, where they were kept from running away by a regime of brutal discipline.

It is telling that the ending of the slave trade, after decades of stalling by Brazilian officials, spurred economic development in the Center-South. This occurred as foreign capital poured in seeking investment, especially in transportation, in response to the growing prosperity of the Paraíba Valley coffee plantations. Slavery reigned supreme, but gradually the economy diversified. Between 1850 and 1860 the number of corporations boomed—ventures in manufacturing, railroads, insurance, mining, savings banks, and land settlements. The first railroad opened in 1854; the first telegraph system started in 1857. Not only did new rail lines link mines and plantations to Brazilian ports, but a suburban train, the *Dom Pedro II* (later *Central do Brasil*) connected Rio de Janeiro to working-class districts beyond the city's limits. Foreign engineers brought the first illuminated street lights to the capital in 1854, replacing lamps fueled by foul-smelling fish oil. Street cars pulled by mules (later propelled by electricity) arrived a decade later, as did sewage disposal systems in the major cities. Yet as late as 1889 Rio de Janeiro, the national capital, remained an "old colonial burgh with narrow, dirty streets, poorly maintained houses, peeling hoardings, pot-holed pavements and dusty shops."[3]

Economic cycles displaced one region by another in prominence and profitability. Economic decline in northeastern Brazil, the result of lower prices for sugar produced in the Caribbean and Louisiana, led many plantation owners to sell their slaves south, to the mines, ranches, and coffee plantations of Minas Gerais and São Paulo. The shortage of slaves in southern Brazil was due in large part to the low birth rate among slave women, and to the high incidence of death of slave mothers in childbirth. By the mid-nineteenth century, moreover, many slave owners had manumitted their slave property, less out of charity than as an economic measure, because slaves over the age of forty were less productive. Also, Brazilian slave owners sometimes freed slave women who gave birth to their illegitimate children. The adult manumission rate for women was double that for men. Brazilian society did not know what to do with many of the children born to whites and slave women, and as a result thousands of foundlings were placed in the care of religious institutions. Some churches had revolving doors; infants could be placed outside on a shelf, which was then swiveled to the inside so that the child would be discovered without ever seeing the faces of the people who had abandoned it.

The emperor worked with Liberal Party leaders to implement a gradual program of emancipation of slaves. The Rio Branco Law of 1871 freed children born to slave mothers, although planters could keep them, for a small payment, until they reached the age of twenty-one. It was named for Viscount Rio Branco, José Maria da Silva Paranhos, a conservative in his youth who had been educated at an imperial military academy but whose outlook had become more liberal as he matured into a leading imperial statesman. During Rio Branco's term as prime minister, Brazil reformed and enlarged public education, organized the first national census in 1872, invited foreign investors to build railroads linking rural agricultural regions to ports, created a modern post office, reformed the criminal and civil codes, and promoted immigration from northern Europe. He also oversaw the introduction of the metric system and increased European contacts.

The initiatives to weaken the hold of slavery did not have the desired effect. The provisions of the Rio Branco law were widely ignored: the law made no provision for enforcement. The metric system was not applied universally, and in the hinterland local citizens, probably fearing that fees and taxes would be raised with more accurate weights and measures, smashed metric equipment in marketplaces in riots in the 1870s known as the *Quebra-Kilos* ("smash the kilos"). Economic hard times during this decade made enforcement of reform laws even more difficult.

A second national law regarding slavery in 1885 freed bondsmen over the age of sixty—an age reached by few in the nineteenth century—when productive labor was unlikely. On May 13, 1888, Princess Regent Isabel, acting in the name of her father, Pedro II, who discreetly was traveling, signed the "Golden Law," which was ratified by the General Assembly of parliament. It emancipated all of Brazil's remaining slaves. Abolitionist sentiment had been fueled by embarrassment over the fact that with emancipation of slaves in the United States, Cuba, and Puerto Rico, and of the serfs in czarist Russia, Brazil stood out as the last independent nation in the world where slavery remained legal. Yet Princess Isabel's act was still mostly symbolic. Very few slaves were left; their role in the economy had been replaced with members of the lower class hired for day wages, and by immigrants from around the world induced to come to Brazil by planters and by provincial governments who paid ship passage for indentured workers. But if the abolition decree was largely symbolic, it was powerful enough to bring the monarchy to its end.

A year after the Golden Law, Rui Barbosa, the finance minister and jurist who would write most of the 1891 constitution, ordered the government's slave registers burned, a sign that Brazil was entering into a new era. This was true juridically, but the former slaves and other free blacks remained at the very bottom of the social hierarchy. The abolitionist movement, which had argued that slavery was both immoral and inefficient, vanished overnight, its former leaders giving no attention to the plight of the ex-slaves, who now faced destitution if their former owners turned their backs on them.

One group usually overlooked in the history of slavery were the overseers. They often were Portuguese immigrants, although sometimes free blacks or even "trusty" slaves were given the job of watching and disciplining field slaves. Their onerous jobs positioned the overseers in an awkward position: the slaves they punished hated them—and sometimes murdered them—yet slaveowners frequently did not trust them either. Some overseers managed to acquire their own land and slaves, and some managed to earn the trust of the slaves under their whip.

ABOLITIONISTS

Abolitionists in Brazil differed from their counterparts in the United States in approach and strategies. American abolitionists lived in and appealed to inhabitants of states in which slavery was not present, demanding that the federal government declared slavery illegal. In many cases, they continued their crusade after the 1863 Emancipation Proclamation, protesting against unequal treatment given to blacks (although to ex-slaves in the South, not in their own backyards). In Brazil, the abolitionists lived much closer to the institution, which was nationwide. Abolitionists in the United States portrayed slave owners as brutes; in Brazil, abolitionists were more likely to ascribe savagery to slaves, whom they saw as victimized by the "barbarism" of their African ancestry. In the United States, many abolitionists drew inspiration from Christianity and therefore worked not only to outlaw slavery but to redeem African Americans from poverty. Many abolitionists in the United States worked for black rights, although social barriers restricted progress. Once emancipation was achieved in Brazil, the abolitionists shifted their attention to other causes, including republicanism, and did nothing to help the newly freed blacks prepare for living as free people.

Not all Brazilian abolitionists avoided moral arguments. Antônio Bento, a *paulista* who has been compared to the radical American abolitionist John Brown, denounced slavery on moral grounds. Joaquim Aurélio Nabuco de Auaújo (1849–1910), the son of a powerful landowner and senator, spoke eloquently against slavery as an institution. He hated slavery from the first time he saw it and spent most of his life working for its eradication. A diplomat, he was posted to England and to the United States, permitting him to maintain contact with antislavery groups. He was an eloquent orator and wrote fiercely, mincing no words during a time—in the middle-nineteenth century—when society expected criticism to be indirect and subtle.

Slavery [Nabuco wrote] corrupts everything, robbing working people of their former virtues: diligence, thrift, charity, patriotism, fear of death, love of liberty. The slave, while still a fetus, feels the contortions of the mother under the lash. Its blood becomes corrupted. When one feels its pulse, one senses the horrible treatment of the poor black woman. In this situation of [advanced pregnancy], so grave, so much in need of assistance, she is afforded no respect, not even rest. The owner is compromising two lives. The mother rises to perform service, work, suffers the pull of the infant on her breast on one side and the whip on the other.[4]

In sum, Brazilian abolitionists wrote and spoke as individuals; there were few abolitionist societies or organizations. Many of their arguments against slavery were made not on principled grounds but against the economic costs and impracticality of the institution; for instance, European immigrants, considered far more desirable than African bondsmen, would be dissuaded from coming to Brazil. Once abolition was achieved, the abolitionist cause ended abruptly. Attention shifted to encouraging overseas immigrants; no voices were raised warning of the difficulties the ex-slaves might face if abandoned to fend for themselves.

Slavery had a few escape hatches: individuals could purchase their freedom or be manumitted—although in many cases the freed slaves had to remain in "voluntary" servitude until the master or his wife died. Other slaves ran away. Most, however died in captivity. In contrast to most of the rest of Latin America, which abolished slavery in the early nineteenth century, Brazil retained slavery as a legal institution until 1888. Emancipation brought cries of joy from the 5 percent of Brazilian blacks still in bondage in 1888, but it was accompanied by legislation and social practices that served to limit drastically opportunities for blacks and to keep them subservient.

REPUBLICANISM

As the nineteenth century neared its end, pressures for a republican government began to mount. The political system under the Empire had always been dominated by the landholding oligarchy; the two political parties, the Conservatives and Liberals, simply represented broad factions within the oligarchy. The Conservatives were centered in the older plantation oligarchy, including northeastern sugar producers and interior *fazendeiros* (ranchers and agriculturists), while the Liberals centered in the coffee-growing regions of Rio de Janeiro and São Paulo. There were few ideological differences between the political parties, which had been organized in the 1830s. Conservatives and Liberals shared distrust (in some cases contempt) for the mass of the population, a circumstance underscored by the fact that as late as 1889 only a tiny number of children—3 percent of the school-age population—was enrolled in school. Nor did the parties differ substantially on economic issues, although the Conservatives tended to favor centralization and more traditional ties to the Roman Catholic Church. Liberal Party members were "liberal" mainly on issues of trade and the size of government; they were nineteenth-century economic liberals, not political liberals or, in the twentieth-century sense, progressives.

The roots of the monarchy's decline stretched back to the regionalist insurrections of the early nineteenth century and to the Paraguayan War. Elites in the far South, North, and Northeast were too far from the imperial center in Rio de Janeiro, even though the monarchy's administrative practice of rotating officials—from judges to provincial governors—worked to integrate the political system nationally. Being peripheral nonetheless led to disaffection. The aftermath of the Paraguayan War also accelerated trends challenging the status quo. In 1866, a dissident wing split off the Liberal Party and formed a third national party, the Republicans, in 1870. Another rift developed between the bishops of the Roman Catholic Church and the monarchy. This was ironic, because although Brazil's elite fully supported the conservative tone of the church, Emperor Pedro II, the nominal head of the church in Brazil, personally disagreed with the Vatican's crusade in the last third of the century to impose neo-orthodox practice in dioceses around the world. One of the elements of this campaign, called ultramontanism, was to remove syncretistic elements—such as the widespread practice of Afro-Brazilian religion behind the iconography of Roman Catholicism. Pedro disagreed even more vehemently with the Vatican's insistence that it, and not the emperor, had the right to name new bishops and other officials within the church hierarchy. This led to the so-called Religious Question of 1871–1874, a tug-of-war over whether the emperor or the church controlled ecclesiastical appointments. Pedro II won the battle but lost the war: after 1874, the church withdrew its support, which had been taken for granted, of the monarchy.

The monarchy invested in education, but only for the sons of the elite. Daughters were given lessons in sewing and music and were expected to marry and bear children. The Brazilian government funded no comprehensive universities anywhere in the country, maintaining facilities for higher education only in the military academies and in the faculties of law in São Paulo and Recife and in those of medicine in Rio de Janeiro and Salvador. The monarchy established a public secondary school in 1837, later named the Colégio Pedro II, which provided academic preparation in languages and the humanities for youths who on graduation would be sent to a European university or to study law or medicine, and who would then enter the imperial bureaucracy, not practice the professions in which they had been trained. Provinces funded elementary schools that kept children rarely more than one or two years. Imperial senator Teixeira Júnior summarized the attitude of his elite contemporaries about education: "The mass of the population simply needs elementary education." In the early 1850s, only 61,700 pupils were enrolled in primary schools throughout all of Brazil, and only 3,717 in secondary schools. In 1845, moreover, the imperial government canceled its annual subsidies to the provinces for public schools.

The second half of the nineteenth century saw a sharp increase in commercial complexity, as cities grew. Service industries grew, as did factories for canning food (at first, mostly sweetened preserves) and for manufacturing (household goods, and textiles). Banking began to flourish. Business in general was spurred by the changing culture, which no longer frowned on real estate speculation, as was the case earlier. The most successful entrepreneur during this period was Irineu Evangelista de Sousa (1813–1889), the Viscount of Mauá. He was a visionary, lobbying for railroad construction, with the goal of laying track across South America from one side to the other. He also became caught in scandal, however, and came to be mistrusted by the emperor. Pedro resisted many of the reforms urged by Mauá and others, and he blamed foreign influence—especially the influence of the French—for injecting into Brazil a climate of speculation and fiscal instability.

Young army officers, shaken by the illiteracy of their recruits, became converts to the position that education was a major requirement of any program to bring progress to Brazil, but they did not find any such commitment in either the Liberal or Conservative Party. Disgruntled at what they considered to be a lethargic political system, many of them turned to positivism, or scientific sociology, a doctrine of Auguste Comte (1798–1857), a French philosopher. Positivism became influential in intellectual circles mostly in the South as well as in the military academies. Lawyers, journalists, and other professionals joined Republican clubs and established dialogues with the young military officers about their mutual disaffection.

Radical republicans, who demanded sweeping change, contributed to the overthrow of the monarchy, but when the new republic was promulgated in 1889 they saw their influence ebb before a more moderate coalition of leaders, many of them dubbed "eleventh-hour" republicans because of their last-minute conversion to the movement. The faction that prevailed during the early Republic wanted states rights more than anything else, bolstered by liberal constitutionalism, laissez-faire economic policy, and laws to keep the lower classes in line, especially the former slaves, who had been left to fend for themselves after abolition.

Pedro remained a popular, even beloved, monarch throughout his long reign, but in the 1860s his former political allies began to waver. Army officers resented cuts in the military budget after the end of the Paraguayan War. Pedro alienated the Catholic Church by openly practicing Freemasonry, not permissible under Catholic doctrine, and by arresting two bishops for defying him over the issue. Positivists urged the substitution of a republic for the monarchy. Slave owners opposed the laws that were moving Brazil closer to abolition, and when emancipation was signed into law in May 1888, the die was cast. A year and several months later, on November 15, 1889, a civilian-military coup forced Pedro to abdicate. He sailed to England, leaving Brazil in the hands of Army general Manoel Deodoro da Fonseca.

THE NEW BRAZILIANS

The lack of industrialization and the survival of African slavery during the nineteenth century discouraged immigration, although foreigners did come to Brazil, mostly to urban areas and to the remote hinterland, where they established themselves as peddlers or shopkeepers. One group, however, was attracted to Brazil for the same reasons that kept others away: landowners from the defeated Confederate States of America emigrated to southern Brazil in the late 1860s in a desperate effort to preserve their way of life. Emperor Pedro II had favored the cause of the Southern states and may have aided the emigrant families in obtaining ship passage to Brazil. About 150 Confederate families settled near Campinas in São Paulo province, a few hours west of the city of São Paulo. There they founded a hamlet, Americana, centered on four hundred acres of land purchased by a Confederate colonel, William Norris. The community's members preserved their use of the English language well into the next century, although eventually the Confederates became Brazilianized.

As coffee prospered, southern planters, especially the *paulistas*, pressured their provincial governments to recruit immigrants from Europe to work as *colonos*, or agricultural colonists. Some 250,000 immigrants came under state or private sponsorship in the year 1882, their passage paid for in exchange for a contract that obliged the immigrants to work off their debts for a period of years. Northern provinces also sought to attract immigrant workers, but unattractive conditions and the fact that the region's destitute poor would work for almost any wage scared away would-be immigrants, who probably did not number more than two hundred in that same year.

Some immigrants, especially from Germany, Italy, and Poland, as well as Basques (who first had settled in Uruguay), found ways to come to Brazil on their own, settling in the far south, where land was available and the climate similar to Europe's. Many factors contributed to a boom in immigration to Brazil after 1880. Before the last stages of slavery, few prospective immigrants who knew anything about Brazil were attracted to a land where there would be competition for work from slaves. This changed after abolition in 1888. Planters lobbied for and received government subsidies to bring field hands from Europe, especially to São Paulo and to the states of the south, where labor was relatively scarce. Under these auspices, thousands of Italians, Portuguese, Germans, and Poles came to Brazil as indentured agricultural workers obliged to repay the cost of their ship passage and debts accrued in company stores on the agricultural settlements. Japanese were also brought to the Amazonia and to the South to labor as *colonos*. Many worked the agricultural season from planting to harvest and then—because the seasons were reversed—returned to Europe, but others, and in increasing numbers, stayed.

They brought their families with them and settled, first under contract until they paid off their debts, and then on land that they acquired. They saw Brazil as a place of opportunity, but one in which they faced hardship. German settlers called the land *Urwald*, a tropical forest in which they could starve if things did not go well, because Brazil offered no safety net in case of failure. Trees had to be cleared, sources of accessible water found, and the land worked with simple or even handmade tools. Few immigrant settlers could afford horses, mules, or steel plows. Conflicting and overlapping land claims made possession of the land difficult. Local bandits and other enterprising opportunists often saw the newcomers' vulnerability and took advantage of it. This—and the immigrants' fierce identity with their own heritages—reinforced cultural survivals. The immigrants retained their own languages, schooled their children in them, and eventually published newspapers, organized burial associations, fraternal organizations, and social clubs. The Brazilian nation, then, as it approached the twentieth century, was in reality a cluster of separate groups, differentiated by ethnicity, culture, and economic status. Immigrants could hope to scratch their way to better lives, but for the vast majority of mixed-race Brazilians as well as for the descendants of the recently liberated slaves, poverty and lack of facilities for education or health care remained the norm, even as the elite dramatically transformed its urban places in the image of Western Europe.

Brazil's growth as a nation was accompanied by a human assault on its virgin lands and forests. Depredation was worst along the coast in the formerly vast Atlantic Forest. Here, large-scale coffee cultivation and the quick exhaustion of agricultural land encouraged planters to employ slash-and-burn cultivation. Usually it was cheaper to abandon old farms and fell the trees from adjacent lands than to restore the fertility of the soil. Deeper into the interior, economic necessity made any possibility of conservation impossible. A full-grown jacaranda tree, which produces the hardest mahogany-like wood in the hemisphere, eventually fetched on the open market the equivalent of seven thousand dollars, in rural places where the usual income rarely exceeded fifty or sixty dollars a month. Conservation of natural resources was an idea that, in the nineteenth century, had not yet been born, and Brazilians were no more aware of its eventual costs than anyone else.

NOTES

1. Roderick J. Barman, *Brazil: The Forging of a Nation* (Stanford; CA: Stanford University Press, 1988), 5.

2. Contemporary newspaper report, n.d., quoted in *A Presença Británica no Brasil (1808–1914)* (Rio de Janeiro: Editora PauBrasil, 1987), 37.

3. Max LeClerc, *Cartas do Brasil* (São Paulo: Companhia Editora Nacional, 1942), 46.

4. Joaquim Nabuco, *O Abolicionismo* (London: Abraham Kingdon, 1883), 55.

4

The Republic (1889–1930)

The transition from monarchy to republic in 1889 dramatically altered the structure of Brazilian government. The republican constitution of February 24, 1891, created a dual federalist structure that abruptly terminated the Empire's centralized authority. It guaranteed autonomy for the old provinces, which were renamed states, and it left for the Union only general matters affecting the nation as a whole. Brazil was formally named "The United States of Brazil." The positivist motto, "Order and Progress," was emblazoned to Brazil's handsome new blue, green, and yellow national flag.

Under the 1891 constitution, states raised funds by taxing exports of goods to other states. This meant that the few states that produced surplus food—entirely in the south of the country—prospered, while the other states suffered terribly. States needing loans to finance improvements or debt payments had to negotiate individually with foreign banks and governments at high interest because of their lack of collateral, and poor states had no collateral on which to back borrowed funds. States even raised their own militia forces—in the late 1920s São Paulo even had its own air corps—and hired foreign military advisors from France and Prussia to train their troops. Positivist influence among republican leaders resulted in the formal separation of church and state in 1890, a separation that was more or less ignored as the years passed.

The coup that created the Republic provided a stage upon which the military would remain ready to intervene for at least the next ninety years. From 1889 to 1930, the military would overthrow two constitutional governments and intervene in the states on several occasions to oust political adversaries or maintain allies in control. In the mid-1890s, competing factions within the armed forces more than anything else permitted civilians to regain the government. Naval officers angry at what they considered to be neglect by the federal government rose in revolt in 1893–1894 and further divided their service. Deodoro was a not overly effective president, and his successor, Floriano Peixoto, became increasingly unpopular and isolated.

Meanwhile, the *paulista* landowning oligarchy, in collaboration with the dairy-producing agriculturists in the neighboring state of Minas Gerais, cemented a shared power arrangement that would become known as the *café com leite* (coffee with milk) alliance. The *paulistas* were as new to political powers as the generals, but their rise was inevitable, because of the surging growth of their state's economy. They rose to power after backing Floriano Peixoto against the naval rebellion, which had had the support of monarchists who sought to bring down the Republic. The São Paulo Republican Party was the best organized in the country, and the military liked the fact that the *paulista* entrepreneurs valued stability as the key to profit.

Cities in prosperous states used foreign loans and public funds to create handsome boulevards, stately public buildings and mansions, street lighting and urban transport, monuments and statues, running water and sewers, and a gamut of institutions devoted to the fine arts and culture. Rio de Janeiro in 1890 had more residents than Madrid or Paris—and it would double its population thirty years later. São Paulo was riding a sustained commercial and industrial boom, although in 1890 its growth was only in the beginning stages. Newspaper editors debated whether their country should forge closer ties to the United States or remain closely connected to Europe, especially to Great Britain. The leaders of Brazil wanted protected access to United States markets, especially in sugar, and sought a military alliance with Washington to reduce traditional reliance on London.

Efforts to bring "civilization" (in the words of boosters) to urban places, however, were usually more cosmetic than structural; the lower classes, residing on the periphery of the glittering symbols of progress, were as often as not victims of modernization. Affluent Brazilians ignored the plight of the poor, whether urban—often living in shantytowns and tenements in close proximity to their stately homes—or in the rural hinterland.

The Republic unfolded in an atmosphere of optimism bordering on euphoria. Many of those who had opposed the emperor as a relic applauded warmly when the aging monarch departed. The new federal system was seen as a model of efficiency, a kind of late-nineteenth-century government downsizing, in which the states would govern their affairs and set their economic policies. Even so, the transition from empire proved rocky. Internal political crises plagued the Republic from its inception. General Deodoro da Fonseca, a national hero but a dispirited and impatient political figure, served as the Republic's first chief of state, but he recoiled from governing actively. When he attempted to dissolve Congress in November 1891, he was unceremoniously ousted. His successor, Marshal Floriano Peixoto, aggressively used his executive powers in a Cromwellian manner to attack the surviving influence of the vested landowning class. Peixoto also quelled an uprising in the southern city of Desterro, the capital of the state of Santa Catarina, with such brutality that the repression was remembered with disgust generations after. The man empowered to carry it out was a colonel, Moreira César (1850–1897), a manic-depressive military commander of brutal stripe. Not only did César order the execution of rebel leaders, but after the city capitulated he mockingly changed its name to Florianopolis, a name that survives today.

The armed forces yielded power in November 1894 to Prudente José de Morais Barros, a civilian and a *paulista*. The rural planter oligarchy, now firmly centered in rural São Paulo, consolidated its power through an unwritten agreement with agricultural elites of other states, especially the plantocracy in neighboring Minas Gerais. The coming to the presidency of a *paulista* affirmed the ascendancy of São Paulo, its growth propelled by rising coffee exports, a growing industrial capacity, and a demographic explosion fueled by the steady arrival of both European immigrants and of migrants from the hinterland, including thousands from the northeastern states devastated by worsening droughts in the 1870s and 1880s.

The failure of the radical positivist wing of the republican movement to gain power resulted in the continuation of the Empire's neglect of education for the mass of the population. States in the federation, left to their own fiscal devices, funded when they could schools of higher education—mostly schools of law and, on a much more meager scale, poly-technic schools as well as agricultural extensions. States also ran schools to train teachers. These normal schools were usually in decrepit build-ings, taught by unqualified instructors. Their graduates, almost always single women, were paid pitiful salaries once they graduated and found teaching jobs. When state budgets faced retrenchment, as they did in Rio de Janeiro in 1904, funds for education were cut by half or more. When this happened teachers were not paid at all, and many schools closed.

The military academies and the state secondary schools followed the positivist curriculum of the Colégio Pedro II (later renamed the Ginásio Nacional), emphasizing mathematics and science. Federal policy toward public education addressed the former neglect of the needs of the great bulk of the population. In 1890, the new Minister of Instruction, Postal and Telegraph Service, Benjamin Constant, the leading proponent of pos-itivist education in Brazil, established twenty-two single-grade primary schools in the Federal District and six more that taught two grades. Pri-vate schools received subsidies if they agreed to educate fifteen poor children, usually taken from families who could not afford tuition or from orphanages. In the courts, juridical distinctions were made between categories of minors: "children" were those of good families, integrated into affluent society. The rest were *menores*—a word with a pejorative ring—or worse, *desvalidos* (underprivileged, literally "worthless").

CANUDOS

During the first decade of the Republic, a traumatic conflict, the Can-udos war, took place in the backlands of the state of Bahia, which in 1897 exploded into national consciousness. Latin American society in the nineteenth century had given rise (as it would in the twentieth) to an array of religious expressions and movements. Some of them were small, communal-based, millenarian experiments with apocalyptic underpin-nings. That is, rather than believing that the millennium would heal and reform society, they emphasized the imminence of divine judgment and the final destruction of the world. One such was Canudos, or Belo Monte, a religious settlement founded by a pious lay Catholic mystic, Antônio Vicente Mendes Maciel (1830–1897), known to his followers as Antônio Conselheiro (the Counsellor). Belo Monte took form on the grounds of an abandoned cattle ranch owned by the Jeremoabo clan in the parched backlands interior of the state of Bahia.

The region was afflicted by a severe climate and generally inhospitable terrain, which intimidated visitors. The backlands conjured up images of backwardness and inhospitability of place and people, although on the whole its dry climate was neither intolerable nor oppressive. The backlands residents were not peasants like the sedentary rural peoples of the Andean highlands or central America. Most rural backlanders, though they lived as renters or sharecroppers under miserable conditions, retained a certain freedom of movement and a grudging spirit of self-reliance. Before 1893, few outsiders passed through the Bahian *sertão* except en route to the São Francisco River, to the north.

Conselheiro's followers willingly accepted his prescriptions for life. At Canudos residents were assigned work and lived according to a set routine that must have brought a comforting sense of security, structure, and direction to men and women whose lives had been traumatized by deprivation and by the vicissitudes of drought, disputes between clans, and economic uncertainty. Many ordinary citizens of the backlands questioned the secularized republican order. It is untrue that the backlands residents of Canudos were driven by crazed religious fanaticism. It was economic depression, residual effects of crippling drought, increased use of the state police to enforce political demands, and the disappearance of the monarchy and its traditional prescriptive authority that combined to make the structured life promised by Conselheiro seem powerfully desirable.

Nationally, influential citizens, committed to the secular and modernizing vision of the Republic, dreaded the prospect that the stubborn independence shown by the *Canudenses* might spread and ultimately incite regionalist insurrection. This never happened. What the elites refused to comprehend was that Conselheiro's words were rhetorical, not a summons to aggression. His followers withdrew to Canudos to await the Day of Judgment. They kept to themselves and did not proselytize. Conselheiro's hatred of the Republic was real enough, but at least in the early days of his settlement he and his lieutenants managed to ally themselves with local landowners and other members of the backlands elite, on a purely pragmatic basis.

The nature of Conselheiro's ministry in rural Canudos and the physical exodus of northeasterners to join him in his self-proclaimed "holy city" doomed his movement to intervention by the state. Prophecy coupled with diatribes against sin played a regular part of lay Catholicism as communicated to backlanders not only by Conselheiro during the wandering phase of his ministry but by many others in the region. The Canudos episode occurred at the height of the Vatican's ultramontanist campaign to restore orthodox practice throughout the world. Lacking Brazilian-born priests, the coastal church hierarchy had sent for European-born ones; these men, conservatively trained and speaking French or German or Italian, not Portuguese, were assigned exactly to the remote places where penitential folk Catholicism had taken its greatest hold. The foreign priests were aghast at what they found: superstition, popular flagellation cults, and widespread disuse of Latin. For his parts, Conselheiro an educated man familiar with the work of church missionaries in India and Asia, treated his flock with austere compassion. One of the main elements of his teaching was the apocalyptic Portuguese-language *Missão Abreviada*, written by the Portuguese priest Miguel Couto for use among the heathen. A clash between lay missionaries like Conselheiro and the priests was inevitable, but the harshness of their response—to label him a dangerous heretic—in some cases had the effect of encouraging men and women to seek refuge in his settlement.

Conselheiro's "New Jerusalem" grew rapidly, until it contained more than five thousand mud huts below a ring of hills and low mountains. Its population of twenty-five thousand (at its height in 1895 probably closer to thirty-five thousand) made it the largest urban site in Bahia after Salvador, the capital, seven hundred kilometers to the southeast. Canudos drained labor from several states, especially from the Rio Real in southern Sergipe and Inhambupe in Bahia. The depletion of surplus labor from surrounding regions as well as exaggerated tales of religious fanaticism spread by visitors led local elites to demand intervention. When Conselheiro stubbornly held firm, the decision was made first to disarm the "rebels" and ultimately to destroy their city.

After two punitive expeditions of government troops were sent to Canudos to arrest Conselheiro and dismantle the community were routed by *jagunço* (backlands fighters) forces, the national government sent Colonel Moreira César, the scourge of Desterro, to lead the third assault. Moreira César had risen rapidly within the army but was a flawed tactician, and he allowed his troops to be ambushed and destroyed. In the days before the final battle, in which he himself was killed, he suffered an epileptic attack, reportedly telling the physician who attended him, "Doctor, be advised that I am without nerves. My state is such that I can enjoy neither pain nor pleasure." Word of Moreira César's death in battle was received with extreme consternation across the country; reporters chronicled Canudos's defenders as savage primitives, a threat to the republican order.

As a result, the Army command organized a fourth expedition, made up of troops from nearly every Brazilian state, federal troops, local *jagunços* dragooned into service, ex-slaves, and heavy artillery, including cannon purchased from Krupp in Germany. The campaign was personally conducted by the Brazilian minister of war, at a safe distance from the front. Even Conselheiro's stalwart defenders could not hold out against the cannon barrage and from weeks of encirclement of the holy city. The end came in October 1897, when Canudos was pounded into submission by a furious assault. Male captives had their throats slit, often with family members forced to watch. The body of Antônio Conselheiro, who had died of dysentery some days before the fighting ended, was exhumed; soldiers severed the head and displayed it on a pike in parades held in several coastal cities. The Republic took credit for the victory, benefiting from the fact that the final campaign had been reported by newspaper correspondents who had traveled to the front and submitted dispatches daily via telegraph to their newspapers. The community's 5,200 homes were burned to the ground. The few surviving women were evacuated to the coast, where they were made servants (and in some cases, prostitutes); some of the surviving children were "adopted" by onlookers or otherwise taken as trophies of war.

The remarkable tenacity of the faithful who did not flee but resisted to the end may be explained by theories of "density" of popular culture. Social psychologists have also suggested that belonging to or joining a group that demands great sacrifice tends to give great prestige to its members. This seems to fit with what we know about Canudos under Conselheiro's leadership. The determination with which what outsiders considered primitive efforts to block change were pursued may be seen as a form of coping or even assertiveness. Group cohesiveness under Belo Monte's utopian framework was reinforced by Conselheiro's teachings that the faithful, not the outside world, would be redeemed.

THE REPUBLIC MATURES

Although traditional interpretations of the Republic emphasize its extreme federalism and the weakness of the central government, in fact in 1892 (and at various other times under the Republic) the national treasury amassed a higher percentage of the nation's revenue than before 1889. This occurred even though the state of São Paulo, bursting into dominance as a result of coffee exports and rapid industrialization, took in three times the revenue it had under the Empire. The greater autonomy of the states, on the other hand, led to widening gap between the have and have-nots. São Paulo was able to spend more on education as time passed than some of the northeastern states had available, after their debt payments were made, to spend on public works, education, health, salaries, the police, and the courts. Rio de Janeiro state, adjacent to the federal capital and the site of Brazil's first coffee boom, but now long decadent, spent only 0.5 percent of its budget on primary education. The percentage of literacy among the population of the prosperous Center-South and South more than doubled in the generation following the fall of the monarchy, whereas in much of the rest of Brazil, because of state insolvency and the burgeoning rate of population increase, literacy actually fell during the republican period.

Economic Growth

The coming of the new century—and, especially, the impact of World War I—saw Brazil, with the rest of Latin America, drawn closer into the world marketplace. Of course, Brazil's fortunes had always been linked to international conditions, from the merger of the Portuguese crown with Spain's in the seventeenth century, to the gold rush in the eighteenth, to the surge in foreign investment in railroads and other infrastructure in the nineteenth, when coffee became king. World War I, however, accelerated this dependence. The war abruptly cut off trade and blocked imports of needed replacement parts for machines. When it ended, France and Great Britain withdrew their capital investments which were only partially replaced by capital from the United States. The effort by London banks and investment houses to recover their financial assets created deep despair through Latin America, although in the long run it also helped to spur local industrialization—a process called "import substitution" by economists. Rivalry between the United States and the weakened European powers created a temporary vacuum that benefited Brazilian banks and opened opportunities for lawyers, brokers, and manufacturers in the Brazilian upper classes. The elite, historically rooted in control of the land, now broadened its membership and shifted to an urban base.

One result of the export boom and of the political stability brought about by the gentleman's agreement among state elites to share power was that the period between 1902 and 1912 saw the most rapid economic growth in Brazilian history. Impressive economic growth occurred not only in Brazil but in neighboring Argentina and Chile, based on high prices for agricultural and mineral exports. Rising Brazilian coffee prof its, moreover, encouraged wealthy planters to invest in industrial enterprises, especially in textiles, processed foods, and building materials. Most of the industrial workforce was made of women, who toiled not only in cloth factories and as seamstresses but in the informal economy, producing hammocks, lace, embroidery, baskets, hats, sandals, and a myriad of other products sold at local markets and in some cases to middlemen for distribution in urban centers. A high percentage of industrial workers were immigrants. Brazilian manufacturers favored foreigners over native-born *caboclos* and blacks, who were relegated to jobs as menial laborers or to such arduous work as the killing floors in slaughterhouses. Brazilians from all walks of life were affected by the changing economic climate. Inflation made keeping up with the cost of living more difficult, and the boost to industrialization given by World War I effectively cut off imports of manufactured goods and caused prices to rise sharply.

By 1920 immigrants constituted more than half of the labor force in manufacturing and over 58 percent of transportation workers. The foreigners, however, were often literate in their own languages if not in Portuguese, and they brought with them anarchist and anarcho-syndicalist ideas from Spain and Italy. The immigrants found themselves in an industrial system where management routinely fired men if they could be replaced by women and children, and provided neither training nor safety equipment nor a living wage. Despite the dangers—employers sent thugs to beat and intimidate would-be trade union organizers—immigrant workers responded positively to the alternative vision that anarchism provided: a new moral order, decent wages and housing, enlightened attitudes toward women and life without greed or excessive profits.

Even in the face of violence and the probable loss of their jobs, some workers courageously stood up against intolerable conditions. Scattered strikes occurred, culminating in the southern city of Porto Alegre in 1906. There, workers in a number of factories staged a walkout that lasted twenty-one days and was so effective that it became known as the "1906 General Strike." A broad spectrum of workers participated, many of them female. Still, political stability and fervent lobbying by the government to attract foreign investment to permit the modernization of the country's leading cities yielded economic progress and transformed the richest parts of the country, though the vast majority of Brazilians lived in near-absolute poverty.

The currency remained stable, without inflation, but in 1914 the treasury began to issue unbacked banknotes to cover spending deficits, resulting in rapid erosion of the *mil-réis*. The war years accelerated labor conflict. Strikes were called with greater frequency, and they were often broken up by club-wielding policemen called out by employers. Industrial workers, perhaps emboldened by the greater demand for manufactured goods during the war, became increasingly strident and willing to press their demands. Postwar inflation, rising prices, and news of Bolshevik victories in Russia further fueled labor conflict, especially in São Paulo but also in other large cities. Unfortunately for the workers, employers won out. Strikes were crushed with brutality, and anarchist leaders were imprisoned and frequently deported. The large numbers of willing replacements among the urban unemployed, many of them migrants from the rural interior desperate for jobs at any wages, dealt employers the upper hand. Politicians, officers of the armed forces, and the hierarchy of the Roman Catholic Church accepted the repression as the necessary cost of preserving economic progress and minimizing social conflict.

Social Development

By the presidential term of Francisco de Paula Rodrígues Alves (1902–1906), the Republic had stabilized under elite rule committed to investing the country's revenues from export agriculture in modernization of the cities and social control of the lower classes, who were considered unruly or worse. "We recruit policemen from the scum," one saying went, "and we train them to keep the rest of the scum in their place." The Republic sought to regenerate the nation on the model of Western Europe, so the elite built grand opera houses (including one in Manaos, a thousand miles up the Amazon River) and imported Italian singers to perform. The Academy of Letters had been inaugurated in 1897 on the exact blueprint of the French academy, even to the point of calling its new building in Rio de Janeiro *Le Petit Trianon*. British engineers and administrators played soccer (and organized factory soccer teams for workers, giving birth to Brazil's national craze) and constructed in several cities equestrian facilities and boating clubs. Decades later the clubs would be taken over by Brazilian elites, who would retain the English names "Jockey Club" and "Yacht Club" as symbols of borrowed cachet.

Rodrígues Alves's administration worked assiduously to attract foreign investment and European immigrants. His foreign minister, Baron

Rio Branco, successfully pressed Brazilian claims on territory disputed with Brazil's neighbors. He selected diplomatic aides for their European appearance and manners, therefore making the point among European diplomats that Brazil, unlike the other countries of Latin America, was not a nation of half-breeds. He invited foreign dignitaries—including Georges Clemenceau, Anatole France, Sarah Bernhardt, and Theodore Roosevelt—to see Brazil's progress at first hand. The government hosted the 1906 Pan-American Congress in Rio de Janeiro, in the ornate Monroe Palace, with its thoroughly Europeanized Beaux-Arts facade, and followed it by a world's-fairlike international Exposition in 1908, whose pavilions trumpeted Brazilian achievement.

At the same time, the Republic underwent a dramatic shift in demographic character. Under the Empire, the nation had been overwhelmingly rural; cities housed the agencies of governments and carried on commerce but mostly served as places where wealthy landowners built stately mansions for themselves and their families. By 1930, however, tens of thousands of rural men and women had migrated to cities and towns. Historians have tended to romanticize the urban boom, pointing out the dynamic aspects of industrialization, city beautification, and the construction of opera houses, social clubs, restaurants, and, in Rio de Janeiro, gambling casinos. But urbanization carried a heavy price. Marginalized families were displaced when the tenements in which they lived, in tiny subdivided rooms, were torn down to make way for wide boulevards modeled after those of Paris. The working class was forced to relocate on the far outskirts of the city, where public transportation, if available at all, often ate up half or more of daily wages. The poor understood what was happening to them, and sometimes they resisted.

For six days in November 1904, mobs of *cariocas* (residents of Rio) rebelled against the high cost of living and against the city government, which had decreed that all residents must be vaccinated against yellow fever, under a program administered by Oswaldo Cruz of the Pasteur Institute. Accurate stories of smallpox, plague, malaria, and yellow fever in Brazil had hindered recruitment of European immigrants, and the vaccination program was designed to improve health conditions and therefore improve Brazil's attractiveness to foreigners. The turmoil, which became known as the anti-Vaccine Riot (although the mobs directed their ire as much against the municipality's massive program of slum eradication and relocation) damaged Brazil's image. The riots also represented concerted action by radical opponents of Rodrigues Alves to precipitate a coup. Taken together, the events shook the Old, or

First, Republic, as the period is known, and came close to toppling the national government, although stability was quickly restored. Historical accounts have painted the participants in the riots as mulish Luddites, resisting the advances of science and medicine. More recent research stresses the broader nature of the protests and the fact that citizens, stretched to the breaking point, finally lashed out against the government and its clients in the elite.

Once the turmoil ebbed, however, the administrations of the federal government and of the municipality of Rio, the capital, returned to their programs of urban renovation. Engineers Francisco Pereira Passos and André Paulo de Frontín oversaw the modernization of Rio's port to facilitate commerce, and they built handsome thoroughfares and boulevards reminiscent of Haussmann's Paris and Edwardian London. Similar projects were started in burgeoning São Paulo, although that city's urban renaissance flowered somewhat later. What the reformers wanted, in the words of Jeffrey Needell, was "a 'civilized' city not only as a statement of welcome to European capital and labor, or as a celebration of national success and potential, but as kind of school for Brazilians and as a means by which Brazil could transcend itself as a country of color and colonial backwardness. In a local context in which the state's finances were invigorated by London credit and ensured by domination of international coffee and rubber exports, as well as the continued export of sugar, cotton, and tobacco, and in a global context shaped by the continued triumphs of the European world at the time, there was no doubt regarding the lesson and the goal."[1]

Political Life

For most Brazilians, especially outside of the large cities and away from the coast, the Republic changed little in their lives. This was not the case for the citizens of southern Santa Catarina, especially the inhabitants of the capital, Desterro, who were put under a cruelly repressive regime of military occupation. Civil conflict raged in Rio Grande do Sul between Federalists and Republicans, but it followed generations-old fault lines in the state elite and was resolved by the end of the 1890s. The richer, more populous states, Minas Gerais and São Paulo, dominated the political system, alternating control of the presidency by unwritten convention known as the "politics of coffee" (São Paulo) and of milk (Minas, a dairy producer). National politics were played out through the republican parties of each state, whose alliances with local, mostly rural bosses (*coronéis*) gave control of voting in exchange for patronage. In 1909, Nilo Peçanha became the first person of mixed-race origins to become president, but he was a member of the elite; nothing he did showed that he was sensitive to racial matters.

In Rio Grande do Sul, the state's republican party (the PRR) remained supreme, but only after the violent internal civil war. The longtime head of the PRR, Júlio de Castilhos, prevailed, although for decades his state was the only unit of the federation to have two parties with ideologically different programs. He then imposed a quasidictatorial regime, based on positivist and corporatist principles. Castilhos passed the helm of the state to his successor, Borges de Medeiros, who retained the Castilhos plan for bringing progress to the state. The program was based on a strong state apparatus, the absence of effective opposition, and a commitment to education and economic development based on the collective good, not that of individuals or interest groups.

This system not only succeeded but its influence on young and rising *gaúcho* figures (including a law student named Getúlio Vargas) strongly colored their outlook when they came to power after 1930. *Gaúchos* innovated in labor relations and public education. Rio Grande had supported public schools as early as the 1830s, and by the 1872 and 1890 censuses its rate of literacy ranked at or near the top among all provinces and states. A normal school was started in 1878, and it was well funded, unlike most such schools elsewhere in Brazil. Castilhos and Medeiros wooed religious institutions—not only Roman Catholic but also Lutheran, to which many German immigrants belonged—to share responsibility for education with the state. State funds went to both public and private schools. The state encouraged rigorous curricular requirements and offered wide opportunities, including industrial and technical training. All students studied physical education and took military drill. The promise to provide good quality education to all students in the state was not universally applied, but in no other unit of the federation did so many opportunities exist for youths from all walks of life.

In 1917, Brazil declared war on Imperial Germany and joined the Entente powers. More than anything else this was a gesture, to assert Brazil's stature in hemispheric diplomacy; for decades Brazil had been overshadowed by its rival Argentina, which by the turn of the century had become one of the wealthiest countries in the world and whose diplomatic efforts were usually backed by Great Britain, its major trading partner. These events, however, were not understood by the average Brazilian. Local and national news dominated the press, especially because every political party and faction had its own newspaper, and citizens who could read seemed captivated by political lore. The 1891 constitution had carried forward the Empire's principle of representative democracy, even if almost all candidates came from the elite and advocated policies with few differences meaningful to the majority of the population.

The early Republic brought nominal universal male suffrage, making public opinion more important than ever. Still, fewer than 3 percent of the population voted as late as 1930. Elections were staged and manipulated, with frequent fraud by the incumbent political machines in the states. There were no national political parties. When national interests clashed with state or local interests, the former usually prevailed—as during the administration of former war minister Hermes da Fonseca (1910–1914), who ordered naval ships to bombard the city of Salvador, Bahia, to oust the governor from office.

During the Republic, every major city had more than a dozen daily papers; even small towns of a few thousand inhabitants, most of them illiterate, boasted three or four rival broadsheets. Some brought their readers international news, using telegraph services from abroad. This was a boon to those who wanted to keep up with the outside world, since Brazil had always been isolated by geography. Most of the other newspapers were more gossipy than informative, although intellectuals sometimes moonlighted as journalists, thereby interjecting spry and informed writing on a level not often seen, for example, in the press in the United States. Censorship, always exercised by Brazilian authorities when they felt like it, continued to operate—Rio's *Correio da Manhã* was closed down from August 1924 to May 1925—and the courts upheld the right of the government to require prior censorship of all published material.

In 1926, the *cruzeiro* replaced the *milréis* as the unit of currency; it was defined on the basis of its worth in gold. The government enacted legislation to create a monetary agency, the Caixa de Establização, to coin gold and to retire all paper money, but the Great Depression and the 1930 revolution ended the plan. By 1930, one-half of Brazil's federal budget (as well as the budgets of almost all the states) stood in deficit. There had been only one budget surplus between 1907 and 1930, in 1927.

The Elite and the Downtrodden

Despite economic ups and downs, elites felt comfortable with the political system, which was nominally democratic but for all practical purposes permitted state republican machines to govern with a firm hand, allied with rural bosses, or *coronéis*. At the national level, the federal government was controlled by the politicians of the key units of the federation: São Paulo, Minas Gerais, and Rio Grande do Sul, and the city of Rio de Janeiro. The elites were composed of members of old families, most of them longtime owners of rural property. They favored measures to develop the country economically, when the projects served their home locales, and they disputed with one another over patronage and government revenues. On the social front, however, they closed ranks. Trade unions were considered communistic: "Labor," President Washington Luis Pereira de Souza said when he was governor of São Paulo, "is a matter for the police." The presidential cabinet had no ministries for labor, education, health, or social welfare. Government functioned according to positivist principles, based on a kind of noblesse oblige, tolerating no dissent and believing that the masses needed to be led by enlightened leaders for their own good. In one crucial way, however, Brazilian positivism differed from its counterparts in Argentina and Mexico. There, positivists saw public education as the key to progress. Brazilian positivism emphasized technology and order, relegating education to an abstract goal never implemented.

Given this outlook, it is clear why the 1920s were a time of complacency and seeming harmony. But there were signs of discontent, especially among groups excluded from the circle of power. Labor militants organized workers in a handful of industrial and craft trades, precipitating police crackdowns and deportation of many labor leaders, who for the most part were immigrants from Italy or Spain. The Brazilian communist party organized in the early 1920s, a tiny cadre of dreamers inspired by the 1918 Russian Revolution who spoke about proletarian revolution but who for the most part did not understand the mentality of Brazil's lower classes, for whom ideological rhetoric held no meaning.

Elite custom abhorred race mixture and forbade marriages among persons of different races. Everyday interaction among persons of different racial backgrounds however, was more frequent than, for example, in the United States; Brazil had no laws separating the races, only unwritten rules that did not humiliate, as they did in North America. The poorest Brazilians represented a melting pot, with much interracial contact and some intermarriage. The lowest classes represented a democracy of poverty: there were poor whites, and poor people of mixed race, and poor blacks. Immigrants, however, who arrived in Brazil mostly from Europe and also from Japan during the early republican decades, tended to remain within their own ethnic communities, their resistance to immediate assimilation reflected by the fact that they tended to retain their languages and customs. In the absence of free public schools of any quality, they often sent their children to private schools. In the South, the language of instruction was often German, Polish, or Italian. More affluent Brazilians married within their own social circle, with the result that the elite remained Caucasian, with the occasional addition by marriage of a foreign administrator or technician stationed in Brazil.

Educated Brazilians celebrated the official version of Brazil's history, and they were willing to display some degree of openness to new cultural trends (for instance, 1922 witnessed the success of the avant-garde Modern Art Week in São Paulo), not to social reformism. Still, not only did nearly every newspaper and magazine commemorate the elite's version of progress, but professional associations—from the Engineering Club to the Congress of South American History, to the Bar and Press associations, to the National Academy of Medicine—sponsored international congresses in homage. Life for those with education and social standing was good.

SIGNS OF DISCONTENT

Regions peripheral to the economic progress of the 1920s and frustrated at the lack of federal assistance continued to chafe at the imbalances of the federal system. Within the military, a small group of idealistic cadets and junior officers objected to what they saw as a sellout to foreign interests as new foreign investment was invited in after World War I. A spontaneous barracks revolt at Copacabana Fort in Rio de Janeiro gave birth to the nationalistic *tenente* movement, which electrified the public and by 1930 would bring the Republic to an end.

Artur Bernardes took office as president in November 1922, after a fraudulent election. His opponent had been Nilo Peçanha, the head of a faction backed by the oligarchies of Rio de Janeiro, Rio Grande do Sul, Pernambuco, and Bahia. Divisions among the elite divisions offered the only opportunity for contested elections, but in this case the Minas–São Paulo incumbents held on to power while the armed forces, especially young and idealistic officers and officer candidates, seethed. An explosion came when cadets at Rio's Copacabana Fort raised a foolhardy revolt against their commanders in defense of what they considered to be the military's honor. Most of the young men were gunned down, but the handful of survivors became national heroes. On July 24, 1924, on the anniversary of the Rio uprising, cadets and young officers in São

Paulo and Rio Grande do Sul rose in revolt again, this time retreating to the rural interior and regrouping as a guerrilla force. The rebel band became known as the Prestes Column, after its highest-ranking officer. During the ensuing years it crisscrossed Brazil, travelling more than twenty-five thousand kilometers through fifteen states between October 1924 and February 1927, when, pursued by Brazilian forces, the *tenente* fugitives slipped over the Bolivian border at San Mathias. Their trek had started in Santo Angelo, in the northern part of Rio Grande do Sul near the border with Santa Catarina, with 1,500 volunteers. They had passed through Mato Grosso, Minas Gerais, Bahia, Goiás, and every single state in the Northeast, reaching the sea at Mossoró in Rio Grande do Norte. They had been always on the run but had always had time to speak with the impoverished inhabitants of rural towns and the countryside. There were 620 men at the end; they left their arms (ninety Mauser rifles, four heavy machine guns, and eight thousand rounds of ammunition) in San Mathias and dispersed. Some members of the Column never returned to Brazil. Benetido Barradas, for example, was twenty-nine when he fled Brazil, suffering from disease contracted in the interior; he would die in poverty in San Mathias at the age of ninety-five, of the same ailment. Luis Carlos Prestes escaped into Bolivia with many of his fellow officers. He then surfaced in Montevideo, the headquarters of the local Soviet Comintern, and unlike any of the other *tenentes*, joined the Communist Party. He was then taken to Moscow, where he was named the head of the Brazilian Communist Party in absentia and feted as a proletarian hero. He would return to Brazil, with tragic results, in 1935 with his wife Olga, a German communist and fellow fighter for the antifascist cause.

Generally, individual states remained responsible for public education, and most did little about it. Many states had no free secondary schools throughout the years of the Republic, and rates of literacy remained as low as those in the poorest countries of Europe and Latin America, despite Brazil's relative prosperity in the republican years. Brazil boasted only one modern comprehensive university, founded in Rio de Janeiro in the 1920s with the merger of existing independent faculties. Brazil's constitutional federalist system resulted in the rich states' becoming richer and the poor, poorer. The Republic was not, as some have suggested, a period of laissez-faire; in fact, both the federal and state government pioneered social legislation and other measures that affected people's lives. The main difference from the Empire was that administration was now decentralized. This in turn abetted regionalist senti-

ment—and, in parts of Brazil distant from the federal capital and shut
out of political influence by the coalition of the powerful states of the
Center-South and the Federal District—contributed to the revolts on
the geographic periphery that by the end of the 1920s so destabilized the
regime that it could not withstand the shock of the Great Depression and
fell to a military coup.

THE 1920s AND 1930s

The 1920s, then, saw a modicum of the legislative innovation that
would burst on the scene during the 1930s under Getúlio Vargas, much
as Franklin D. Roosevelt's New Deal was anticipated by measures in
New York State prior to his presidency. In 1923, the Brazilian congress
enacted the Elói Chaves Law, considered the starting point of the later
system of social security for workers. The law's system was based on
contributions from employees, companies, and the government, and it
was initially for railroad workers. In 1926 it was extended to dock and
maritime workers, and in the late 1930s to white-collar, industrial, and
transportation workers. Yet the representative federalist system, founded
on the fiction of representative democracy as specified by the 1891 constitution, failed. When world prices for agricultural exports plummeted
after 1929, the system showed itself to be hollow and inflexible. It barred
the door to persons excluded from the inner circle of the "best" families,
of clan groups linked by marriage and by business ties back to the old
plantocracy.

Society remained dominated by the agricultural elite, although rural
family groups had diversified, forming *panelinhas*, or networks, in which
family members became prominent in government, the professions, commerce, the armed forces, and industry. Hierarchy prevailed, though no
new titles of nobility were granted after the end of the monarchy and
the elite invariably married within its own ranks. The exception was
successful foreigners—sometimes engineers, or architects, or entrepreneurs—marrying into local elites. An example of such a marriage occurred in Belo Horizonte, the new capital of Minas Gerais, where a Czech
immigrant named Kubitschek married into the influential Oliveira family. The couple's son, Juscelino, eventually became governor of Minas
and, during the 1950s, president of Brazil. Non-Brazilian families that
did not intermarry with elites had opportunities to become wealthy, but
they less often achieved elite status—and therefore were tacitly excluded
from the inner sanctums of power.

Most members of the upper classes considered a "whitened" population the prerequisite for future national progress; this view was a product
of the pseudo-science of eugenics, popular in the late nineteenth and
twentieth centuries in Europe and North America. Many fretted about
what would happen to former slaves as they aged: the 1890s, in fact,
saw may states enact vagrancy laws designed to permit officials to jail
or run out of town beggars or others found within municipal limits without employment. One result was increased racial prejudice and a hard-
ening of racial lines. In Bahia, for example, during the late Empire most
schoolteachers had tended to be men of color, but under the Republic
the jobs were given to white women, usually unmarried. In small towns,
families of mixed racial origins were often barred from social clubs that
in some cases had admitted their parents and grandparents. This new
behavior was not universal, however, and never was written into law.

In the cultural realm, the period after the close of World War I witnessed a maturation of artistic expression, characterized by a determined
emphasis by many artists and writers on celebrating Brazil's unique heritage. The modernists, influenced by the avant garde movements of European Dadaism, mocked traditional elite culture and became the "bad
boys" of high culture. Historians and essayists searched the past to il-
luminate the present, although some of them preferred to dwell on past
glories rather than contemporary realities. Some saw the glass as half
empty, not half full. Paulo Prado, for example, scion to a wealthy *paulista*
coffee clan, carried forward the pessimistic explanations of the
nineteenth-century eugenicists, convinced that Brazil's colonial heritage
of slavery, plantation life, and race mixture was responsible for what he
termed Brazil's "sadness." Few championed the role of coffee as the economic force that had brought riches and spurred economic development
in the Center-South; analysts like Caio Prado Júnior a distant member of
the Prado clan, emphasized in his magisterial economic histories coffee's
negative associations with slavery and plantation society. The 1920s for
Brazil paralleled the experience of the United States but with greater
distance between the prosperity of the cities and the destitution of the
countryside. Elections sent members of the elite to the legislature and to
the presidency, and Brazil's economy prospered to the extent that prices
for export commodities remained high.

The Wall Street crash of 1929 sent tremors though the world marketplace, and coffee prices plummeted. This shock had an immediate political effect, as Brazil prepared for what was expected to be another fixed
and uncontested presidential election. São Paulo coffee producers, anx-

ious to retain control of the national government as a hedge against further economic dislocation, now backed out of the gentleman's agreement with the political leaders of Minas Gerais, who expected to be handed the presidency in keeping with the policy of rotating *paulistas* and *mineiros* in office. As a result, the 1930 presidential campaign witnessed a split in the elite, the formation of an opposition coalition made up of the states of Minas, Rio Grande do Sul, and northeastern Paraíba, and a successful effort by the opposition, which called itself the Liberal Alliance, to recruit the support of the *tenentes*, still exiled in Argentina and Uruguay but very much part of the nation's political consciousness.

Brazil in 1930 remained mostly rural, but its capital cities were growing rapidly. Urban residents, sensitive to the fact that rural bosses controlled politics and that the middle class had little say in government, flocked to the Liberal Alliance banners. Brazil stood poised to enter a new era characterized by political reform, economic change, and nationalism.

NOTE

1. Jeffrey Needell, "The Domestic Civilizing Mission: The Cultural Role of the State in Brazil, 1808–1930," *Luso-Brazilian Review* 36:1 (Summer 1999), 1–18.

5

The Vargas Era (1930–1954)

The First Republic (1889–1930) was dominated by oligarchies who controlled the state political machines, which in turn kept themselves in power by not enlarging the electorate. Under this system, the dynamic units of the federation (namely, São Paulo, Minas Gerais, the Federal District, and to some extent Rio Grande do Sul) controlled the federal government through their control of cabinet positions and the bureaucracy. The elites cared little for democracy or popular mobilization, although the country went through the charade of empty electoral contests, in which only a handful of men (women were not permitted to vote) cast ballots. Coffee planters dominated; industrialists were mostly left to fend for themselves. Nevertheless, substantial changes did occur. Landowners and factory owners, needing cheap workers but not inclined to pay wages to the descendants of the slaves who had been freed in 1888, subsidized the immigration of European laborers. Most of these immigrants were settled in agricultural colonies, where they had to work for years to pay off their debts; eventually many migrated to the cities of the Center-South, finding menial jobs in factories, as artisans, and in commerce. Some of the immigrants, many of them from Spain or Italy, brought with them socialist and anarchist ideas, implanted labor militance among their fellow workers, and led a series of strikes—almost all of which were quelled, often with violence. Fearing accelerated labor strife, employers regularly fired laborers suspected of being agitators, and in 1924 the Brazilian government established a special police organization, the Department of Political and Social Order (DOPS), to infiltrate unions, spy on dissenters, and preserve public order.

On October 3, 1930, in spite of his clear defeat in the presidential elections earlier in that year, Getúlio Vargas took control of the government by a military coup. Like Brazil's independence, the 1930 revolution was welcomed by the majority of the population. Crowds thronged to the railroad stations where Vargas's train stopped en route from Rio Grande do Sul to Rio de Janeiro. Most educated Brazilians had resented the attempt of the *paulista* oligarchy to keep power for themselves, and they rallied to the new leader's call for nationalistic reform and social legislation, much of which, those who closely followed politics knew, was patterned after laws in force in Vargas's home state.

Because the ousted President Washington Luís had controlled the election apparatus, his claim to have won all but three states garnered little popular support. Vargas's Liberal Alliance, a coalition of opposition politicians, rebel *tenentes*, and nationalists who advocated a return to centralized government to end São Paulo's dominance, had offered the incumbent several opportunities to compromise, but he had refused. Led by Oswaldo Aranha, like Vargas born to a powerful clan along the border in southern Rio Grande do Sul, the insurrectionary movement had gathered steam when Vargas's vice-presidential candidate, João Pessoa, was murdered—although the motive was not political—and when the old *café com leite* partnership broke apart. Vargas would be in power, in two separate periods, for twenty years—until 1945, and again from 1950 to 1954, when he put a pistol to his heart and took his own life at dawn of the day the armed forces were to oust him for the second time.

Who was Getúlio Dornelles Vargas? Universally known to Brazilians as "Getúlio" or "Gegê," he had been born to a powerful *gaúcho* clan and had risen within the dominant state Republican Party. He entered politics around the time of the First World War, when the state's older generation of partisan leadership was aging; many of his friends and fellow students acceded with him to positions of significant national leadership—civilian and military—during the 1930s and after.

Although he rose in politics as a loyal party hack, whose advancement depended on the good graces of a powerful state political machine, he showed the ability to be flexible. The main difference between Vargas and his political mentors—Júlio de Castilhos and Borges de Medeiros—is that he became willing to open the political system to new groups, principally members of the nascent middle class. In addition, he was a good listener, ultimately more comfortable with back-room deal making than trying to hold all power himself and suppressing opposition. In a patronage arrangement with the *paulista*-run government, Vargas was named to the cabinet as finance minister, even though he had no training or experience whatsoever in fiscal matters. When he was named as the opposition candidate for the presidency in 1930, his candidacy was dismissed universally as merely a symbolic gesture to preserve his state's independence; he even wrote a personal letter to the outgoing president more or less apologizing for his actions. His personality reflected a paradoxical combination of traits: he lived simply, yet he surrounded himself with cronies, some of whom were flamboyant, corrupt, or both. He was believed to be an agnostic, yet he worked closely with the hierarchy of the Brazilian Roman Catholic Church, effectively ending the separation between church and state that had been in effect since 1889.

VARGAS AS CHIEF OF STATE

Vargas and his advisors knew that the success of his new government would depend on the restoration of economic stability in the face of the world economic crisis. The country's entire gold reserve had disappeared in the fourteen-month period after September 1929. Ordinary Brazilians did not feel the pinch of the Depression as much as the middle class, because the poor always had lived at subsistence levels. Vargas maintained the delicate price controls that held down prices of basic foods, mostly wheat, milk, and beans, although his government did little to create jobs as unemployment rose sharply above even its usual high level. Currency-exchange controls were imposed in 1931 and were never completely removed. The right to issue currency was taken from the Banco do Brasil and transferred to the treasury in 1933, and the government ran budget deficits year after year. The *cruzeiro* was changed back to the *mil-réis* in 1932 and devalued by 40 percent. The rate of inflation worsened throughout the 1930s; by 1940–1944 it stood at 86 percent. Even during the Depression, then, hardship was worsened by chronic inflation.

Given these difficulties and the restlessness of the professional and business elites at the arbitrary measures taken by the provisional government, which held dictatorial powers, Vargas did his best to shore up the quality of urban life. The regime established new cabinet ministries to deal with urban issues and devoted considerable effort to the needs of urban workers. In the end, however, as Gabriel Bolaffi has noted, the government's urban activities were few and of little significance, "episodic achievements" based on "exceptional political circumstances."[1] Shantytowns grew in almost every major city during the 1940s and after, and millions of destitute northeasterners and other migrants from the hinterland streamed to the cities of the Center-South in the vain hope of finding industrial employment and housing. Before the 1930s, buildings in deteriorating neighborhoods had been subdivided and turned into tenements to provide housing for the poor, but migrants could afford to pay no rent at all; they had to build shacks out of scrap wood, tin, and cardboard on unused land, usually in the most unhealthful places, and without any running water, police protection, or sanitation.

Vargas's Liberal Alliance platform had promised to emphasize education at all levels, including vocational training. His regime started out in 1930 to reform education; some of his most hard-working and idealistic officials were educators. By the mid-1930s, however, their plans were drawing fierce opposition from traditionalists, including the hierarchy of the Roman Catholic Church, which considered progressive education to be communistic and supported only a limited form of vocational training provided to workers who were in highly skilled trades and also completely docile. This training was not implemented until the mid-1930s, and it was based on the premise—not altogether incorrect—that Brazil had to import industrial know-how and technology. After 1937, Vargas adopted a more nationalistic stance and backed away from the notion that Brazilian development should rely on foreigners.

Vargas delivered on many election campaign promises, but he did so in ways that made most of them meaningless. He gave the vote to women, for example, following the lead of a handful of northern and northeastern states during the late 1920s. The number of eligible voters rose from 1,291,548 in 1912 to 2,659,221 in 1934, reflecting the addition of women to the pool, but there were no direct national elections to the presidency or the federal legislature during Vargas's fifteen years in office before his ouster in 1945. By then, further population growth and the reforms subsequently enacted in the 1946 constitution had raised the number of eligible voters to 7,459,849, 20 percent of the population. As late as 1960, only 23 percent of the population was eligible to vote, a consequence of the high birthrate (and consequently the large numbers of Brazilians younger than the voting age of eighteen).

Unlike the United States, where racists in the southern states and elsewhere intimidated moderates by threatening blacks with violence, in Brazil neither formal segregation nor organized racist vigilante groups existed. Indeed, Brazil's new left- and right-wing groups welcomed nonwhites as members, although the ranks of both movements were heavy with Brazilians of foreign origin. Skin color as well as social status, however, did influence the way Brazilians were treated: well-to-do whites were rarely arrested by the police for any offense, whereas when poor Brazilians were picked up, even in the absence of formal charges, they expected to beaten, sometimes savagely.

Still, although unwritten attitudes and rules governed interracial behavior and cities remained highly segregated along economic lines, race discrimination never became a legal issue. During the 1920s a young sociologist named Gilberto Freyre, who had studied at Baylor University in Waco, Texas (the site of more lynchings of blacks than any other United States town or city), would return to Brazil and, during the 1930s, publish books and give talks in which he argued that Brazil's relaxed racial atmosphere, and what he claimed had been the benign ways in which masters treated slaves before emancipation, had created a "Tropical China," a diverse society with a promising economic future that lacked racial discrimination. For the large majority of Brazil's destitute and illiterate underclass, overwhelmingly nonwhite, this was in some ways a moot point, but by the late 1930s intellectuals delighted in embracing Freyre's theories about "racial democracy" and other interpretations, which were largely myths. After all, by arguing that all races are equal but that each one had its own place in the social hierarchy, Freyre offered a way to preserve the status quo, whereby discrimination in Brazil was seen as based on class and income, not biology.

To achieve his goals, Vargas set out to dismantle the old political system. He replaced entrenched state administrations with political interventors, most of them *tenente* military officers from the victorious Liberal Alliance military campaign of 1930. The idea was to bring in administrators loyal to Vargas's policies, not tied to local interests; in some cases, notably in Bahia and Pernambuco, the interventions for a time had the desired effect. Powerful São Paulo, however, bristled under the interventorship of João Alberto Lins de Barros, a dour and tactless officer who refused to cater to the sensitivities of the defeated *paulista* incumbency. In 1932, chafing under what it considered a military occupation, the state of São Paulo raised the banner of revolt, demanding a return to constitutional rule and the ouster of Vargas. Only the reluctance of other states to join the revolt prevented Brazil from breaking out in nationwide civil war for the first time in its history.

The roots of the conflict were economic as well as political. São Paulo had dominated the Republic because of its huge coffee exports and growing industrial and commercial base. *Paulistas* had shared power with the neighboring dairy state of Minas Gerais, expecting to rotate power. When São Paulo violated that agreement in 1930, putting forward a *paulista* (Júlio Prestes) to replace the outgoing president (Washington Luis Pereira de Souza, also a *paulista*), Minas Gerais and Rio Grande do Sul had defected to form the opposition Liberal Alliance. The worldwide depression that had wiped out demand for coffee made things worse and exacerbated tensions.

The São Paulo revolt was led by a coalition of conservative landowners and industrialists. Nearly the entire *paulista* population supported and joined the struggle. Young men from all classes flocked to enlist as volunteer soldiers, and women mobilized themselves to raise money, serve as nurses, and safeguard the home front. The armed conflict lasted from July to September 1932. A campaign to collect gold and jewelry to pay for armaments obtained by September 87,120 wedding rings and other articles valued in the millions of dollars.

Vargas's federal forces prevailed, but he wisely pardoned the leaders of the revolt and took over the state's war debt. Within a year he decreed that a constituent assembly would be called, on paper a fulfillment of the *paulistas'* goal. In 1934, the assembly ratified a new constitution for Brazil, a hybrid of holdovers from the republican era and provisions borrowed from experiments with corporatism (a form of fascism) in Europe. The members of the constituent assembly, none of whom had been elected by the people, then "voted" for Vargas to remain in office as constitutional head of state for a four-year term. To assuage the *paulistas*, who had advocated an outright return to pre-1930 arrangements, he made it clear that his government would give the state ample autonomy. This arrangement remained in force even after 1937, when Vargas and the armed forces canceled the scheduled presidential elections and proclaimed the Estado Novo dictatorship, which lasted until 1945.

Politics in Brazil during this period were affected not only by local events—and by the continued impact of the Great Depression—but by the winds of ideological conflict in Europe. Foreign influences had always entered Brazil freely: the conspirators in Minas Gerais in the 1780s had been inspired by the French Enlightenment, and Comtean positivism had closely influenced military officers and civilians in the second half of the nineteenth century. Immigrants from Spain and Italy had brought with them anarcho-syndicalist ideas as well as radical trade unionism, and intellectuals in 1919 in Rio de Janeiro founded the Brazilian Communist Party, inspired by V. I. Lenin and the Comintern. Fascism, as applied in Italy by Benito Mussolini, appealed to certain intellectuals in Brazil, and others turned with interest, especially in the aftermath of Hitler's rise in Germany, to the growing strength of nationalism and authoritarianism not only in the Reich but in Portugal, Spain, Romania, Poland, and among the followers of the French Catholic thinker Jacques Maritain. Brazil's Roman Catholic Church, which had followed a staunchly conservative line (rejecting European Catholic movements, for example, favoring Catholic labor unions and other organizations seeking social justice), felt comfortable with Vargas. He in turn restored all privileges that had been taken away by the 1891 constitution, which had separated church and state. He permitted for example, the return of Catholic chaplains in the military, the use of crucifixes and crosses in state buildings, and friendly relations with the Vatican.

IDEOLOGIES IN CONFLICT

The *tenente* movement that had fought to bring Vargas to power in 1930 contained factions committed to right-wing nationalism (and not adverse to continued military dictatorship). A second faction was led by Luis Carlos Prestes, who had gone to Moscow from his exile in Uruguay and, during the early 1930s, had been named the titular head of the Brazilian Communist Party. In October 1932, the Brazilian far right organized the Integralist Party, a movement dedicated to fascism; its members marched in military formation wearing uniforms of forest green with white armbands marked with the the the Greek letter sigma (Σ), the mathematical symbol for the sum of all parts. At a distance, the Σ looked very like the swastika—a distinction not overlooked by the Integralist *führer*, a nationalist writer and intellectual named Plínio Salgado, who wore a Hitler-style mustache. The left, for its part, organized local groups of militants, which in early 1935 organized nationally into the National Liberation Alliance (ANL), headed by a leftist admiral, Hercolino Cascardo, acting as surrogate for Prestes, who was believed to still be in the Soviet Union. The years 1934 and 1935 were marred by violent clashes between Integralists and leftists, with the police sometimes joining in on the side of the rightists.

In November 1935, the clandestine Communist Party, nominally led by *tenente* hero Luis Carlos Prestes but in reality closely directed by Soviet agents operating out of the Comintern office in Montevideo, launched a military insurrection to overthrow the Brazilian government. All three of the attacks occurred in army barracks; they involved communist militants, ANL fellow travellers, and soldiers and noncommissioned officers enlisted to the cause. In Natal, in Rio Grande do Norte, the rebels raised the red flag over the barracks and issued various manifestos declaring the liberation of the oppressed from international domination; in Recife fighting flared in various parts of the city; in Rio de Janeiro it broke out at Praia Vermelha, a military station in residential Urca. Loyal troops put down each of the outbreaks easily and arrested most of the participants. The folly of the communists, who apparently believed that the masses were ready to rise up against Vargas, gave hardliners and pro-fascists justification for inducing the government to suspend civil rights under a state of national emergency. Under the new National Security Law, thousands of persons were held and jailed, often under shocking conditions. Many of those jailed were only nominally connected to the ANL or to leftist causes and had certainly not been involved in the insurrection. Prestes and his German wife, Olga Benario, and several Comintern agents were captured early in 1936. He was sentenced to prison; his Jewish (and pregnant) wife was deported to Nazi Germany, where she perished in a death camp in 1942. The agents were tortured savagely, in some cases until they died.

The civilians and military leaders behind the imposition of dictatorship in November 1937 openly borrowed from European fascism. The name Estado Novo itself—the New State—was taken from the fascist regime of José de Oliveira Salazar in Lisbon. The principles of the dictatorship were also borrowed, more from Mussolini's Italy than Hitler's Germany, in terms of nationalism, government organization, and contempt for liberal democracy. The Estado Novo's makers, in their way, were highly idealistic and considered themselves visionaries. This is how Francisco Campos, the author of the constitution of November 15, 1937, explained the need for a revolutionary new order:

> The nation is not simply a concept hanging in the air. Men construct their country in the manner birds built their nests, as termites silently construct their cities, as rivers silently find their path. Each

one of these builders bring to their task effort, work, sacrifice, and tenacity, whether rooted in instinct or in will. . . . Vigilance must never be ended. . . . This is the lesson and the warning of our time: nations stand in peril. This is no time for dissention, for agitation, for internal discord. . . . Beneath our flag, each Brazilian is a soldier, and regardless of his vocation or his profession, his soul must be that of a soldier, ready to follow, ready to obey, prepared for privation or sacrifice.[2]

Vargas's propaganda agency bathed the country in sea of motivational rhetoric. "Do not be deceived," proclaimed press baron Assis Chateaubriand, "Getúlio Vargas is one of the common people. He uses his political position to promote the public good. His most important victories have been achieved at the side of the people; his interests are national as well as social." Chateaubriand concluded, "His different governments have been rooted in the goal of constructing a permanent place for the people, the great mass of the population, seeking to emancipate them from partisan oppression and from the avarice of militant politicians."[3] Other spokesmen lauded the Estado Novo as "an act of courage," a "work of art." The initiative was brilliant to the extent that it created a common language of praise, a common bond of citizenship. Yet that citizenship was hollow: free speech and the rule of law had been taken away, representative democracy buried, and the country turned into a dictatorship, however mild for most Brazilians and wrapped in pageantry and blue, green, and yellow flags and banners.

The Estado Novo regime closed the door on the hallowed Brazilian tradition of state autonomy, with a major exception: the state of São Paulo. No legislation exempted the *paulistas* from any laws or requirements; the matter was simply understood privately on both sides. Vargas, the pragmatic politician, knew that he had to give the *paulistas* what they had been demanding since 1930, at least in economic matters. Vargas also knew that he had to work for national unity. To the sound of drums and bugles, Boy Scouts ceremoniously lowered the state flags at a public square in the federal capital of Rio de Janeiro and raised on each flagpole the Brazilian ensign. Democratic pretense was dropped. There were no elections, no congress, no independent judiciary. To legitimate the New State, Vargas charged the propaganda machinery, centered in the new *Departamento da Imprensa e do Propaganda* (DIP), to instill national pride and teach Brazilians that they were part of a national family. Using public schools as his chief forum but also orchestrating newspapers, magazine, newsreels, and radio programs—all subject to strict censorship by the regime—Vargas attempted to imprint appropriate patriotic values in the hearts and minds of citizens, whom he now addressed as the *povo*, "the people." His portrait placed in every school and public building, Vargas was extolled as the Father of his Country. One primary school textbook explained the Estado Novo's philosophy in the form of a catechism:

"What is government, papa?"

"[Government] is an organization that directs and orients the destiny of the country, attending to its needs and its progress. Everybody needs a guide, a governor, a director who makes things run smoothly."[4]

Most members of the elite went along, and some were very enthusiastic. Many blamed what they considered to be the country's condition of backwardness on lack of organization—and on the unwillingness of the Brazilian people to work hard. They endorsed programs that as publicists for the regime explained in European fascist terms, were to impose efficiency and improve moral and national pride (the issue was rarely seen as one of poor education, low wages, or lack of jobs). They found themselves stirred by pageantry, by flags and banners, and by government programs that claimed to be "recovering the national past." Many were disenchanted with formal representative democracy—not that it had been given much of a chance—believed that by supporting Vargas Brazil could move forward industrially without threats from the communists and leftist sympathizers, and that social change could be accomplished incrementally, without dislocations. Government-imposed social peace, then, appealed both to conservatives and to practical businessmen.

A major turning point in the social policy of the Estado Novo regime came on January 26, 1942, when Vargas created by decree the National Service for Industrial Training (SENAI); four years later, General Eurico Dutra, elected president after Vargas's ouster by the military in 1945, created the Industrial Social Service (SESI). Both agencies represented something new for Brazil, in that although they were established by the government they were to draw their funding from the private sector. These training programs were narrow in scope: almost no women, for example, were offered instruction. Progress was also limited by the attitude of their managers, who feared labor independence and who borrowed from corporatist conceptions of common identity between workers and industrialists. As a result, "good" workers were rewarded, but workers who did not want to be treated as children drifted away. In all, skilled workers benefited in some ways (improved sanitary conditions, better instruction), but wages did not go up very much, and the training programs were offered only to the most skilled, a tiny percentage of working-class Brazilians. In 1945, the British consul in Porto Alegre, stepping down after long-service in Brazil, remarked in this final report: "The rich are richer than ever and the poor are poorer."[5]

Vargas's rotund shape and habit of speaking plainly, with ordinary gestures, endeared him to the public. One observer remarked, recalling having seen Vargas for the first time in public in 1930 as a small child,

> I was struck by how short he was. . . . The crowd went wild with adulation. . . . An enormous mass of people. Their spontaneous shouts made me think that I was in Italy, at the Venetian Plaza, watching one of the fascist rallies. This was the first impression I had of him. Later, as time passed, my view of him changed. It became evident that he was an opportunist, cold, capable of doing anything to hold onto power.[6]

Severino Fama, a businessman who considered himself a socialist, objected to the repressive side of the Estado Novo. He later recalled:

> Getúlio was intelligent, extremely perceptive, but also a demagogue who knew how to manipulate the masses. His self-assumed posture as "Father of the Poor" was based on Mussolini's *Carta del Lavoro* and shaped to Brazilian conditions. There was no freedom of expression, the press was controlled by the DIP, and the papers printed only what the regime wanted them to.[7]

Working-class people saw him less critically. A factory worker expressed himself in this way:

> Getúlio Vargas was everything to me. I never permitted anyone to say anything bad about him. Whenever he spoke on the radio I was thrilled. . . . I didn't understand anything about politics, but when I learned he would be speaking I told my mother that I wanted to hear him. I was always excited, even when I didn't understand

what he was saying, because I knew that he always gave us benefits, my work papers, I thought, I am a worker, and he has given
me so many benefits.[8]

IMPENDING CHANGES

World War II seemed to Brazilians to be very far away, although several thousand Brazilian soldiers fought in Italy and thousands of U.S.
armed forces personnel were stationed in Brazil, building air bases to
defend against a possible Axis invasion, flying antisubmarine patrols
over the South Atlantic, and otherwise helping produce rubber and erad-
icate disease in the Amazon. To win Brazil as an ally as the Second World
War approached, Washington had promised large amounts of military
and economic assistance, and although Nazi Germany took over the lead
from the United States in exports to Brazil between 1935 and 1937, by
1941 the need to enlist Brazil as an ally to obtain its rubber for arms
production, and to operate military bases on Brazilian soil had led the
U.S. State Department to make important trade concessions.

The Americans persuaded Brazil's government to create a "Rubber
Army," work brigades organized to plant and harvest rubber trees in
the Amazon. Brazilian rubber production had fallen as the result of
epidemic plant disease to six thousand tons in the mid-1930s, less than
one-half of 1 percent of world output. U.S. Agriculture Department technicians visited the Amazon in 1941 and 1942 and determined that rubber
cultivation could be boosted with sufficient manpower. The result was
the largest mobilization of unskilled labor in Brazilian history, almost all
of it peasants from the parched, unproductive Northeast. The U.S. Army
provided several dozen tanks and pledged two hundred million dollars
in military equipment, some of which was delivered only after war's end.

By 1945, rubber production had risen to 118,715 tons. The effort to
increase rubber production continued for another two years, after which
time revived rubber production in Southeast Asia and a switch to syn-
thetics by the automobile industry made Brazilian rubber uncompetitive.
Some recruits to the rubber campaign died from disease, but on the
whole working conditions, under the watchful eye of U.S. Army and
Rockefeller Foundation technicians, were better than before the war.
Many of the workers settled in the Amazon and were able to acquire
land and raise families. (In recent years a number of Brazilian journalists
have circulated stories that as many as thirty-one thousand of the fifty-
five thousand "rubber soldiers" between 1943 and 1947 died, but the

allegation remains one of those canards that are equally impossible to prove or disprove.)

The war interrupted shipping and therefore closed overseas markets. To some extent that fostered industrial expansion, although difficulties in importing machinery and spare parts limited gains. Vargas-era social legislation brought new benefits to certain working-class Brazilians, mostly members of skilled labor unions, although the Estado Novo did not permit independent labor unions to function. So cynical were Brazilian workers about the official unions, run by *pelegos*, government honchos, that despite the offer of attractive benefits (pensions, training, union-run vacation properties) most workers did not join. Most of Vargas's other social policies (including a minimum wage, pensions for workers, a commitment to school construction, and health care) proved immensely popular among the population—because of this legislation and of his attention to working class citizens he became widely known as "Father of the Poor"—but the failure to follow through on many of his reforms meant that they promised more than they delivered. Still, millions of hardworking Brazilians earned protected government jobs through the creation of a relatively independent civil service. Millions more, especially in the large cities, benefited from the improvements in infrastructure (modernization of transportation, expansion of radio networks, opening of some schools and hospitals) made possible by the influx of capital from the United States.

The war cut off Brazil's traditional Western European sources of loans and investment capital. For a time during the late 1930s, when Vargas was playing off Washington against Berlin, the German Reich almost became Brazil's leading trading partner, and British and French capital fled back to Europe. By 1942, the year Brazil declared war on the Axis in return for promises of massive American military and technological aid, the United States, whose role had been relatively minor, suddenly emerged as Brazil's major partner and source of investment. The American share of Brazilian trade jumped from 24 percent in 1938 to an average of 55 percent in the early 1940s and remained at that level.

During 1944 and 1945 Vargas not only pledged a return to democracy but personally courted members of the Left, whose leader, Luis Carlos Prestes, had languished in prison under harsh conditions since his arrest in 1936. Believing that elections would come as soon as the war ended, Vargas pointedly shifted the emphasis of his public statements to Brazilian workers, the family, and the middle class.

When the war ended, life for most Brazilians changed in many ways.

The country's Estado Novo constitution was increasingly an embarrassment: the war had been fought to preserve democracy, but Brazil's government was still authoritarian, with fascist trappings. The armed forces—chafing not at his authoritarianism but at his self-styled populism, which they considered demagogic—carried out a bloodless coup d'état. For the first time since he rose to power in 1930, Getúlio Vargas no longer ruled Brazil as head of state; he was sent back to his Rio Grande do Sul ranch, where he received a steady stream of visitors, dabbled in politics at the state level, and bided his time for a return to power. His nationalistic programs had not penetrated very deeply into the nation's hinterland; nor had opponents of his regime, including university students in São Paulo and Rio de Janeiro, allowed themselves to be intimidated.

In 1946 presidential elections took place, and a constitutional convention was held, which produced a new national constitution. It enlarged the electorate, made voting compulsory, and restored many of the functions of representative government that had been canceled under the Estado Novo, including the right of habeas corpus—guaranteeing, at least in theory, due process and legal rights for each citizen. It kept Vargas's social legislation, although it relaxed somewhat the powers of the central government.

The presidential election, which pitted one general, Eurico Dutra, against another, Eduardo Gomes, resulted in victory for Dutra, a short, bland man who looked physically like Vargas and governed without fanfare (Dutra, who had expressed fascist sentiments during the Estado Novo, had so tempered his policies that he became the preferred presidential candidate of the U.S. State Department). Nonetheless, changes brought about by the transition from wartime to peacetime and by the impact of United States military aid began to emerge. The military air bases, turned over to Brazil in 1945, served as the basis for the creation almost overnight of a modern domestic airline system, making travel between cities possible in a matter of hours, trips that had taken days or longer over Brazil's miserable prewar system of roads. The Estado Novo's radio network remained in place, but commercial networks, headed by the powerful media chain *Diários Associados*, took over predominence.

The postwar years ushered in a spurt in prosperity as wartime shortages ended, construction of apartment houses and private residences increased, and Brazilians imported thousands of automobiles from Europe and the United States. States and to some extent the national government took on responsibility for road building and construction of dams and port facilities. Brazil still lacked an adequate railroad system, but other forms of transportation, especially air travel, helped achieve a greater degree of economic integration. In 1947 a new plant at Volta Redonda, built with government funds and large grants from the United States Export-Import Bank, began to produce steel. This cut Brazilian reliance on costly imports and spurred construction of factories and residential units.

The accelerated government role in construction, however, had social consequences. The lure of jobs to the Center-South attracted tens of thousands of men from the Northeast and other distant areas. Voluntary communal labor, whereby neighbors helped one another to raise roofs, dig wells, and mend fences, diminished, because the government now provided more of these services (if, that is, a community was allied with the incumbent state faction or local political boss, not the opposition). On the whole, political violence decreased, abetted by a newly autonomous press (censorship was abolished with the Estado Novo in 1945).

Although Vargas had worked diligently to assert a sense of nationalism and to forge national unity and economic independence, World War II had brought Brazil much more significantly under the influence of the United States than ever before. Movie theaters and radio spread American popular culture; young Brazilians grew up on a steady diet of Disney characters and American westerns. Elites who had traditionally scorned the United States for its materialism and much preferred French, British, and even German culture, found American influence distasteful— Brazilians hooted Carmen Miranda when she returned to Brazil after becoming Hollywood's greatest success, for having sold out. Even they, however, could not resist the opportunities made possible by growing U.S. economic investment.

THE END OF AN ERA

Vargas's second chance came in 1950, when he was democratically reelected to the presidency. The 1946 constitution had ended censorship and led to an atmosphere of heady optimism. Interest groups, including industrialist associations, landowners, and workers, jockeyed for benefits. In 1953, labor unions, their members angered by economic hardships and runaway inflation caused by rapid post-war expansion, called a successful general strike that led Vargas to appoint the Labor Party's João Goulart as labor minister (in an effort to court worker support). Still, shortages persisted, and inflation continued to eat away at purchasing power. When Goulart broke with Vargas and demanded that the minimum wage be doubled, Vargas moved to distance himself from the labor unions, which conservatives considered radical and threatening. Vargas removed Goulart from office, but by early 1954 Vargas had apparently decided to abandon his characteristic appeal for industrial progress based on a controlled labor environment; in his 1954 May Day address to the nation he announced that the minimum wage would be doubled. He appealed to workers for their votes, reminding them of the power of their numbers. This angered employers, who felt that not only was Vargas's caving in to demagoguery but that they could not afford to pay higher salaries. It was one more instance of Vargas backing himself into a corner.

Financial instability and ever more vitriolic attacks from his political enemies crippled Vargas's presidency and drove him to despair. His main adversary was Carlos Lacerda, a newspaper publisher and formerly, as a university student, a member of the communist youth movement. By the 1950s Lacerda had changed political coloration and become a strident nationalist. On August 5, 1954, at an anti-Vargas rally, a gunman attempted to assassinate Lacerda, managing only to shoot him in the foot but killing Lacerda's bodyguard, air force major Rubens Vaz. Investigation by the armed forces implicated Vargas's own fiercely loyal bodyguard, Gregório Fortunato. This imposing black man had been convinced by people around Vargas that Lacerda was a threat, and he seems to have acted in outrage. To what extent the shooting represented a broader plot is not known. Vargas himself knew nothing of the plot but now found himself further isolated; he became a virtual recluse at the presidential palace in downtown Rio de Janeiro's Catete district. On the evening of August 24, 1954, Vargas retired to his bedroom and fired a pistol into his heart, killing himself instantly.

Vargas's death came hours before a military coup would have removed him from office. From 1930 to 1945 he had governed as a dictator, only to be removed by the generals. His suicide stunned the country and was met by an outpouring of public grief. Millions thronged the streets of Rio de Janeiro as his coffin was carried to Santos Dumont airport to be flown to his beloved home state of Rio Grande do Sul for burial. The suicide shocked his enemies as well as his supporters and led to a period of caution lest political and labor instability provoke massive strikes or military intervention. For a period of some years, the volatile political climate calmed down. Vargas's vice president, João Café Filho, was sworn in as president. In spite of his reputation as a leftist, derived from his days as a member of the National Liberation Alliance in 1935, and as an opponent of the Estado Novo, he governed cautiously; he prepared the way for peaceful national elections in 1955.

The Vargas years had seen the first efforts among Brazil's black and mixed-race citizens to address the needs of that community. Nonwhites numbered more than half of Brazil's total population, but only a minuscule percentage had achieved middle-class status. Nevertheless, on October 12, 1931, an assembly of more than a thousand in the city of São Paulo had approved by-laws for a new association, the Brazilian Negro Front. This was less a civil rights organization—the leaders were too cautious to speak up against discrimination—than a cultural group seeking to bring to national attention some of the cultural activities launched during the previous decade to champion Afro-Brazilian cultural expression. Negro Front leaders had sought social and economic progress and hoped that Vargas would be receptive to the needs of their community.

This had never happened. Vargas championed a kind of color-blind nationalism in keeping with the official myth that Brazil was a racial democracy. All Brazilians were equal before the law, this view went, so it would be wrong to single out individual groups as having special needs. Vargas's government in this sense had carried forward the laissez-faire attitude of the Old Republic, ignoring the obvious fact that nonwhites in Brazil so often lived wretched lives and lacked opportunities for education and employment. A few black militants had reacted in frustration by offering to organize a black legion to fight as volunteers on São Paulo's side in the 1932 civil war, but the initiative was not welcomed, and the effort died. Individual blacks had joined (and were accepted into) the fringe ideological groups that emerged during the mid-1930s—the fascist Integralist Party on the far right and socialist National Liberation Alliance on the far left—but both of these movements were closed down by Vargas in 1938 after the Estado Novo coup, under his ban on political organizations. The Brazilian Negro Front itself had won official recognition by the Supreme Court on November 10, 1937, the day of the Estado Novo coup. It was nonetheless closed six months later by Vargas's decree banning political groups, although its activities had been purely social and cultural.

The Estado Novo, moreover, had reinforced the elite's perception of the Brazilian people as childlike and simple. With all newspapers, magazines, books, newsreels, and radio programs censored, regime officials had manufactured an image of the Brazilian population as docile and hard working. Roguish behavior had been tolerated among men and sensuality praised among women, but it had remained explicitly forbidden under pain of arrest to write or speak publicly about poverty, illiteracy, malnutrition, or destitution, conditions under which a majority of the population lived.

Vargas had left many institutions untouched, including Brazil's 1916 Civil Code, a conservative legal document that reinforced patriarchal social relations, declaring husbands the legal heads of their households and leaving married women virtually without rights. He had left charity work in the hands of the private sector, although he turned them into semipublic agencies by giving them subsidies. During the 1920s, a number of *paulista* factories had pioneered the concept of "workers' villages" (the Vila Operária Maria Zélia, for example), in which workers were given housing and provided a comprehensive program of social benefits, including schools, infant-care centers, chapels, and soccer teams. The archdiocese of São Paulo had maintained a Metropolitan Catholic Workers' Central, with local agencies in the working-class neighborhoods of Moóca, Penha, Bras, Barra Funda, Itaquera, Ipiranga, and Lapa. The organization built children's playgrounds, showed films, and sponsored classes for women in hygiene and domestic skills. The city of São Paulo had established a bureaucratic agency responsible for children's recreation; in January 1935 it came under the jurisdiction of the new Department of Culture and Recreation.

The Estado Novo had been porous enough to permit independent private associations. In 1942, for example, neighborhood associations emerged in several São Paulo cities to promote urban improvements. After 1945, more private groups had organized, challenging the notion that only the state could propose change. The newly legal Communist Party had established "Democratic Committees" as alternatives to official *sindicatos*, first in Belém and then in other cities. Worker committees were organized in several industries to sidestep the official unions, which continued to be controlled by the government. The year 1946 had seen the creation of the Popular Campaign against Hunger, which published lists of merchants who charged excessive prices for basic food. After Vargas's election in 1950 a wave of strikes, marches, and other protests had demanded that he raise wages and combat inflation and soaring prices. Three hundred thousand workers struck in São Paulo in 1953, and nearly half a million marched in rallies in São Paulo and Rio de Janeiro. In cities, people enlisted in the national Campaign against the High Cost of Living.

Men had benefited more than women under Vargas's legislation. The laws were written by male bureaucrats for the good of male wage earners and their dependents. It had always been assumed that men headed families and that families were natural; legislation aimed at helping women who were not part of families or even worked to supplement family income was never considered, although women made up more than three-quarters of teachers and dominated white-collar commercial and retail jobs. Although Vargas's decrees were color blind, persons of mixed race (if not pure blacks) were more likely to gain employment in the government than in the private sector, where hiring practices openly excluded non-Caucasians. Many citizens of color had owed their higher economic status to the changes ushered in by Vargas's programs, if not to any conscious effort by Vargas to assist persons of color—although he became a hero to them. Photographs show that blacks had participated in Vargas-era rallies and activities, but typically not in significant numbers.

Vargas had been the first Brazilian head of state to place women on his political agenda. He had given them the vote, a hollow gesture since there were no direct elections between 1933 and 1945. DIP propagandists paid homage to motherhood and the role of women as homemakers, but the regime had done little to enforce regulations prescribing work conditions for women. The government's lip service to women and its commitment to the traditional value system tended to smother impulses to mobilize feminist activities. As a result, Brazil had failed to develop a women's movement of any significance. Vargas had drawn legitimacy from his country's tradition of social hierarchy and paternal authority, embodied by his role as benevolent father.

The Estado Novo had wooed the middle class by symbolically coupling home, politics, and morality. By appealing to white-collar employees and professionals and their families, Vargas and his advisors had hoped to build a stable base of support among these men and women who were neither connected to the old politics, dominated by the landowning class, nor linked to the lower class. By emphasizing order, education, and discipline, Vargas's propaganda had assuaged the fears of the middle class of downward mobility. Members of the middle class responded warmly. Many of its members had felt helpless as partisans of the Right and Left clashed in the mid-1930s. The imposition of the

Estado Novo had been frightening too, especially to intellectuals and those touched by the loss of free speech. But Vargas had taken pains to demonstrate that his regime would be fairly benign to those that supported it, and by the early 1940s the government had even begun to permit mild forms of dissent. Especially in São Paulo and Rio de Janeiro, where the emergent middle class achieved the highest standard of living, subtle changes were at work. The middle class had expected to have schools for their children, to enjoy access to health care, and to be able to compete for jobs on the basis of merit, not connections. By promising all this Vargas not only consolidated his support but gently created the preconditions for the eventual restoration of working democracy. Much of this was a sham, however: the middle class had accepted a bargain that brought them the illusion of protection by the agencies of government—after all, the schools and the health facilities were never adequate—in exchange for denying themselves an active role in politics. Vargas's social legislation, much of which was to remain in place in the middle 1990s, had remained limited in scope and uneven.

For example, when the minimum wage had been introduced in 1940, eligible workers in Rio de Janeiro received the equivalent of $131 a month. This was a generous amount, although it is telling that workers continued to stay out of officially sanctioned labor unions, which not only guaranteed the minimum wage but offered benefits. (The national monthly minimum wage was to rise the equivalent of $252 by 1954 but thereafter go into free fall, bottoming out at $120 a month in 1992.) Moreover, a good proportion of the population had not earned the minimum wage, which was pegged lower outside the Center-South. On the other hand, Vargas had used his wage policies to lessen traditional reliance on the export sector, strengthening the hand of the industrial elite and urban workers. The minimum wage had affected both supply and demand, in a complementary way.

Employers had regularly ignored the rules, claiming that they would have had to close otherwise. More than anything else, this is why Vargas's sweeping social and labor legislation had failed to change very much although Vargas had remained popular among the working-class Brazilians he so ardently courted. They, in turn were to become the basis of his successful run for the presidency in 1950. Industrialists and employers did not care whether Vargas's rhetoric was progressive or corporative: they had simply intended to block any reform that interfered with their profits. Virtually all of the strikes between 1931 and 1936, from Rio Grande do Sul to Pará, and all the limited strikes and work stoppages that took place between 1936 and 1940, had been to win rights and conditions guaranteed by law but not provided. The Companhia de Tecidos Paulista, in Pernambuco, forced workers—large numbers of them women and children—to work twelve-hour days in spite of eight-hour-day legislation. The same had been true for many mills in São Paulo, where fourteen-hour days were not uncommon. There had been many ways of getting around regulations. Sociologist Janice Perlman tells the story of a sixty-year-old migrant who waited six months to obtain his papers, only to be told by a manager that he could have the job if his work card was not signed, so that the firm would not have to pay social security benefits, pensions, sick-leave, or overtime rates. The man accepted the job, working a twelve-hour shift, four hours over the legal maximum, at half the minimum wage, and without protection. Those without work papers fared worse. Police regularly stopped busses, raided shantytowns, and demanded to see documents; those without them were charged with vagrancy.

Vargas imposed few taxes on income or on inherited wealth, and charitable philanthropy remained very limited. Nor did the Roman Catholic Church, historically relatively poor and socially very conservative, have a major impact in social relief. Banks never were given incentives to provide credit for small lenders to start businesses or build housing. The federal government established an independent monetary authority, with limited powers, only in 1946, and Brazil's Central Bank would be fully established only in 1964.

Many of Vargas's initiatives had produced little more than paperwork and moral self-congratulation. He had lauded public school teachers as the "little, overshadowed heroes of daily life," but he did little to improve their wages. Almost all teachers had been underpaid and underqualified; most lay teachers were paid little more than manual laborers. Their salaries were sometimes paid months late. At the secondary level, Brazil had had fewer than a dozen tuition-free secondary schools. Vargas's educational reforms had varied enormously from state to state, although his National Educational Plan, which called for free and semi-mandatory public education, was made part of the 1934 constitution. In Rio de Janeiro, Anísio Teixeira took dramatic steps to professionalize education, expand matriculations, and to improve schools, but he had been fired as being too liberal after the ANL was closed in 1935, in a wave of anti-intellectualism. São Paulo achieved progress in this area mostly under its own auspices, under the unwritten arrangement its elite had made with Vargas after 1932 to let the state carry out its own programs. The drive to modernize Brazil had led Vargas to create free, comprehensive universities, but few nonelite youths who did not attend private secondary schools could hope to pass the rigorous *vestibulares* (entrance examinations).

The contention that Vargas's reforms actually accomplished little— that programs were shallow and limited in their impact—is borne out by the allocation of fiscal resources under Vargas's tenure. Despite his constant and growing emphasis on the need to elevate the condition of the poor, the fact is that while his government claimed to allocate between 5 and 10 percent of the national budget to public education, it is likely that a good portion of the funds were either never delivered to needy school systems or, worse, misappropriated or stolen.

Determining to what degree the improvements in the lives of ordinary Brazilians came about from government action rather than evolutionary change is of course difficult. During the 1930s and 1940s, many countries with different kinds of governments acquired social security systems of comparable scope. Vargas never eliminated the role of the states, many of which, especially São Paulo but also Minas Gerais and Rio Grande do Sul, initiated or maintained social programs of their own. In the stagnant municipality of Cunha, in São Paulo's Paraíba Valley, the state built during the 1930s schools, a health service, a pediatric center, an agricultural station, judicial and police facilities, a state bank, statistics and records agencies, and a meteorological station—all entities that affected the lives of its citizens in direct and indirect ways every day. World War II boosted exports, brought in hard-currency reserves, and increased the power of industrial labor unionists. Import substitution stimulated manufacturing, although the interruption of shipping made it nearly impossible to obtain needed tools and metals.

Analysis of social and economic conditions reveals unexpected findings. Of a thousand students entering first grade in 1942, only 155 completed three years of primary school. In 1995, sixty-five years after Vargas swept into power at the head of a victorious coup that soon declared itself to be revolutionary, and forty-one years after Vargas's death, Brazil's infant mortality rate stood at 51.6 per thousand, almost ten times worse than Spain's, a country surpassed by Brazil a decade earlier in aggregate economic output. That conditions were even worse in preceding decades, when Vargas's social legislation was enacted, hints at the magnitude of the problems faced by government planners and at the shallow impact of the Vargas-era programs. At the end of World War

II, life expectancy in southern states was eight years higher than the national average and sixteen years more than in the long-depressed Northeast. Vargas had done little for the poor regions of the country.

His suicide in 1954 produced outpourings of grief that matched in intensity and scope the shock felt by most Americans at the death of Franklin D. Roosevelt in 1945. Even though Vargas had not provided very much, and even if the archaic hierarchical structure of the Brazilian oligarchy had remained completely intact, he had been the first politician to extend dignity to the Brazilian people. The contrast between the political spirit of the Old Republic, which had despised the common people, and the uplifting rhetoric of Vargas's radio broadcasts, speeches, and public appearances in even the most remote reaches of the vast country, was striking. Vargas really had become the father of the poor in the minds of the mass of the population. For nationalists, the stridency of his admonition against imperialism and foreign interests, which dominated his suicide letter, made him a prophet and seer.

Yet Vargas's laws were never intended to close the vast gap between rich and poor. Only laws based on concepts of distributive justice could have brought real change, but this was alien in concept to Vargas and the upper classes. Vargas's reforms raised the quality of life for millions but distanced the lives of millions even further from those of the affluent. They modernized Brazil, but they did not do much to enlarge the domestic market, to deal with underemployment, to facilitate the acquisition of land, to provide technical training, or to remove the pariah status of men and women doomed by lack of opportunity to grinding poverty. The period between 1939 and the early 1970s was to yield increased real wages for industrial workers (industrial wages rose 60 percent between 1939 and 1975) but a decline in real wages and living conditions for unskilled workers, the vast majority.

NOTES

1. Gabriel Bolaffi, "Para uma nova política habitacional e urbana," in L. do P. Valladares, ed., *Habitaçõ em Questão* (Rio de Janeiro: Zahar, 1980), 50, cited by Edesio Fernandes, *Law and Urban Change in Brazil* (Brookfield, VT: Ashgate, 1995), 17.

2. Franciso Campos, *O Estado Nacional* (Rio de Janeiro: Livraria José Olympio, 1938), 256–57.

3. *O Jornal* (Rio de Janeiro), 1939. Clipping file, Arquivo Nacional, Rio de Janeiro.

4. Paraphrased from Luiz Amaral Wagner, *Nosso Brasil* (São Paulo: Nacional, 1938), 19.

5. Memorandum, Ex-Consul McRae to Foreign Office, on board the S. S. *Boskoop*, June 1945, in Public Record Office, London, Foreign Office, 371/44807, AS 3388/52/6.

6. Anonymous public official, interviewed by Cecília Vita, São Paulo, cited by Maria de Lourdes Mónaco Janotti, "O Imaginário sobre Getúlio Vargas," in *História Oral* 1, no. 1 (June 1998): 94.

7. Severino Fama, interview with Claudia Padilha Furlai, São Paulo, in *História Oral*, 1, no. 1 (June 1998): 99–100.

8. Anonymous worker, interview with Rita de Cásia Rossi, São Paulo, cited in Janotti, *História Oral*, 97.

6

Dictatorship and Democracy
(1954–1998)

The political aftermath of Vargas's death brought enormous changes to Brazil, although it is difficult to ascertain to what extent they resulted from internal events and to what extent they were inevitable by-products of modernization and the burgeoning world economy. By the 1950s Brazil's government had bureaucratized at the national, state, and local levels to a degree that would have been unheard of a generation earlier United States air bases built for hemispheric defense during World War II had become the basis for a modern civilian aviation industry, compensating for the nation's lack of railroad tracks and paved highways and making possible contact with even the most remote parts of the country. Brasília, the new national capital carved out of the forests of central Brazil, rose out of nothing as the result of a massive airlift that flew in thousands of tons of cement, steel, and supplies. By the late 1950s television programs were available in every major city, complementing a network of sophisticated national newsmagazines and major newspaper that broke down (but did not completely eliminate) the barriers that formerly had isolated one Brazilian city from another.

During the Juscelino Kubitschek administration in the late 1950s, critics seeking fundamental social change—land reform, higher wages, alignment with Cuba, redistribution of income—began to be heard. The result was to some an exhilarating experience in free expression, but to others it seemed an ominous threat, a kind of rabble-rousing that would bring about social instability. The movement for social change was played out in the cultural arena as well as in the political. In 1960 filmmakers launched what became known as the Cinema Novo (the New Cinema), following the successful release in the late 1950s of films by Nelson Pereira dos Santos and others exploring the harsh underside of Brazilian life and the sufferings of the poor. The first phase of the Cinema Novo lasted until 1964, with films on rural poverty, hunger, religious alienation, and economic exploitation. They included Glauber Rocha's *Deus e Diabo na Terra do Sol* (1964) ("Black God, White Devil"), a searing film in three parts set in the drought-ridden Northeast, and Carlos Diegues's *Ganga Zumba* (1963), which brought up the issues of race and violence.

Thirty-six percent of Brazilians could not read and write, although by the 1970s the country's leading universities—centered in São Paulo and Rio de Janeiro—boasted world-class professors in law, letters, social science, the natural sciences, and medicine. More Brazilian women worked in the professions (though not in the business world) than in the United States, but as late as the 1970s married women could not leave the country without their husbands' permission, even if they were legally separated, and women could not press charges against their husbands for physical abuse unless the husband gave his consent. The 1970s saw raised feminist consciousness about women's role in Brazilian life. Most feminist writers, however, were restricted to Marxist categories and analysis. As a result, lower-class women in the millions went on with their lives of deprivation and hardship while upper-class women debated theoretical points. The voluntary associations that did seek to help poor women tended to be sponsored by the Roman Catholic Church, evangelical Protestant groups, or by mayoral administrations in urban areas.

The armed forces continued to stand in the wings, intimidating political leaders with the threat of intervention. In 1930 the military had overthrown the officially elected government in favor of Vargas's popularly defeated Liberal Alliance. Coups had taken place again in 1937 and 1945; in August 1954 another one, to oust Vargas for a second time, was stopped only by the bullet by which Vargas took his own life. Rumors of new coups flew during the presidency of Vargas's successor, João Café Filho, and his successor, Juscelino Kubitschek. They increased after 1960, when reformist Jânio Quadros took office, and they rose to fever pitch when Quadros's leftist vice president, João Goulart, returned from a trip to communist mainland China to assume the presidency. On March 31,

1964, the rumors came true at last, with the ouster of Goulart and the imposition of a military dictatorship, which would last until 1985.

Lack of a sense of any need for inclusion kept the political system closed and prevented democracy from developing. Under the colonial system and the Empire, Brazilians—at least at the local level—probably had more say in their own affairs than under the Old Republic, when state political machines had controlled virtually everything, or under Vargas, when elections had rarely been held despite his laws enlarging the electorate. Insufficient opportunities for public education preserved the rigidity of the class system, whereby young men from the elite went to the nation's few universities and on graduation stepped into positions of leadership. The only way for young men not either well connected or from the powerful regions of the country to gain an education was to attend one of the country's several military academies. There they received excellent schooling, often superior in quality to that received by the elite *bacharéis*, as college graduates were called. This reality had fueled the *tenente* movement of the 1920s, led by cadets and junior officers disdainful of professional politicians and their narrow interests. Vargas's revolution brought many of the *tenentes* to power, although by 1930 they were divided among themselves, and by 1935 nationalistic officers who favored corporatism and fascism had risen to power in the military.

The causes for the civilian-military coup that now overthrew still another constitutional Brazilian government had many causes. Vargas's effort to promote national integration, industrial development, and benefits for skilled workers had sped Brazil's maturation as a modern nation. The influx of migrants from the depressed hinterland had accelerated urban growth: by 1960, most Brazilians lived in cities. Improved transportation and communications made distances shorter, at least for those who could afford air travel, automobiles, telephones, and television sets. Café Filho, vice president and a former leftist, assumed the presidency after Vargas's suicide, although the armed forces considered ousting him. Juscelino Kubitschek, the governor of Minas Gerais, won the 1955 presidential election on a platform promising national development and democracy. The economy buoyed by foreign investment, Kubitschek oversaw the construction of the new national capital of Brasília, spurred the growth of the automobile industry, and shepherded the country through a maze of growing-pains. When Kubitschek stepped down in 1960, however, the country faced an enormous foreign debt and labor unrest. The 1960 election was the first in Brazilian history where the incumbent turned over power to the opposition party, in this case led by *paulista* reform candidate and governor Jânio Quadros. Quadros's victory came less from party strength than from his personal popularity and his promise to sweep Brazil clean of corruption and inefficiency. His principal opponent was Marshal Henrique Teixeira Lott, Kubitschek's war minister. Lott was defeated at the polls, but his vice-presidential candidate, leftist João Goulart, won election.

REFORM AND REACTION

Before his inauguration, Quadros departed on an extensive trip abroad, in which one of his stops was Cuba, just a year after Castro's revolution. Journalists, who had been sympathetic to him during his campaign, began to emphasize his personal eccentricities. Congress balked at his proposed reforms, none of which were enacted. He applied an austerity program to stabilize the currency, an unpopular measure. Guanabara (Rio de Janeiro) governor Carlos Lacerda, who had supported him, began denouncing him angrily, in the same tone as Lacerda had used to attack Vargas in 1954.

Seven months after he had taken office, the mercurial Quadros abruptly resigned. It is speculated that he hoped that Congress and the armed forces would seek his forgiveness and give him additional powers to deal with the growing crises, but the country remained silent, and Quadros forlornly flew into exile. Goulart, more outspokenly leftist than Quadros and therefore anathema to the military, was in the People's Republic of China when Quadros resigned, but he was permitted to return and take the oath of office as part of a deal that made him president under a parliamentary system limiting his executive powers. The first part of Goulart's presidency was rather successful. He assumed a moderate posture and worked quietly behind the scenes to restore the presidential system. Voters in 1963 restored the presidential system by a five-to-one margin.

But the economic situation deteriorated ominously, exacerbated by Goulart's efforts to keep workers' wages on a par with the soaring cost of living. To stabilize the economy in a long-term manner, Goulart would have had to enact austerity measures similar to those that had helped bring down Quadros, and the militant labor unions and the left-wing press would not allow him to do so. This united the rich and the upper-middle class against him, and his efforts to mobilize the mass of the population failed. By mid-1963, armed forces officers were beginning to conspire against him, with the full moral support of influential property owners, industrialists, bankers, and the U.S. State Department (since 1959 vigilant against another Castrolike takeover in the hemisphere). These were the years of the John F. Kennedy–Lyndon B. Johnson "Alliance for Progress," an international economic development program established in 1961 by the United States and twenty-two South and Central American nations. Much of its funding was channeled to Brazil's Northeast to combat poverty and the influence of the threat of Francisco Julião's Peasant Leagues, which sought to take unproductive land from wealthy owners and give it to landless peasants. There were seventy-six million Brazilians in 1963, most of them under twenty-five years of age, and many observers feared that the masses might be stirred by demagogic promises to abandon their traditional posture of docility in the face of hardship. By 1960, the electorate had grown to encompass almost one-quarter of the population.

During 1963 and early 1964, Goulart moved steadily farther to the left. Radicals loyal to the president took control of the leading labor unions. In public statements, Goulart attacked multinational corporations and what he called the imperialist activities of the United States. What stood in the way of Goulart's radicalism, however, was what political scientists have dubbed the "system." Oliveiro S. Ferreira explains it this way: "Although it has no clear-cut constituents, it is comparable to an organism which reacts as a whole, as though by reflex, when one of its vital organs is threatened."[1] Philippe C. Schmitter offers another way of understanding the quandary:

[D]espite obvious differences in interest and attitude, the *sistema* was formed by sedimentation, not by metamorphosis. Intersectorial flows of capital and entrepreneurial talent, inter-elitist family contacts, generalized fear of the enormous latent potential for conflict of such a weakly-integrated society, heterogeneity within the rural, commercial, industrial, and proletarian classes—all have helped seal the compromise. The success of this non-antagonistic pattern in turn ensured a continuity in the political culture and a reinforcement of those attitudes stressing the avoidance of conflict, dialogue, ideological flexibility, tolerance and compromise.[2]

According to this view, the "system" reacted in self-defense when Goulart violated the rules of the compromise and attempted to appeal directly to the masses. When noncommissioned officers led by sergeants mutinied in Brasília in September, he refused to condemn them, infuriating the military command. Governor Lacerda, whose vitriolic attacks on Goulart were growing in intensity now, forged an alliance against Goulart with the governors of the other two most powerful states—São Paulo's Adhemar de Barros and Magalhães Pinto of Minas Gerais.

On March 13, 1964, Goulart and his brother-in-law Lionel Brizola addressed, in an open square in Rio de Janeiro, a crowd of some hundred thousand workers and supporters. To many listening to the speeches on radio or television, it seemed that the president had gone too far, demanding land reform and the nationalization of private oil refineries. Brizola demanded that Congress be dissolved and that worker and peasant "assemblies" be substituted to speak for the people. Adverse reactions to this and other developments took many forms, including an escalation of the press campaign against the government and the organization of middle-class protest groups. The largest of these groups, the "March of the Family for God and Liberty," organized by a nun, Sister Ana de Lourdes, held an anticommunist parade of what supporters claimed to be eight hundred thousand women in São Paulo. The leaders of the march issued a proclamation, which read, in part:

This nation which God gave us, immense and marvelous as it is, faces extreme danger. We have allowed men of limitless ambition, without Christian faith or scruples, to bring our people misery, destroying our economy, disturbing our social peace, and to create hate and despair. They have infiltrated our Nation, our Government Administration, our Armed Forces and even our Churches with servants of totalitarianism, foreign to us and all consuming. ... Mother of God preserve us from the fate and suffering of the martyred women of Cuba, Poland, Hungary and other enslaved Nations![3]

On March 31 and April 1, 1964, the leadership of the armed forces ousted the president and drove him into exile in Uruguay. Left-wing officers, who had supported Goulart's government, stood by mute. The coup, which its makers called a revolution, drew almost no opposition, although it was bitterly received by university students, progressive intellectuals, and labor officials. The middle and upper classes, however, welcomed the declaration by the military that it would stay in power until national reconstruction was achieved. Strikes were banned, a censorship apparatus was put into place, and arrests were carried out (at first, only of active militants—later, of many people simply on suspicion of being leftist). The military leadership remembered that the armed forces had withdrawn after intervening in 1945, 1954, 1955, and 1961, without accomplishing much change in the political system, and they were determined never to let it happen again. In language that was over-simplified and exaggerated at the same time, supporters of the coup rationalized what had been done. One analyst wrote (in an unintentionally ironic reference to the "Brazilian way," and using the label the coup's makers claimed for it, "revolution"):

Brazil was saved by a genuine people's revolution, by its concerned patriots working in law abiding and moderate groups. In the very Brazilian way, however, the climactic phase of the revolution was accomplished by military action. The Brazilian military had proven once again to be the trusted "guardians of the nation, the true protector of the people and defender of their will." They are much respected for their great loyalty and dedication of their duties and for never showing the tendency to grab power.[4]

The day after the coup, the leaders of the March of the Family held a massive rally of support in the streets of Rio de Janeiro. They called the rally "The March of Thanksgiving to God" and later claimed that more than a million citizens had lined the streets. The presidency of Brazil was temporarily given to Raneiri Mazzilli, the president of the Chamber of Deputies. Two weeks later the Congress rubber-stamped the armed forces's "nomination" of a military president, Marshal Humberto Castelo Branco, to serve the remainder of Goulart's term. Castelo Branco's image was that of a reserved, personally honest, and austere man, and he was not unpopular. The son of a career army officer from northern Ceará, he articulated the reasons for the coup in reasonable language and was warmly received abroad. One of his first moves, however, was to remove from office fifty-five deputies, seven state governors, 122 military officers, and 4,500 government employees. Hundreds of citizens were imprisoned without habeas corpus or legal defense. Leading politicians linked to Goulart, including Quadros and Kubitschek, were stripped of their political rights. Other figures, like progressive archbishop Dom Helder Câmara, became "nonpersons," kept out of the newspapers and the media, and under surveillance. Because Goulart was considered an heir to Vargas's populism, even the late president-dictator, still popular among older Brazilians, became to some extent a nonperson.

Agents of the political police ransacked the headquarters of student associations, labor unions, left-wing newspapers, and the homes of militants. The contents of libraries were stuffed into canvas mail sacks and taken to police headquarters and scoured for communistic books; quantities of Cuban and Russian textbooks, scientific publications, and works of ideological propaganda were seized. The definition of "communistic" was very broad: it was enough to have a copy of John Gunther's *Inside Russia* (published when Brazil and the United States had both been wartime allies of the Soviet Union) to be labeled a subversive and subject to arrest. The military government announced that in the Northeast two farms had been bought with money sent by Fidel Castro and set up as training centers for Brazilian guerrillas, and that in São Paulo the Communist Party had printed up large supplies of postage stamps, bank notes, and pamphlets, with the portraits of Lenin, Joseph Stalin, and Brazilian Communist Party chief Luis Carlos Prestes.

With the congressional opposition purged, the military realigned with remaining legislators into two new party blocs, the right-wing ARENA (Alliance for National Renewal) and the moderate MDB (Brazilian Democratic Movement). Wags called them the "Party of Yes" and the "Party of Yes, Sir!" The military-era Congress did little but rubber-stamp what the military wanted, including the 1967 constitution, with its authoritarian provisions.

Castelo Branco completed his term and stepped down. He was followed on October 3, 1966, by General Artur Costa e Silva, who five years before had refused to accept João Goulart's invitation to become army chief of staff. Costa e Silva, like Castelo Branco, governed by decree but in consultation with civilians, and he limited repressive measures to a relatively small group of persons openly linked to the Goulart administration and the left wing. In August 1969, however, Costa e Silva suffered a stroke and was replaced by another general, Emiliano Garrastazú Médici. By 1969 tensions had increased and the atmosphere had become more confrontational. At the local and state level, police and military officers, often acting on their own, stepped up arbitrary arrests of persons they considered subversive, and reports began to surface of brutality and torture. Under Médici, repression at the national level also worsened. Small groups of left-wing militants had taken to the streets, robbing banks, kidnapping prominent persons (including the U.S. ambassador, who was released with others in exchange for the release of political prisoners). The political police and the intelligence agencies of each of the military services carried out mass arrests and drove thousands of others from their jobs or into exile. As ever, whether one was tortured, murdered, or simply allowed to leave the country depended on one's personal and family connections; it helped to have a cousin or brother-in-law who was a colonel. While Brazil's repression was not as savage as that under the military dictatorships in neighboring Argentina or Chile, it was terrible for those caught up in it, and it helped produce a generation of apolitical university students and intellectuals.

The military government launched a public relations drive that was in some ways a caricature of the nationalistic efforts of Vargas's DIP. The army's *civismo* campaign, however, was no lighthearted effort, with Walt Disney characters and pageants; during the 1960s and 1970s the armed forces and their civilian agents used intimidation to teach patriotism. Billboards overlooking city streets showed a hand holding a work permit, and a warning in large letters: "Without proper documents you are nothing!" Military and police censors drove newspapers and book publishers out of business and tightly censored the Brazilian movie industry, theater, and popular music. Television networks constantly carried government propaganda. Bumper stickers were distributed with slogans like "Brazil: Love It or Leave It." The campaign frowned on dissent and preached unconditional loyalty to the country and to its military leaders. This sort of propaganda, and the carrot-and-stick techniques used by authorities to reward cooperation and squelch dissent, made people cautious. They lacked the stimulus and the experience needed to mobilize political concern. The chilling warnings against dissent and in favor of patriotic loyalty hammered home in the government's propaganda campaign came through loud and clear in the selection titled "The Maximum Norm of the Exercise of Liberty." Consider this excerpt from a textbook required for all secondary school students:

Brazil, to us in 1973, in the tenth year of the Revolution, is an enormous land distinguished by its greatness among the nations of South America; it is a land of hope, destined for power and for world leadership. Its population of 110 millions form a western people forever united in pride and bravery. We are known for our generous character and Christian values; we love this country because it is ours; we triumph in its progress. We speak the same language and are united behind the same flag. Our history has been made by exemplary men, lovers of their country, who shed their blood to defend it. [We possess] resources of prodigious wealth. Here there are no volcanoes, hurricanes, cyclones. We have land in abundance, mineral and petroleum wealth, enormous rivers to produce electric power, forests, raw materials to contribute to industrial progress. . . . The very map of Brazil appears in the shape of a human heart. It is a heart that encompasses treasures of rich natural resources above and below the ground. Through its great rivers—the São Francisco and the Amazon—circulate its lifeblood; extensive networks of highways form its arteries. It is a virgin heart, trembling with hope, a heart which incorporates blood from the Indian, Latin and African races. . . . This is my country; I am proud to call myself Brazilian. . . . We Brazilians know that teamwork is more effective than individual effort. . . . To subordinate our own freedoms to the common good is the maximum norm of the exercise of liberty in the social order.[5]

Courageous investigative reporting as well as inquiries by foreign human rights organizations and the Brazilian Catholic Church revealed scores of hideous abuses. Agents of the Second Army's OBAN (Operation *Bandeirantes*) and São Paulo's DOI/CODI (Internal Operations Department) conducted tortures so brutal that most victims died or were permanently impaired. Torturers often kept the nature of their work hidden from their own families, but except for those with sadistic personalities it took a toll on them as well. The agents wore hoods or even fake hairpieces and beards to mask their appearance. Victims were grabbed from their homes during the night and immediately hooded so they could not see who had kidnapped them. The dictatorship institutionalized the torture apparatus by creating a nationwide network of information and training—in some cases with active consultation with the U.S. FBI and other military and police agencies. The U.S. Agency for International Development (USAID) supplied field radios that were used to administer electric shocks.

Sociologist Martha K. Huggins, based on a decade of research and interviews, describes how Brazilian agents of the dictatorship perfected methods of torture that combined psychological and physical terror and that almost always broke their victims unless they died first. One of these methods was the *geladeira*, or "refrigerator," a five-by-five-foot concrete box without windows encased within a larger room, from which agents tormented their victim around the clock. The words in quotes come directly from the records of the Brazilian security police:

Oxygen was introduced only through tiny holes in the walls. For the first five days of incarceration, the prisoner was nude and hooded, his or her arms tied behind the back. Food was withheld and no sleeping was allowed. The captive had to defecate and urinate on the floor of the cell; every movement was monitored through closed-circuit television. During the day, the victim faced beatings—especially the "telephone" torture, in which objects were smashed with great force against the ears. The captors administered electric shocks—"in the fingers, hands, feet, genitals, stomach, chest, and arms." "During the night, bone-chilling sounds were played with the objective of 'destructuring' the captive's personality. Diabolical sounds . . . seemed to penetrate the head like a corkscrew."

The torturers subjected their prisoners in the *geladeira* to cycles of heat and cold, noise and silence, first "lowering the temperature inside the box and playing loud recordings of aircraft noise over the speakers and starting the strobe lights blinking." Then the cycle went on to "heat up [the box] to about 115 degrees, all lights turned off . . . [to create] dead silence." Once this cold/loud/hot/silence relationship had been established, the combinations were reversed until in some cases "weeks of constant exposure to a changing constellation of sense patterns . . . causes . . . a total nervous breakdown."[6]

Most Brazilians did not know to what extent suspected subversives and other opponents of the regime were being brutalized, although citizens tended to avoid walking by police stations, from where screams were often heard. The military government was popular with foreign governments, and especially with the United States, whose officials praised the military regime for restoring stability and promoting economic progress based on foreign investment. Abandoning Goulart's populist nationalism, the military regime welcomed foreign corporations to Brazil. Enforced labor peace, coupled with generous tax and other concessions, produced an industrial boom from 1967 to 1973 that was praised by economists as Brazil's "economic miracle." The boom was based on a combination of local, international, and state capital, anchored by a docile labor force paid pathetic wages and stripped of the right to strike. The gap between rich and poor in Brazil—always present—stretched until Brazil became one of the least equal countries in the world with respect to income equity.

The surge in prosperity for those at the top gave many if not most educated and affluent Brazilians an attractive incentive to look the other way and endorse the military regime. Both middle and upper-class Brazilians showed willingness to sacrifice the apparatus of representative democracy for guided economic development and prosperity. Only a handful of attorneys and spokesmen for the Catholic left protested the cancellation of civil rights, although some courageous individuals—including the university sociologist Maria Isaura de Queiroz—risked their own safety to help publicize the names of persons arrested without charges. Most middle-class Brazilians accepted the economic progress that accompanied military rule, dubbed the "economic miracle" by analysts, as a substitute for freedom.

Defenders of the dictatorship argued that state security was more important than individual rights. Right-wingers—civilians as well as military—argued that the Brazilian people were not ready for democracy. By the mid-1970s, however, the hard-line officers were beginning to cede power to career military officers who had less stomach for repression, and under the presidency of General Ernesto Geisel steps were taken to curtail military rule. Democracy was finally restored in 1985, twenty-one years after tanks rolled out into the streets of Brazil's major cities.

Although the coup that overthrew João Goulart represented a coalition of civilians and military officers, once a general had become head of state some of the civilian supporters of the regime realized that their own political prospects were abruptly ended. Carlos Lacerda, whose implacable opposition to Vargas in 1954 had contributed to the crisis that had provoked the president's suicide, held strong ambitions to be elected president himself after 1964. At first the military regime agreed to hold elections in October 1965, but it soon canceled plans for them. The only viable candidate besides Lacerda was former president Kubitschek, but Kubitschek was stripped of his political rights soon after the generals took power. Lacerda himself was declared persona non grata in December 1986, when the repressive arm of the government increased in the face of guerrilla terrorism and kidnappings carried out by elements of the far Left. Lacerda had used the same tactics that had furthered his career as a politician; in April 1964 he called General Artur Costa e Silva opportunistic and a would-be dictator, and when Costa e Silva in fact became dictator he punished Lacerda.

Under the repressive stage of the "national security state," as the armed forces named their regime, censorship was tightened, all freedom of speech curtailed, and opponents silenced, some of them arrested and subjected to brutal treatment in prison, including systematic torture. The military blandly set out to root out "the enemy within"—citizens considered subversive because of their past record of activism or their magazine subscriptions, or because their names appeared in the address book of some other suspect dragged in and arrested. Most well-to-do Brazilians continued to support the regime, however. Opening the country to foreign investors boosted the economy, despite the OPEC oil crisis of the mid-1970s and many were alarmed at the prospects of armed opposition to the government.

Most opposition to the military regime was expressed nonviolently, in the arena of popular culture. Cinematographers, especially directors identified with the Cinema Novo movement, predicted in their films that the dispossessed would rise up against their tormentors; after 1968, however, the climate changed abruptly. Most of the Cinema Novo filmmakers were forced into exile, mostly to Europe. Movies criticizing the regime were forbidden. Filmmakers in Brazil filled the void by turning out cheap, titillating sex films (*porno-chanchadas*) or allegorical works under the banner of the broader cultural movement known as *tropicalismo*. The films fooled censors by obscuring their message. Two of the cleverer tropicalist films were by Pereira dos Santos: his 1969 *Azyllo Muito Louco* ("The Alienist"), based on Machado de Assis's classic work "The Psychiatrist" but deeper down a condemnation of the military regime; and his *Como Era Gostoso Meu Francês* ("How Tasty Was My Little Frenchman"), suggesting that Brazilians should metaphorically cannibalize their foreign enemies but at the same time indicting the government for its genocidal practices against Brazil's surviving indigenous tribes. The tropicalist movement then entered a final phase, in which films mocked society: André Luiz de Olivera in his "Meteorango Kid: Intergalactic Hero" (1969) and Júlio Bresane's "Killed the Family and Went to the Movies" (1970). Most successful in making statements against the regime was Joaquim Pedro de Andrade's 1969 adaptation of the Brazilian modernist classic *Macunaíma*, a parable of identity and empty patriotism.

Tropicalism's main venue was popular culture, especially popular music. It was created by a group of composers and performers—Caetano Veloso, his sister Maria Bethânia, Gilberto Gil, and Gal Costa—who left Bahia in the late 1960s for Rio, the center of the commercial music industry. Rather than take a stand against the military government (which invariably led to censorship and often arrest), they dazzled their audiences with sophisticated lyrics and music that challenged listeners, mostly affluent youth from the upper-middle class, to seek personal liberation and reject the conformity of Brazilian life.

The military period gave rise to three distinct forms of popular expression in Brazilian music, two of them contemptuous of the dictatorship. The first, represented by the singer Roberto Carlos, avoided political themes completely, selling millions of records, influenced by soft American rock, about love and middle-class concerns. The second group was made up of protesters openly contemptuous of the military. Leaders included Geraldo Vandré, a country-folk singer from the Northeast, and Chico Buarque de Holanda, a deft composer and singer who first tricked the censors but then was labeled a subversive and forced into exile. The tropicalists made up the third wave. Their music used outlandish performance art and relied on esoteric allusions and confusing lyrics to make powerful statements condemning both the complacent left and the military right, attacking commercialism, populist politics, and American imperialism. The music was creative and fertile, but it failed to reach the masses, who presumably could not afford to buy the tropicalists' music or attend their concerts, and who favored less jarring, more traditional forms of musical expression.

On the far left, militants struck back as coercion tightened. Beginning in late 1967, urban terrorists—their ranks a mixture of hardened operatives and mostly idealistic, middle-class students— began to rob banks to raise funds to finance their operations. In one well-known (but botched) action in September 1967, depicted by the 1997 film *Four Days in September*, a small group of urban terrorists who called themselves "MI-8" kidnapped U.S. ambassador Burke Elbrick and held him for ransom. To release Elbrick, the regime freed and sent into exile a handful of imprisoned leftists, but as soon as the exchange had been made officials savagely increased the repression. In November 1969, troops shot and killed Carlos Marighella, a leading communist who, with compatriot Carlos Lamarca, had led a band of guerrilla terrorists in the rural interior. Most of these guerrillas were by 1970 shot or captured, to die in captivity. Military president Emiliano Garrastazú Médici (1969–1974) governed during the harshest years of the repression. They were symbolized by the enactment on December 13, 1968 of Institutional Act No. 5, a decree that considerably strengthened the government's repressive powers.

Another by-product of the declaration of guerrilla warfare by the far left was the increase of brutality and of the frequent use of torture by police and armed forces agents. The Department of Political and Social Order (DOPS) operated throughout Brazil, as did agents of the Navy, Air Force, and Army. Because civil rights, including the habeas corpus, had been stripped by the Institutional Act, citizens could be unceremoniously dragged out of their homes and led away; relatives often had to spend months or years relocating their family members, sometimes to learn that they had died. Like their Argentine counterparts under that country's military dictatorship, agents perfected brutal forms of torture, resulting in the deaths of many. Extralegal vigilante groups, often composed of off duty policemen, also used violence against their victims, persons they decided were subversive or criminal and could be more efficiently dealt with by assassination than through the judicial process.

STIRRINGS OF PROTEST

Under the dictatorship the press was controlled and journalists intimidated and mistreated. Journalists were required to apply for credentials to cover political stories, and these papers could be detained on a whim, sometimes because of the bad feelings of one military officer toward a newspaper or a reporter. Many editors and reporters were detained; in 1967 Hélio Fernandes, the owner of Rio de Janeiro's *Tribuna de Imprensa*, was imprisoned at the harsh Fernando do Noronha penal colony because he had published an unflattering obituary of former military president Humberto Castello Branco, who had died in an airplane crash. One of the ugliest events was the arrest of São Paulo newspaper and television reporter Vladimir Herzog, who was apprehended by officers of the Second Army and tortured to death within hours of being interned. Officials claimed that Herzog had confessed to being a communist and then committed suicide, but photos released to his family showed that his body had been beaten savagely and that he had supposedly hanged himself while on his knees. Tens of thousands, including São Paulo's Cardinal Evaristo Arns, attended the ecumenical funeral service at the cathedral, but the army remained impassive.

Examiners from the Catholic archdiocese of São Paulo later revealed that two-thirds of the persons arrested and imprisoned during the dictatorship had been members of outlawed political organizations—including some responsible for acts of terrorism. The remaining third however, had included students, labor activists, progressive members of the clergy, and working journalists.[7] Thousands more, including most of the faculties of the social sciences and humanities at Brazil's leading universities, fled the country. Some found teaching posts in the West, including sociologist Fernando Henrique Cardoso, who was hired at Berkeley. Others washed dishes in Stockholm, Paris, Toronto, or New York; a few sought refuge in Salvador Allende's Chile, only to be caught by the dragnet that swept up leftists after the socialist president's over-throw and death. Imprisoned in Santiago's huge soccer stadium, they were interrogated not only by Chileans but by agents of the Brazilian military; not a few of them received harsh treatment or simply "disap-peared."

Under the presidency of General Ernesto Geisel (1974–1979), the armed forces, some of whose leaders had grown frustrated at the difficulty of governing and of managing the economy, agreed to phase out authori-tarian rule and gradually restore civilian democratic rule. Some military officers felt that the repression had broken the back of the small leftist militant movement in Brazil, and others heeded the outcry against tor-ture and state violence from the international community. Primarily, however, this occurred because of a split within the military command between so-called "hard-liners" and a group linked to the National War College and to the policies of the first military president, Castello Branco. The latter, known as the *castellista*, or Sorbonne Group, worried about Brazil's negative image abroad; they advocated not a new strategy but a return to more conciliatory forms of control, similar to those of Vargas's Estado Novo of the 1930s. Under the administration of Geisel's successor, General João Baptista de Oliveira Figueiredo (1979–1985), this policy was renamed *abertura* (opening).

In 1985 civilian government was restored. Tacredo Neves, a well-liked professional politician from Minas Gerais who during the 1940s after Vargas's ouster had worked to restore democracy, and who had taken a stance of mild opposition to the military regime, was overwhelmingly elected president in March. The election was brokered by machine pol-iticians, but it had the support of the population. Tragically, however, Neves was in failing health, and days before his inauguration he died from complications following intestinal surgery. The vice president–elect was José Sarney, a minor politician from northern Maranhão and yes-man to the military. He entered the presidency for a five-year term char-acterized by economic instability.

To many, the most important thing about the 1964–1978 military dic-tatorship was not its crackdown on dissent and its curtailment on civil rights but the fact that it restored stability ("order") and achieved sig-nificant economic gains ("progress") resulting from foreign investment. If authorities persecuted progressives and some moderates in their an-ticommunist zeal, many were willing to overlook such excesses; they believed that the country in 1963–1964 had been teetering on the edge of a Castro-style revolution. More typical of the reaction of educated Brazilians was that of Boris Casoy, the editor in chief of the *Folha de São Paulo*. The basis for his support of the regime was his fear that the far left would take power, that the world as he knew it would crumble. "The guerrillas weren't against the dictatorship," he said, "they were against our way of life. . . . Deep in my heart, I supported [the regime]."[8] Others disagreed, arguing that the worst terror was from the right, not the left, but most Brazilians saw things the way Casoy did and therefore went along.

An unspoken characteristic of the military repression was that like so often in Brazilian life, some received favored treatment because of who they were. Well-connected newspapers like the *Estado de São Paulo* were permitted to express their dismay at censorship by printing recipes or selections from the classic Portuguese epic poem *The Lusiads* in lieu of columns deleted by police censors. Less prominent newspapers—*O São Paulo*, for example, and *Opinião*—were not permitted to use such devices. It was widely believed as well that some intellectuals were not arrested or in general received better treatment because they had protectors (sometimes family members) in high places in the military. Roberto Faller Sisson, one of the leaders of the left-wing National Liberation Alliance in 1935 and a militant leftist all of his life, was put under house arrest after 1964 but never harassed; when it came time for the annual dinners at the Naval Club that brought together surviving members of his *turma* (class), the former naval commander was permitted to attend and participate in the camaraderie.

Political events were complicated by the fact that in 1981 a severe recession had hit, a consequence of the second international oil price crisis (1979–1980) and of the rise of international interest rates in 1979, spurred by the U.S. Federal Reserve. The recession lasted for two years, slowing the process of democratization. The rapid growth that had propelled Brazil forward since the end of the Second World War stopped, and the external debt crisis worsened. The "economic miracle" of the 1970s had generated a huge external debt—the largest in the developing world. Changes in Brazilian society frustrated efforts to turn back the recession by traditional means. The absolute decline in the rural population, for example, led to deep structural changes in rural production— to the benefit of agro-industrial producers but to the detriment of millions of lower-class families living precariously on the edge of starvation. Half of all households in Brazil lived below the poverty line; twenty-four million Brazilians still could not read, and workers—if they were employed—had to toil four and a quarter hours to earn enough to buy a kilo of black beans, the staple of the Brazilian diet.

FIRST STEPS TO REDEMOCRATIZATION

Democracy returned to Brazil fitfully. Under the armed forces' policy of gradualism, elections had first been permitted at the municipal level, then in the states, and nationally only after several years. Some of the more outspoken opponents of the dictatorship were still in exile, and the press and the media for the most part expressed themselves with great caution, lest censorship crack down on them again. In the 1980s (as after) how one measured progress often depended upon the beholder. To proponents of economic development, it meant new crops, aggressive production for foreign markets, increasing transfers of capital into agriculture, mechanization, improved yields, and a decline in rural labor requirements. Medical and health care facilities continued to be clustered in affluent neighborhoods, where residents paid for health services, rather than in poorer districts or in the rural interior, where few could afford to pay for medicine, physicians, or hospital care. To watchers more concerned with social health, the changes meant more migration of uneducated and untrained workers to the crowded cities of the industrial south, fewer opportunities for employment, depressed wages, and the incapacity of small farms to compete. Some Brazilians during these years left for other countries—to Paraguay, for example, where foreign agrobusinesses and the newly opened Itaipú dam offered jobs; or to the United States, which attracted educated middle-class Brazilians unable to obtain good jobs at home owing to lack of family connections and willing to work in New York and Miami as restaurant workers or taxi drivers in order to save enough money to be able to return to Brazil and start a business.

The stage for the full restoration of democracy was a new federal constitution enacted in 1988. Enacted after partisan negotiation influenced both by regional bloc lobbying and populist demands for social change, the lengthy document, in the words of political scientist Riordan Roett, "created a time bomb in national politics by transferring a significant share of national income to the states and municipalities, while leaving responsibility for major social programs with the federal government, which now had vastly reduced revenues."[9] Because the old system remained in place, the shift widened opportunities for corruption and mismanagement, and hindered efforts at country-wide solutions to social needs.

The 1989 election of Fernando Collor de Mello (1990–1992), the first directly elected president since Jânio Quadros in 1960, raised hopes for dramatic change, but this was not to be. Collor, a relatively obscure politician from the small state of Alagoas, used his media connections and a brash electoral campaign to sweep in to office. He promised to kill the "inflation tiger" with a single shot, in his words, and to bring Brazil into the ranks of first-world nations. He won the presidency in 1989 with 30.5 percent of the vote in the first round and 49.9 percent in the runoff, beating the Workers' Party candidate, Luis Inácio da Silva, by four percentage points. Once in office he set out to liberalize trade, privatize government cartels, and deregulate the economy. His reforms, however, were obscured by his arrogant personal corruption, overwhelming evidence of which was published by the nation's newsweekly magazines, which now, more than newspapers, used investigative journalism to monitor abuses in the political system. Collor had come to office with a number of advantages—his youthful, dynamic image, for one, and his openness to change—but many disadvantages as well. He had no major political base, although he was supported by the powerful Globo telecommunications empire. He had little credibility with bankers, industrialists, or other members of the elite, no links to labor unions, and no respect from the armed forces. Somewhat like Bill Clinton in the United States, Collor had found himself unable to convert his lofty campaign rhetoric into workable politics.

Collor went through three cabinets, none able to deal successfully with Congress or refrain from infighting. Three cabinet members also fell under investigation for corruption. Public opinion became more restive; during congressional debates over whether Collor should be impeached, millions filled the streets demanding justice. The president faced increasing attacks in the media for his abuses of patronage and for his (and his wife's) extravagant lifestyle. For a while, he managed to fend them off, claiming that he was being victimized as an outsider by the political establishment. He had attempted to reinvent Brazilian government, and one thing he had done effectively was centralize the traditional practice of patronage, making himself the recipient of graft that traditionally had been spread across the government. Even more sordid were the adventures of Collor's henchman, Paulo César "P. C." Farias, his principal agent in extorting and collecting tens of millions of dollars (and perhaps more) in kickbacks. Farias fled the country in his private plane as investigators closed in, and he lived the life of a lavish playboy as Brazilian law enforcement agents fumed. Finally, he was returned to Brazil, where he faced trial, during which he lived in a luxurious form of house arrest. A long and angry impeachment trial that lasted throughout much of 1992 led to Collor's forced resignation in December of that year. The Senate found him guilty and deprived him of his political rights until the year 2000. Collor retreated to Alagoas, where many considered him a victim, and he subsequently took up residence in various cities, including Paris, until finally settling into a mansion in Miami. From there, aided by press aides and others in his entourage, he launched a publicity barrage aimed at restoring his credibility as a candidate for Brazil's presidency at the end of his political-rights suspension. In 1996, Farias was shot to death in his bedroom with his mistress, Susana Marcolino. Later, authorities revealed that he had been killed not by robbers, as had been claimed, but by Susana, in an apparent act of murder-suicide.

It is telling that although Farias's life ended in violence, the successful campaign to oust Collor had been entirely nonviolent. Citizens had displayed their concern peacefully, demonstrating, in the words of an apt observer, "that very restraint and non-violence to which the dominant class and the state had long made false claim."[10]

Collor's removal elevated the vice president, Itamar Franco, to the presidency. Franco was a machine politician from Minas Gerais who had never traveled outside of Brazil and who seemed to want to be little more than a caretaker until the next election. He might have done more: the 1988 constitution had given the president a very large role in legislation, including the right to issue provisional-decree laws (*medidas provisórias*) that had the force of law for thirty days. Because they could be reissued, they often remained in force indefinitely: up to May 1995, the four presidents since the return to civilian rule had issued 1,004 such decree laws, 604 of which had been repeatedly renewed. The new constitution did not empower the judiciary to invalidate laws as unconstitutional.

Franco resisted implementing Collor's policies, although he adopted some of them under different names. The Collor-Franco experience so soured public opinion on presidential politics that legislators enacted legislation for a plebiscite on a possible change in government structure. The ballot held three choices: presidentialism, a parliamentary system based on the French system of "prime minister presidentialism," and a restoration of constitutional monarchy—a solution favored by a handful of traditionalists who had never abandoned their support of the Bragança dynasty. The plebiscite was carried out in April 1993, with a victory for presidentialism. Only a quarter of the voters opted for parliamentarism, and a handful voted to fulfil the dreams of the monarchists. The defeat for parliamentarism was seen as a sign of low public confidence in the Congress, since legislators would under that system select the nation's chief executive.

NEW BEGINNINGS

The Franco administration's main accomplishment was the March 1994 monetary reform, called the "Real Plan" (after the new currency unit, the *real*) and pursued by the finance minister, Fernando Henrique Cardoso. Five previous economic plans had failed, each using interventionist measures, such as price and wage freezes. As a result, inflation worsened, reaching 2,500 percent in 1993 and jumping 500 percent in the month of June 1994 alone, at one point reaching 5,200 percent. The Real Plan linked the new currency to the dollar, opened the economy by lowering tariffs, slowed government spending, and imposed high interest rates to cool down the economy. The official rate of inflation fell below 5 percent in 1997. The plan bolstered foreign confidence in Brazil's economy and encouraged investment, leading to sustained inflows of capital that kept the value of the *real* at unprecedently high levels.

The plan's success made Cardoso's own popularity soar, and he was elected to the presidency in late 1994. Cardoso, a brilliant sociologist who had written widely on economic dependency and race relations, was inaugurated on January 1, 1995. Although a former Marxist who had been exiled by the military regime, he had earned a reputation as a progressive centrist when he had been a senator from São Paulo. As a presidential candidate, he ran with the backing of traditional conservative machine politicians against the candidate of labor unions and the Left, Luís Inácio da Silva ("Lula"), a metalworker and union organizer who had migrated from the impoverished Northeast with his family. He had risen to the leadership of the Workers' Party (PT), which had achieved electoral victories in some important cities, especially in the industrialized Center-South.

Cardoso defeated "Lula" after a spirited, media-based campaign with 54.4 percent of the 94,782,000 total votes. As soon as he took office, Cardoso set out to revise the statist 1988 constitution, address fiscal imbalances, attract foreign investment, back away from economic nationalism, and reduce the enormous public sector. His administration represented a breakthrough in several ways. The election of a former exile proved that Brazil had embraced a new political climate in which the taint of leftist views did not prevent conservatives from backing former opponents of the military regime. Cardoso was Brazil's first "modern" chief executive, because of his political experience and position on key issues of reform—in contrast to his civilian and military predecessors, whose backgrounds were much more limited.[11]

The sixty-six-year-old Cardoso, moreover, was ready to bring Brazil into the market economy. His program attacked statism, government-run monopolies in mining and energy, telecommunications, internal shipping and ports, natural gas, and chemicals—all products of Vargas-era nationalism. Even Petrobrás, the enormous petroleum agency, was forced to permit competition from private companies. Foreign capital received the same legal status as domestic capital.

Cardoso's early proposals sailed through Congress in 1995, but a second round of broader reforms—including proposals addressing the tax structure, pensions, health care, and retirements—slowed sharply, as they became mired in political infighting. A coalition of retired government workers, unions, and bureaucrats blocked reforms of the pension system that would have ended the practice of paying up to 120 percent of working salaries, continually adjusted for inflation, to persons earning $100,000 a year or more while retired "regular" workers earned pensions worth three hundred dollars a month. In anticipation of coming pension reform, thousands of professors at state and federal universities took retirement under the old system, many of them simply switching universities and taking new positions elsewhere while drawing one hundred percent of their old salaries. Cardoso himself had been forced to retire in 1968 by the military government, and on his return he had sought a political career; others in his cabinet took early retirement at full benefits after only twenty or twenty-five years in government service, only to move on to second and third careers while still collecting their pensions. A presidential proposal for minimum retirement ages of sixty-five for men and sixty for women was shouted down by lobbyists and thousands who had benefited from the extremely liberal pension statutes.

The early retirements within the university teaching profession had enormous consequences, and it cast doubt on how long the traditional framework of Brazilian higher education would survive. That system had been tuition-free but for all practical purposes had been limited to affluent youths whose families had provided them private education to prepare for the difficult *vestibular* entrance examinations. Now it tottered amidst lengthy and frequent strikes by students, staff, and faculty, with continued inadequate funds for university facilities and programs.

Much of Cardoso's support among progressives rapidly evaporated as he threw in his lot with rural political bosses and moneyed laissez-faire businessmen and financiers. Breaking with the decades-long tradition of economic nationalism, Cardoso moved to privatize major state-owned utilities and businesses; his second term, he promised, he would be devoted to deregulation. Some of the privatizations were immense. Companhia Vale do Rio Doce, an energy producer, was sold for more than three billion dollars. Cellular phone rights in the city of São Paulo went for an astonishing $2.6 billion to a broad telecommunications consortium. Telebrás, valued at $130 billion, was the largest telephone company in Latin America. Its sale yielded more than six times the revenue of the second-largest privatization, the Vale do Rio Doce power company, sold in 1997. The sale of Telebrás benefited consumers immediately: the cost of obtaining a new phone line dropped from $1,200 to sixty-six dollars. Most of the privatization proceeds were earmarked for debt reduction and for education. In the past, however, spending for education has meant funds for construction of school buildings and roads, not to train or pay teachers or to equip buildings once completed.

At the same time, Brazil's economy enjoyed the initial results of the successful inauguration, in March 1991, of the Southern [Cone] Common Market, the Mercado Común del Sur, MERCOSUR in Spanish and MERCOSUL in Portuguese. The bloc originated in part as a response to the success of the European Union as well as to the creation of the North Atlantic Free Trade Agreement (NAFTA) in the aftermath of difficulties in completing the Uruguay Round of the General Agreement on Tariffs and Trade (GATT). Each of the trading blocs lowered tariffs between member nations, promoted travel and investment, and initiated plans aimed at facilitating economic integration.

The regional common market had originated in 1986, when presidents Raúl Alfonsín of Argentina and José Sarney of Brazil signed accords for a bilateral trade arrangement. This was a historic breakthrough: for generations, each nation had feared the other, deploying large portions of their armed forces to the border with one another, and competing for leadership within Latin American diplomatic circles. Both countries were emerging from nasty dictatorships, and the economic integration effort was couched in language that committed each country, as well as any others that wished to join, to consolidate democratic gains. But economic conditions deteriorated thereafter in both countries, and the trade initiatives stalled. Capital-goods trade between the two countries stood at lower levels in 1988 than in 1980.

Still, the slow pace of reform and the seemingly pragmatic accommodation to Cardoso's political allies angered those who had expected a more aggressive social agenda. In January 1998, in the midst of an important Senate committee vote to reduce social security benefits to help reduce the federal deficit, irate protesters from a left-wing labor union smashed through a bullet-proof door to the committee chambers, interrupting the vote. The president of the Senate, Bahia's Antonio Carlos Magalhães, Cardoso's ally, was quoted as telling policemen to clear the demonstrators out even if it meant shooting them. Seven hours later, Congress passed the bill. Cardoso, a foreign newspaper reported, had achieved another victory for Brazil's standing in the global economy. To some, these painful measures were necessary. Because of generous retirement laws and bloated bureaucracies, many of Brazil's twenty-six states were spending 70 to 90 percent of their revenues on salaries. To others, the belt-tightening hurt the working and middle classes, while Brazil's rich, historically insulated from the stresses of inflation and job pressures, simply got richer on their investments in the stock market and currency speculation.

Nor did partisan politics offer sought-after solutions. National political parties, absent since 1889, had returned after 1945 in the form of a three-party system, but in 1964 the system had been stripped of any real significance when the military government banned all opposition as subversive. The military government's two "official" parties yielded to no fewer than thirteen parties after 1985 in the 513-seat lower house of Congress. The 1988 constitution, in effect devised to micromanage Brazilian life, so rigidified the lawmaking process that amendments were required to pass by a 60 percent vote in each house of Congress, each house having between sixteen and twenty-two political parties.

As Brazil emerged from the long shadow of military dictatorship in the 1980s and after, there were signs that the public was no longer content to accept the government's line. In 1988, calls for meetings and celebrations to mark the centenary of the abolition of slavery were met with apathy around the country. In Salvador, the Bahian capital and the nation's center of Afro-Brazilian culture, white scholars and politicians who had been invited to participate in a conference on abolition and its aftermath were booed off the stage; later, their bus was attacked by angry blacks. The explosion of pent-up anger at the lack of progress for Brazilians of color shocked officials, who tried to dismiss the events as an aberration; it showed fissures in the façade of racial harmony. A similar although less violent event took place in October 1997, when hundreds of religious penitents trekked to the site of Canudos, in the Bahian backlands, on the hundredth anniversary of the destruction of that religious haven by government forces. While officials had designated the Canudos massacre as its centenary (the centenary of the community's founding was 1993), the pilgrims, from all over the backlands, showed in their piety that the memory of Canudos as a refuge for the faithful and the downtrodden had survived.

NOTES

1. Oliveiro S. Ferreira, "Uma Caraterização do Sistema," *O Estado de São Paulo* (October 17 1965), 5.

2. Philippe C. Schmitter, *Interest Conflict and Political Change in Brazil* (Stanford CA: Stanford University Press, 1971), 378.

3. Translated and cited by Roberta C. Wigder, *Brazil Rediscovered* (Philadelphia: Dorrance, 1977), 350.

4. Ibid., 352.

5. "Construindo o Brasil," circulated by the Group for Moral and Civic Education, Rio de Janeiro.

6. Martha K. Huggins, *Political Policing: The United States and Latin America* (Durham, NC: Duke University Press, 1998), 166–67.

7. See *Torture in Brazil: A Report by the Archdiocese of São Paulo* (New York: Random House, 1986).

8. Boris Casoy, interview with Anne-Marie Smith, in *A Forced Agreement: Press Acquiescence to Censorship in Brazil* (Pittsburgh: University of Pittsburgh Press, 1997), 153–54.

9. Riordan Roett, "Brazilian Politics at Century's End," in Susan Kaufman Purcell and Riordan Roett, eds., *Brazil under Cardoso* (Boulder, CO: Lynne Reinner Publishers, 1997), 25.

10. Peter Flynn, "Collor, Corruption and Crisis: Time for Reflection," *Journal of Latin American Studies* 25, no. 2 (May 1993): 351–71.

11. Roett, 19.

7

Political Culture

Although nominally representative, Brazilian government remained dominated by oligarchic factions during the monarchy and First, or Old, Republic. In 1894, only 2 percent of the population could vote, and elections were not by secret ballot. As late as 1930, the percentage had risen only to 6 percent, and incumbent state political machines manipulated vote counts fraudulently. Vargas gave the vote to women in 1932, but there were no meaningful free elections until 1946, by which time voters still constituted only 16 percent of the population. This figure jumped sharply in subsequent decades, reaching 22 percent in 1961, 34 percent in 1974, 56 percent in 1989 (including for the first time illiterates and youths sixteen years old) and in 1998, 66 percent or 106 million voters. More than half of these cast their ballots at computer terminals; partisans of the Left protested that this intimidated and confused poorly educated voters, another example of the ambiguity of the legacy of modernization.

BRAZILIAN CREATIVITY

What is telling about the country's psychology—to the extent that there is such a thing—is the resilience of Brazilian culture and its ability to break out into new and dynamic creative directions. This holds both at the levels of elite and of popular culture. In the nineteenth century, educated Brazilians turned hungrily to European ideas but altered them for their own purposes. Comtean positivism, brought to Brazil from France, was adapted by military planners to justify the need for secular technology, and, for better or worse, by civilians anxious to resist what they considered the smothering influence of the Roman Catholic Church. We may not agree with the positivist program, but it represented a uniquely Brazilian adaptation.

Imported culture invaded Brazil during and after the First World War and has reigned supreme ever since. Following the close of the war, Anita Malfatti and other Brazilian artists who had visited and worked in France introduced avant garde culture to South America in the 1922 Modern Art Week. Modernism, too, took on a Brazilian cast when the nation's modernists extolled native themes in architecture, art, and creative writing: novelist Plínio Salgado advocated substituting Tupí-Guaraní for Portuguese as Brazil's national language; Heitor Villa-Lobos blended Bachian fugues with folk airs from the Amazon. Later, the inventive landscape architect Roberto Burle Marx used plants and grasses as living sculpture beside the dazzling sidewalk mosaic patterns crafted under his direction by skillful Portuguese artisans.

The most recent cultural importations include video arcades, found in even the poorest of small towns, American television programs, and the Internet, which is wildly popular among young people. Historically, however, Brazilian culture has to some degree transformed and reinvented those influences to its own rhythm. Brazilian *novelas*, or television dramas, are superior in quality to much of American programming and have been received in Europe and Latin America with enthusiasm. Cultural adaptation has taken its highest form in music, where in the late 1950s and early 1960s creative musicians crafted the understated samba-jazz-pop innovation known as the bossa nova, and where by the 1990s Brazilian music had expanded beyond tropicalism to embrace (and subtly integrate) rock, electronic acoustics, rich and beautiful melodies, Tuvan throat singing, heavy-metal guitar chords, Brazilian funk, wild percussionism, hip-hop, rap, and polyglot samba. "We don't have any preconceptions about any kind of music," said André Abujamra, the founder of the group "Karnak." "Bad music, good music, strange music, we put them all together in a mixer. . . . The mixing of the music and of the culture is in our blood," he said. "I don't have to do research, because my head is already a mix of all the music and traditions and religions of the world." Then he added a Brazilian twist: "We are not world music. We are just born into chaos."[1]

Religious expression in Brazil also embraces combinations of orthodoxy and creativity. For the last several decades, evangelical Protestantism has outstripped all other religious denominations in rapid growth, especially among members of the urban poor. Twenty-five million Brazilians now call themselves *crentes*, or believers. Evangelicals, most of whom are Pentecostals but including also Seventh-Day Adventists and members of the Assemblies of God, Jehovah's Witnesses, and other ecstatic cults, believe in personal salvation through charismatic worship. They emphasize the Holy Spirit, the third person of the Trinity, and lead austere personal lives, observing prohibitions on alcohol and other stimulants, repressing sexuality, and wearing plain clothing. Emphasis on born-again salvation shuns community action and therefore flies in the face of Brazil's unique brand of socially conscious Roman Catholic reformism, including liberation theology, a 1960s movement led by Augusto Boal, Paulo Freyre, Dom Helder Câmara, and others. Evangelical practice has so influenced popular culture that both mainstream Protestantism and Roman Catholicism in Brazil have moved away from social action and embraced worship centered on charismata. Methodists and Presbyterians, for example, have formed their own "renewed" congregations in the Pentecostal mold. As many as eight million Brazilian Roman Catholics, as well, have joined the Catholic Charismatic Renewal (RCC)—in the words of Andrew Chestnut, "a Catholic version of Pentecostalism."[2] Charismatic Afro-Brazilian spiritist cults, including *candomblé* and voodoolike *umbanda*, has not only expanded among the descendants of slaves but has in Rio de Janeiro, Salvador, and in other cities become popular among the white upper-middle and upper classes. Syncretistic blending the adoption of native, non-Christian elements, has occurred as well. Ministers of the Christian Universal Church of the Kingdom of God (IURD) as well as lay leaders at RCC ceremonies practice exorcism of demons—frequently *exús*, impish spirits from *umbanda* believed to inflict bad karma.

Both *umbanda* and evangelical Protestant sects permit children to attend, either as participants or as observers. For parents, this becomes a means to keep their children away from trouble, including teenage pregnancies, glue sniffing, and drug use. Protestant churches hire rock bands that keep youngsters involved throughout whole weekends. Children stay through the night-long *umbanda* rituals, which often are held on

Saturdays. Middle and lower-class parents fear for their children's futures especially as television and films and behavior considered immoral assault everyday life. For them, religious events offer protection against these influences, and the moral guidance that social institutions no longer provide.

The Roman Catholic Church, for the most part staunchly conservative in spite of its activist progressive wing, has been limited in its capacity to fight back against such influences by lack of revenue and by an acute shortage of Brazilian-born priests. Since as far back as the late nineteenth century, most Catholic priests—secular as well as regular clergy—in Brazil have been sent from Europe—from Italy, France, Belgium, Germany, and Portugal. Language difficulties and culture shock at Brazil's historically tolerant acceptance of syncretism in popular Catholicism fostered an atmosphere of tension; in rural Brazil, many nominal Catholics go for years without seeing a priest and without the opportunity to enroll in a Roman Catholic school. In the 1990s aggressive acts by evangelical Protestant figures went unchallenged; in one highly publicized case, Sérgio von Helde, a bishop of the Universal Church, during a program televised nationally on an IURD network, kicked and punched a statue of Our Lady of Aparecida, Brazil's patron saint, to expose what he called the impotence of idolatry. In other instances, Universal Church followers have invaded and desecrated *umbanda* centers, claiming that Afro-Brazilian spiritism is devil worship.

POLITICAL ATTITUDES

Time has never been kind to reformist impulses, especially those critical of the political culture. In the 1930s, pioneering mental health expert Ulisses Pernambucano was tormented by police cars blaring their horns day and night as he lay dying in his Recife home. Nutritionist and food specialist Josué de Castro was twice exiled, under two different military regimes. Educators Paulo Freire and Anísio Teixeira suffered similar fates. One insurmountable problem, according to some, has been the enormous imbalance between what affluent Brazilians demand of government and how much they are willing to pay. Brazilian governments at all levels collect proportionately as much in taxes as do the United States and Great Britain but spend almost all of it on the well-to-do. A Brazilian fiscal gap exists, London's *Economist* has noted, without even the excuse of existing for virtuous reasons.

Brazil's return to democracy was not accompanied by social equity.

Democratization has brought about very little redistributive change. Agrarian reform has been blocked, and taxation remains regressive, favoring the rich over the poor. The health care system retains its emphasis on curative, not preventative, measures. Housing subsidies have been shifted to the middle class. There have been virtually no successful efforts to accomplish structural reform. Only half of the population is integrated into the formal economy. The remainder are marginalized, with low, irregular incomes and little social protection and no retirement pensions. At the same time, professionals and other public employees benefit from extremely generous rules on retirement. Today, beneficiaries retire at the average age of fifty-three, in most cases going on to new careers while continuing to receive nearly 100 percent of their prior salaries. Brazil's public universities have been hit hard by faculty retirements; many of their professors retire and move on to jobs in the country's many new and aggressive private universities. Only the rich can afford tuition in these places, widening still further the gap between Brazil's haves and have-nots.

Some continue to profit from economic and social uncertainty. During the inflation-swept 1950s and 1970s, many upper-middle-class individuals acquired real estate worth much more than they otherwise could have afforded, by creative investments in currency exchange and mortgages. When Fernando Henrique Cardoso's administration pledged to compensate landowners for the seizure of unproductive properties by landless squatters, middle-class city residents began buying deeds to distant rural properties, hoping that they would be "invaded" by the landless (and therefore bring a handsome profit from the government's indemnification fund).

In addition to an effective lack of checks and balances in its governmental structure, the 1988 constitution—a lengthy document very difficult to enforce—has created a confusing set of overlapping responsibilities. Lack of strong national political parties (in 1998 legislators represented a total of nineteen different parties in Congress) made congressional agreement on anything subject to networking and coalition building, made more difficult by a tradition of congressional absenteeism that made it virtually impossible to veto executive actions. Congressional fragmentation has crippled initiatives involving broad economic and social policy, with the result being that only the executive has the power to carry out such initiatives.

After a brief challenge under Juscelino Kubitschek in the late 1950s and the short-lived reformist administration of his successor, Jânio Quadros, the country's corporatist tradition, which had regulated the lives of citizens since the early 1930s, finally began to give way as the military regime faded during the late 1970s, and as protests surfaced. The 1979 strike of metallurgical workers in the industrial belt around the city of São Paulo directly challenged the military regime's corporatist labor policies, and the Workers' Party emerged a year later. Since the 1960s, demands for social justice had been voiced, even during the dictatorship. Groups representing the interests of marginalized groups—Indians, landless peasants, abandoned children, blacks, women, gays and lesbians—emerged. In the realm of filmmaking, groups typically excluded from political discourse now asserted themselves as subjects of documentaries. Sandra Werneck's contribution to a short series of films called *Communion*, for example, portrays the abduction of a film crew in the Morro da Santa Maria favela in Rìo; the kidnapper, pointing a revolver at the filmmaker, makes an impassioned speech about the example of the 1897 resistance of Antônio Conselheiro at Canudos, who, the bandit claims, was defending "against the violence of the state against the poor." Another short film, one of a seven-part German-Brazilian production called *The Seven Sacraments of Canudos*, contains dialogues between moviemaker and documentary subject in the bleak community of Nova Canudos in the Bahian hinterland.

Filmmaking experimentation notwithstanding, Brazil's political system has many rough edges. Hundreds of approved laws cannot be carried out because Congress has not enacted statutes to put them into force. The absence of broad-based national political parties strengthens the role of state governors, who can persuade their federal delegations—even if made up of deputies and senators from a wide array of political parties—to vote together when patronage and revenues for their states are to be negotiated. Election districts are statewide; voters cast ballots either for individuals or for coalitions of parties formed to elect a single slate. Governors hold power over who gets nominated and who gets elected. In the mid-1990s, governors found ways to enlarge their powers even more: by creating new municipalities, or *municipios*, and thus a wealth of new patronage positions, funded from state and federal sources because the new districts are usually too small and poor to pay their own ways. The number of municipalities nationwide increased from 3,990 in 1980 to 4,974 in 1992 and 6,040 in mid-1997.

The generation of Brazilians that came to political maturity during the period from 1964 to 1985 was marked by the repressive military regime. Rather than seeing civilian politicians as heroes, many consider them to be motivated by personal gain. In 1989, a survey taken by political scientists yielded the following attitudes about legislators. "Take care of friends and relatives," 30.1 percent; "Get rich off public money," 44.8 percent, and "Defend constituents' interests," 9.1 percent. Kickbacks on public contracts and looking aside while businesses and corporations keep two sets of books (caixa dois, as it is called, "the second treasury") to avoid taxes have too long been shrugged off as the way things are.

THE CONCEPT OF CITIZENSHIP

Present-day attitudes are derived from the institutions of the nineteenth century. The 1824 constitution defined citizenship and established a parliamentary system that preserved the privileges of the landed elite. Another important moment occurred in the aftermath of the transition from monarchy to republic in the early 1890s. The 1891 constitution, symbolically influenced by French Comtean positivism but in practice dominated by republican liberal constitutionalists, yielded to the acerbic dictatorship of Marshal Floriano Peixoto. He brought with him young military officers who had challenged the old slaveholding elite during the 1880s, but in 1894 he yielded power to a civilian regime run by planters and their new industrial allies. This regime, nominally representative but neither democratic nor inclusive, clearly represented the interests of the elite. The third crucial period, 1930 to 1935, witnessed a nominal opening for new groups, including urban residents, women, skilled laborers, and political groups from the country's periphery. It ended when state intervention suspended civil rights in November 1935, ushering in a dark period of repression and censorship that lifted only in 1945, when Vargas was ousted by the same groups in the armed forces that had put him in power.

The concept of "citizenship" brings with it a fundamental idea of the individual and a set of rules that in theory pertain universally. The reawakening of civil society in Brazil in the 1970s, however, yielded to a democratization process that revealed a lack of consensus and a tenacious survival of traditional brokered politics, an atmosphere in which relationships play a critical role in the conception and dynamics of social order. Reform groups, mostly fragile neighborhood associations and Roman Catholic "Base Communities" (CEBs), have made few meaningful inroads. Brazilian society, much like society in Spanish America (and in North America, in relation to African Americans and other minorities), has not applied the rights of citizens universally. Discussions of citizenship take place on a moral, political and juridical level, whereas the concept in practice is manifest in the social (and behavioral) realm. Being a citizen in Brazil, in fact, means learning where one fits into society. One of the worst things that formerly could be said about someone in Brazil was "he doesn't know his place."

Citizenship rights clash with rules for memberships in social groups. Such groups are defined by different genders, ages, political affiliations, occupations, places of residence, and so on. Persons born into the elite in a society that values hierarchy see citizenship differently than do members of the working classes, the urban homeless, or the rural landless. Ordinary Brazilians have been often treated as *João Ninguems*, nameless nobodies considered unworthy of the protection of the law.

Brazilians must also deal with the lingering reality of a judicial system that shields influential citizens from justice. The constitution itself guarantees softer prison accommodations and pre-trial privileges to persons of high status (jurors, members of the military, persons with a college education). Impunity characterizes the judicial system. *Mineiro* Sérgio Naya, immune from prosecution because he was a federal deputy, admitted in a tape recording at least seven crimes, crimes involving use of grossly inferior materials in a building constructed by Naya's firm. The building collapsed, killing eight. The violations Naya confessed to should bring fifty-three years in prison, wrote two *Istoé* journalists in 1998, "if Brazil were a serious country." If this were Cuba, another deputy remarked, "they would execute him and that would be the end of the story."[3]

Many other transgressions have gone unpunished. The police who bombed the Osasco Plaza in 1969 during an antigovernment rally, killing thirty-nine and wounding more than four hundred, have never been prosecuted, nor have families of the victims received compensation. The same is true for the men accused of massacring nineteen landless peasants at Eldorado dos Carajás in 1996. Vigilante justice against lower-class criminals continues, although it has abated in the last few years. A few politicians have been stripped of their political rights for short terms—including impeached president Fernando Collor de Mello—but virtually no politician or influential person has ever gone to jail for corruption or malfeasance. More than eighty deputies and senators have been charged with fiscal fraud, but only a few were punished. Ambassador Júlio César Gomes dos Santos was accused in 1995 of selling influence, but the attorney general's office was unable to prosecute him, and he won a transfer to Brazil's Food and Agricultural delegation in Rome. According to

Transparency International's Corruption Perception Index, prepared annually in Germany by a public affairs group, corruption worsened in Brazil from 1996 to 1997; Brazil earned a ranking barely less corrupt than Turkey, India, Mexico, and Russia, but well behind Chile, France, and Portugal.

In August 1997, the *Folha de São Paulo*, in collaboration with the World Association of Newspapers and the Inter-American Press Foundation, participated in a worldwide survey of opinion among youths, including in Brazil.[4] Because the questionnaire was administered to students with access to the Internet or attending schools with such access, the results portray attitudes of young people at the upper levels of affluence and status; they by no means typify young Brazilians in the general population. In any case, the profile of these well-to-do young Brazilians is telling.

The Brazilian youths surveyed were urban, lived in stable families with both parents, and attended school. The most striking response of all was to a question about life in general: 73 percent of the Brazilian young people said that they were happy, in contrast to only 28 percent in other countries, and only 2 percent said they were unhappy, versus 25 percent elsewhere. The youths showed a high level of social engagement: more enjoyed activities like sports, music, spending time with friends, and using computers than their counterparts elsewhere. They scored low only in three categories: art, spending time outdoors, and performing volunteer work. Sixty percent claimed to read the newspaper daily, in contrast to only 37 percent in other countries. The Brazilians were more willing to agree with the proposal that newspapers tell the truth, and more convinced that the press delivers a variety of opinions that help individuals make up their minds.

Eighty percent of the Brazilian youths identified poverty as one of the three main problems in their country, compared with only 15 percent of youths elsewhere. Unemployment and corruption were listed next, with urban violence ranked fourth. Two categories—racism and drugs—ranked very low on the Brazilians' responses: 15 percent for racism, for example, as against 37 percent outside Brazil. More than half of the Brazilian youths expressed optimism about their own lives over the next ten years, in contrast to one-quarter of the respondents internationally. Also telling was the response to a concluding query asking "which phrase best describes you." Only 11 percent of the Brazilians said that "I believe that I must help improve the world (versus 23 percent outside); 24 percent said that they would fight to improve problems "important to me" (versus 20 percent outside); and 41 percent said that "it is not worth fighting because I cannot change them" (versus 30 percent outside of Brazil).

Perhaps the greatest challenge to the survival of Brazil's torpid old political culture is its failure to apply the rights of citizenship universally. When citizens' rights are not extended universally, when some citizens are treated as if they have fewer rights because they have been labeled incompetent, aberrant, unpatriotic, or untrustworthy—or simply because they are unemployable or destitute—the circumstances, hard to deny, reveal important insight about the larger society. Political society produces the legal and regulatory framework for economic activity. In the Brazilian case, enforcement of civil society has been uneven, its application governed by unwritten rules and behaviors favoring some to the detriment of the vast majority. Brazilian law requires universal conscription of young men, for example, but virtually no youths from affluent families ever serve in the armed forces. Inherited from the corporatist period of the 1930s and earlier, privileges and exemptions and categories of special status have been written into law and remain in force.

In turn, Brazilians outside of the elite have long felt ambivalent about their relationship to the state. Many Brazilians felt alienated in the 1970s by the dictatorship's manipulated expressions of nationality, especially patriotism, while it attacked those seeking democracy and the rule of law as enemies of their country. The late sociologist (and crusader against hunger) Herbert de Souza ("Betinho") spoke to the issue more directly: "Citizenship has to be won; it is not given to us." Betinho's widely quoted statement challenged the reality of the old elite prescription, "For my friends, everything; for my enemies, the law." For generations, people accepted the truth of another saying, *"Não há justiça p'ros pobres"* (there is no justice for the poor).

Many young Brazilians today, coming to maturity after a long period of military dictatorship, consider rights as something a person earns by conforming to social norms—and loses when one is arrested or suffers hard times. This perspective holds that citizenship does not confer rights; rather, having rights defines being a citizen. A university student in Volta Redonda, in the interior of Rio de Janeiro, said bluntly, "Everyone is a citizen. Only the poor are not citizens." This may not be as contradictory as it may seem. If rights are understood as material in nature, then the destitute are not citizens in the same way as the affluent. Considering rights as temporary explains the long-standing willingness of some Brazilians to assume that they do not extend universally. Considering rights as temporary and specific to situations weakens the fabric of democracy.

One must be careful, however, not to be judgmental. Under Brazil's nineteenth-century constitutional monarchy, more Brazilians voted—albeit in a highly controlled manner—than in most European countries. Universal citizenship is a recent achievement in the West. In Germany, for example, it would be inaccurate to speak of universal citizenship before the Federal Republic, and in the United States it was not until the conclusion of the civil rights movement that African Americans won full citizens' right and protections. In most of Eastern and southeastern Europe, not to mention the rest of the world, universal citizenship is a goal, not a given.

ELECTIONS

Signs that Brazil's democratic system is resilient, on the other hand, are widespread. The peaceful impeachment and ouster of President Fernando Collor de Mello in 1992 was the only successful legal action against a president in the history of Latin America. White-collar crime, never successfully prosecuted in earlier years, has been condemned by public opinion, encouraging prosecutors to seek the arrest and imprisonment of miscreants—although very few have actually been punished for their roles in financial or other scandals.

Facing the need to democratize Brazilian politics and guide the country through the dangerous waters of international finance and trade, President Cardoso enunciated a set of goals based on a "third, or middle, way" approach, not unlike the programs of Tony Blair's Labour Party in Great Britain (more particularly, of Blair's finance minister, Anthony Giddens of the London School of Economics). This program relies on an "essential state," one that regulates, not runs, the economy and that provides social benefits to the people while leaving the economy in the hands of the private sector.

On October 4, 1998, more than 106 million Brazilian voters cast their ballots for president and vice president of the Republic. They also voted for twenty-seven governors, twenty-seven senators (representing one-third of the upper house) and for all 513 federal deputies, as well as 1,045 state deputies throughout the country. Although the constitution barred second terms, a measure pushed through by the Cardoso administration, in a classic exercise of parliamentary maneuvering, waived the rule. Twenty-five percent of all legislative candidates at the state and federal level were required to be women, and more than half of the voters nationwide used electronic voting machines.

Four of the eleven presidential candidates received serious consideration by the press. These included Cardoso, the Left's candidate Luís Inácio da Silva ("Lula"), Eneas Carneiro (a third-time minor-party candidate), and Ciro Gomes, the former reform governor of the state of Ceará and finance minister in 1994. Other former candidates withdrew after back-room negotiations with the administration, including the ambitious right-wing populist Paulo Maluf, the candidate of many business groups in São Paulo, and former president Itamar Franco, who was persuaded to run instead for the governorship of Minas Gerais. The gubernatorial races were much closer than predicted, with runoffs in most states. Foreign business groups, represented by U.S. Chamber of Commerce president William Little, pressured all the candidates to consider a probusiness agenda that included six points: reform of the legal process, evenhanded application of laws dealing with the environment, strengthening the voice of free enterprise, promotion of international trade, more state funding for infrastructure, and more business involvement in the fight against drugs and against crime in the workplace. Foreign investors also insisted on tax reform, a subject that has met with stubborn opposition in Brazil among politicians. The campaign lacked the exuberance of its predecessors in the late 1980s and early 1990s, in part because it was widely assumed that Cardoso would win easily. As the election neared, Cardoso assumed a more statesmanlike posture, although some ungenerous remarks were picked up by the press (he dismissed the popular singer Chico Buarque de Holanda's music as "washed up," presumably because Holanda had endorsed Lula of the workers' Party [PT]; other musicians, including the vanguardist Caetano Veloso, supported Cardoso).

Cardoso followed a middle-of-the-road platform, reiterating his 1993 explanation that he was neither a man of the Left nor a neoliberal but sought to strengthen the democratic process, increase productivity, and bolster the influence in government of consumers, managers, workers, and public opinion. With speculation rife in the light of blunt statements from foreign fiscal experts that Brazil would have to devalue its currency and make drastic cuts in government spending, many thought at the start of the campaign that the Left, led by the PT, would stand a good chance of winning the election. But although Lula gained the highest vote percentage (33.2 percent) of his three presidential races, he still failed to win the support of the lower class, a seemingly odd result for a leftist candidate. Cardoso received 29,137,463 votes, or 51.9 percent of the sixty-seven million total votes cast. The most likely explanation is that Cardoso's success as finance minister in stabilizing the economy and defeating inflation with his Real Plan before his first presidential term had won him the lasting gratitude of voters. Lula ran a campaign explicitly opposed to Brazil's participation in the global economy under neoliberal rules. Cardoso, Lula charged in his speeches, was "irresponsible and subservient to international interests. The people are paying for his policies." Cardoso "may have studied a lot," he added, referring to his opponent's academic career, "but he still has the mind of the colonized,"[5] "No one," charged a supporter of Lula, "defends neo-liberalism today, not in the US, not in Europe."[6] But the Left, although its electoral performance was the best it had ever achieved, did not succeed in conveying this to the electorate.

Partisans of the PT and other leftist parties charged opponents with widespread electoral chicanery to discourage voters. Before noon on election day, radio and television reporters were claiming unexpectedly favorable exit-poll results for Cardoso and his allies. Some claimed that the electronic voting machines—used widely for the first time during the 1998 election—confused voters and caused many votes to be nullified. A young university woman expressed her rage in a message posted to the Internet:

I worked for Marta Suplicy [candidate for São Paulo governor], and also was a poll watcher. One of the things that most revolted me was seeing how so many valid ballots, including those for PT candidates and others, were lost because of falsified claims about the vote results. And there was a mountain of dishonest election ads, and tens of millions of *reais* [the equivalent of dollars] injected into the campaign from unknown sources. In terms of electoral fraud I think things are now worse than during the Old Republic; and the mechanisms for cheating are more sophisticated.[7]

Lula's coalition had included leftists of all stripes. University students and professors seemed to like him—although students traditionally abandon their revolutionary rhetoric when they finish their studies and return to their conservative origins. The MST (Landless Workers' Movement) offered strong support, as well as trade unionists, Guevarist, Maoists, Trotskyites, Leninists, and Greens. Lula, during one speech, offered his support to land occupations and sackings of supermarkets and food warehouses, statements that enraged his opponents. To the candidate these actions were just, because, as one who had risen out of poverty himself, he understood that if they did not take food, people would likely die. His economic advisors demanded a "Roosevelt shock," emergency measures to be taken by the federal government to provide jobs and construct massive public works. They also advocated government-backed "People's Banks" to finance cooperatives, small businesses, and the informal sector. Youths entering the job market would be paid by the government for the first six months while being trained. To pay for this, a 5 percent surcharge would be added on all imports, and taxes on foreign corporations would be raised substantially. As might be imagined, the business community shuddered.

Observers have not agreed on why Brazil's Left has failed so consistently over the years to attract majority electoral support; the fact that most Brazilians barely manage to keep their heads above water would seem to benefit the Left. But the Left has proved unable to win support from more than one-quarter of the nation's voters. Not only has the Left failed to stop its historical internal divisiveness, but it has failed to propose workable programs. The restoration of democracy in Brazil seemed to catch the Left off guard. The PT gained some victories at the city and state level but never learned how to squelch internecine fighting or to reach out to the poorest members of the population. Lamely, candidate Lula abandoned his use of red as his campaign color, switching to white, which he termed the color "of peace and unity." But his running mate, Leonel Brizola, continued to wear his trademark red scarves and conjure up images of doctrinaire radicalism, reminding older voters at least of the Stalinist and Maoist traditions of Brazilian leftism—and of the cruel purges carried out against loyalists, and the embarrassments created by abrupt changes in the party line in Moscow and Beijing.

One reason lies in the experience of PT officials who have won city and state races and have attempted to enact leftist agendas. In Porto Alegre, the city's PT mayor, Tarso Genro, won four consecutive terms and was able in 1998 to turn over his administration to Olivo Dutra, also of the PT. Cristovam Buarque, considered to be an effective mayor of Brasília, was (with Genro) considered a possible successor to Lula as national PT chief. In São Paulo, however, Luisa Erundina, a woman of working-class origin whose parents had migrated from northeastern Paraíba, accomplished little as mayor and eventually lost the support of factions within her own political party. Her stormy term in office demonstrated how difficult it is to translate theory into practice. In Belém, the capital of the state of Pará, the elected PT mayor declared in 1998 that the police were "agents of oppression," restricting them for the most part to their barracks and turning over the streets, in a way, to hordes of street vendors, beggars, and petty criminals. On the whole, experience showed that government in the name of social justice and redistribution of income was less easy once in office than the Left's theorists had bargained for. Given Brazil's like-it-or-not participation in an increasingly globalized economy, the Left's prescription for economic development—to promote domestic production (and thereby create jobs) by raising tariffs and imposing exchange controls—threatened to erode foreign confidence and therefore undermine Brazil's position in the region and in the world.

All of this, then, is a legacy of earlier periods of government, including the long Vargas years. Brazilians consider politics to be about job creation and patronage, not public policy issues of regional or national concern. Many consider patronage to be normal, if not desirable, remembering the successful political career during the 1950s and 1960s of São Paulo's Adhemar de Barros, for example, who never denied what was often publicly said about him: "He steals, but he gets things done."

Weaknesses in the electoral system feed such attitudes. Voters are often bewildered when elected representatives jump from one party to another or form alliances with strange bedfellows in other parts of the country. Most of the small political parties lack consistent ideological platforms; they are known as "catchall" parties, temporary coalitions formed as much to strengthen bargaining stances as for anything else. Only one party, the PT, seems to have a genuine grassroots base, but as discussed, it has been unable to win sufficient votes to carry it over the top nationally. The PT, moreover, lacks internal consensus over how far to go toward socialism if it does actually come to power. Some PT leaders stand near the British Labour Party—which has moved far from its original socialist base—whereas others advocate dismantling the polices of recent Brazilian governments embracing the free market system.

A feature of the Brazilian electoral system that has had a significant impact on the way elections are conducted is an amendment to the 1988 constitution giving sixteen-year-olds the right to vote. Citizens over the age of eighteen, moreover, are required by law to vote, continuing the law in effect since 1946. Given that most Brazilian youths do not complete more than the elementary grades and that the population mean is younger than in most industrial countries, electoral campaigns that are well financed and are therefore able to turn out slick, sound bite–based advertising techniques have a powerful edge. This is how Fernando Collor de Mello, a national unknown, won election with the backing of the Globo television network, and it is a reality that all candidates must reckon with. Another oddity is that in the 1998 presidential and gubernatorial elections newspapers reported that at least 30 percent of the ballots were "invalidated or blank." The potential for fraud in such a system is high.

SOCIAL JUSTICE

How Brazil administers justice is a measure of the extent to which its democracy has reached its fullest potential. Brazil's overburdened justice system has rarely meted out justice impartially. The judiciary is independent, but as a foreign watchdog bureau has noted, it is "inefficient and subject to political influence."[8] Police agencies are divided into two divisions—civil, whose members function as detectives, and uniformed, or "military" police, who maintain order. In past decades state police forces have committed numerous human rights crimes, including playing self-appointed roles as vigilante assassins of suspected miscreants. Police officials regularly beat and torture prisoners, especially if they are from the lower classes, whether or not charges have been brought. Violence against homosexuals, women, and children is often unprosecuted. In the city of São Paulo, 10 percent of all homicides are carried out by policemen. In Belo Horizonte, the Human Rights Division of the Public Prosecutor's Office has reported more than a hundred "disappearances" since 1990. In Rio de Janeiro between 1993 and 1996, half of the 697 shooting deaths by policemen involved four or more bullets; forty of them were execution-style, with the victim immobilized and then shot in the head. Hundreds of bodies were found dumped in poor neighborhoods. Victims were usually young and black. Most of the murders occurred in *favelas*, among the homeless, or in one documented case, in an ambulance carrying a wounded suspect to the hospital.

While violence is routinely directed against the poor, especially when they are suspected of criminal behavior, the military dictatorship of the 1960s and 1970s revealed an underlying strain of brutality among military and police officials against their own colleagues. Colonel Jefferson Cardim de Alencar Osório, a left-wing officer arrested after the 1964 coup, wrote the following harrowing description of his treatment in captivity:

In confinement for more than three months, only now have I been able to write down the events surrounding my imprisonment, in the interior of the State of Paraná, on the 27th of last March. They are facts that on hearing are shocking, especially to one, like me and the other military men who were arrested, have pride in the Brazilian soldier's traditions of loyalty, sincerity, and brotherhood. . . .

I was left with my body immobilized on the grass. What followed was witnessed by a dozen or so recruits, who had been invited to participate in a "show" of hypocrisy and sadism. First, the captain made me turn face down to the ground. Then, with the point of his right boot against my mouth, he yelled: "Kiss the soil that you have betrayed, son of a whore! Communist! Murderer!" Then he ordered me to lift my head up and ordered the soldiers to beat me. Instinctively, I tried to turn my head. Reacting in a way that was truly bestial, the captain gave me such a violent kick with his boot that he loosened several of my back teeth. His rage was still not satisfied. He placed the sole of his boot on my nose while two lieutenants beat my body. When they stopped, the captain said I still needed more. So he picked up a metal fork, forcing me on my back, began stabbing me with it, from my bare feet up to my neck. I thought that he even would stab my eyes. He did stab my head and face. . . . I resisted the tortures with one single thought in my mind: "could all of this be in the name of respect for order, in the name of the discipline of the armed forces, our democracy?" These questions still bother me today.[9]

Even after the military regime ceded power back to civilians in the 1980s, police officials continued to defend their violent methods by charging that crime was out of control and that their forces were outnumbered. They receive terrible pay, and in some places salaries are delayed by municipal budget crises for six months or up to a year. They are poorly educated and inadequately trained. For generations, local residents often have feared police and soldiers more than petty thieves and robbers. Police income has always been supplemented by shakedowns and extortion. When bystanders videotaped a police roadblock extorting money from motorists in the São Paulo suburb of Diadema—an action during which some of the victims were tortured—the police shrugged off the evidence and went unpunished. Eight percent of all arrests, according to a report by the São Paulo ombudsman, involve beating or torture of suspects. Officials regularly ignore outcries from protest groups (including the Inter-American Commission on Human Rights), awarding commendations for "bravery" to many of the officers involved in the allegations. A corporal accused of forty-nine killings in 1996 was named "officer of the year." At Carandurú prison in São Paulo, 111 inmates died after police aggressively broke up a strike of prisoners over overcrowded conditions. "There will be more room now," one guard told reporters as the bodies were being dragged away.

Efforts at reform come fitfully. Legislation introduced in 1996 gave civil courts jurisdiction over intentional homicide committed by uniformed policemen. It also, however, put the police in charge of initiating investigations, rendering it unlikely that abuses would be successfully prosecuted. In 1997, President Cardoso signed a law empowering the government to pay indemnities to families of victims; forty-three such payments were made in 1997.

In rural areas, powerful landowners influence juries and intimidate justices. These landowners often employ strong-arm methods to intimidate the powerless; local magistrates, even when not in their pockets, are often helpless to act against them. Brazilian authorities lack the manpower and the strength to oust encroachers on Indian land or to punish bosses who use forced labor, even by children, on their properties. In April 1996, police killed nineteen landless workers in Eldorado de Carajás in the northern state of Pará. Squatters occupying land are murdered throughout the country, sometimes killed by bullets to their heads while kneeling. Confrontations escalated in 1997 in the wake of land seizures by members of the Landless Workers' Movement (MST); according to international watchdog groups, more than two dozen persons died. Gathering public support, MST leaders became bolder: in Pernambuco, an MST organizer likened his cause to that of the Zapatistas in Chiapas, Mexico, and warned that his followers might take up arms to hold land seized for their use. Observers assumed—and hoped—that this would not occur.

The economy's health tended to be voters' greatest concern. Ordinary Brazilians, initially relieved by the inflation stabilization achieved by Cardoso's Real Plan, had by mid-1997 started to react to continued economic stringency. In August, thousands of protesters took to the streets in several cities. The protest, dubbed "Brazil, Open Your Eyes," was organized by the Workers' Party; it was strongest in São Paulo, where crowds blocked traffic on Avenida Paulista, the heart of the city's commercial and business district. Marchers included landless peasants, factory workers, and government employees. Speakers, including Lula, reminded the crowd that the government had spent billions to bail out failed banks, but white and blue-collar workers were being excluded from the government's vision of a prosperous new Brazil.

The Cardoso administration succeeded in enacting a new voting law in time for the approaching elections. One of the most important changes was the adoption of electronic voting, computerized devices that flash pictures of the presidential, gubernatorial, and senatorial candidates on a screen for voter selection. Experimentation with this method in the 1996 municipal elections had revealed that far fewer ballots were voided and that it will likely reduce the number of blank ballots—estimated as many as 50 percent of those voting in 1994—because of voter confusion (though some blanks were cast as a gesture to protest all the candidates on the official slate). Starting in 1998, blank ballots would no longer be counted in the vote total. In the debates leading up to the vote on electoral reform, the government also blocked efforts for public financing of the 1998 elections. This helped Cardoso, since his main opposition, the Workers' Party, drew on far smaller private resources to pay for advertising and campaign costs.

The 1998 election campaign was carried out with the country, in the words of foreign economic experts, on the brink of fiscal collapse. Two weeks before the October 4 voting date, President Cardoso, in a move to counter international uncertainly, pledged to raise taxes if reelected and to push for congressional passage of social security and civil service reform. The Asian financial crisis prompted capital flight at the level of $500 million a day, with the country's reserves sinking to $47 billion. Social security costs at the federal and state level were so high that in many cases they exceeded half of payroll costs. Tax evasion, which wags called "Brazil's third national sport after soccer and sex," had been difficult to combat, with only 10 percent of working Brazilians paying any income taxes at all, and the 1998 social security deficit exceeded $24 billion.

Sixty million voters participated in runoff elections on Sunday, October 25, 1998, in twelve states and the federal district (Brasília), where no candidate had obtained a majority. Incumbents won in six states and four lost. Defeated opposition candidates blamed members of the president's cabinet for having campaigned for their allies although Cardoso had pledged neutrality. On the whole, Cardoso's cause fared well, although a number of politicians also won who were pledged to oppose initiatives. In Cardoso's lame-duck term, the "costs" of winning congressional support for the harsh fiscal austerity measures required by the International Monetary Fund may well be, in the words of a knowledgeable analyst, "very high."[10]

NOTES

1. Jon Pareles, "A Burst of Brazilian Music," *New York Times*, 19 June 1998, B31.

2. R. Andrew Chesnut, "The Spirit of Brazil," paper delivered at the 1998 meeting of the Latin American Studies Association, Chicago, 1.

3. Eduardo Hollanda and Raquel Mello, in *Istoé*, no. 1484. (March 11, 1998); 24–25.

4. For the results of the survey, see http://www2.uol.com.br/survey/.

5. Quoted by Roger Burbach, "Attacking Neoliberals in Brazil," *The Nation* 267, no. 11 (12 October 1998): 19–21.

6. E-mail, Juliano Spyer, São Paulo, 15 October 1998, to author.

7. Andrea Paula dos Santos, "Enquanto alguns voam outros tentar vorar" e-mail, São Paulo, 16 October 1998, to author.

8. U.S. Department of State, Country Report, Bureau of Democracy, Human Rights, and Labor, January 30, 1998.

9. Cited by Andrea Paula dos Santos, "O soldado-cidadão: militares de esquerda no Brasil (1930–1997)," ms, University of São Paulo, 1998, 16–17.

10. David Fleischer, "Second-Round Election Commentary," *Brazil File* 7, no. 8 (November 1, 1998): 7.

8

Social and Economic Realities

For Brazilians in the country's rapidly growing and affluent middle class, life since the restoration of democracy in the mid-1980s has been good. The quality of life has risen dramatically. Shoppers enjoy elegant and well-decorated malls; families usually have more than one car; everyone has a color television set; trips abroad are inexpensive and can be charged by credit card. A continuing urban construction boom has created high-rise concrete forests, complete with swimming pools, twenty-four hour security, and handsome landscaping. More Brazilian women have professional careers than ever before; they have filled the ranks of architects, engineers, managers, physicians, dentists, and lawyers. Middle-class families have full-time domestic servants; many have second homes at the shore or in the mountains. They send their children to excellent private schools, then to the best federal universities, which are tuition free. Middle-class Brazilians are frequently well read, knowledgeable about economic matters, and conversant about national and international events. It is a sophisticated world, vibrant and always engaging.

The bottom portion of the population continues to live in hardship, but Brazilians with jobs live better than ever before. Nationwide, the illiteracy rate fell from more than half the population in 1940 to only 17 percent in 1998. Infant mortality dropped by two-thirds—as did the number of children per family, from more than six in 1960 to 2.5 in the late 1990s. With a median wage of four hundred dollars a month, working-class families, especially where several persons work, can today afford a television set and a car, although not a new one. During the 1990s, more families than ever have been able to afford to purchase simple homes, although the majority rent. Factory workers are a small minority of the work force, and persons engaged in agriculture rarely achieve middle-class levels.

Many Brazilians agree that education remains one of Brazil's greatest challenges. The system requires that students take comprehensive examinations that test memorized facts. More than half of all entering students fail their first-grade examinations and are held back; 32 percent of all students are at least four years older than their age/grade level, a prelude to their dropping out. In 1997, only one in ten pupils who had entered first grade completed secondary school. Forty percent of students in São Paulo, the wealthiest and most economically developed state, failed their first year of high school. Public school teachers received salaries ranging from three to five hundred dollars monthly. The poorest fifth of Brazilian adults had only 2.1 years of schooling, and the richest 20 percent—an equally shocking statistic—had completed only 8.7 years of school. Seventy percent of construction workers in Brazil could not read or write in 1997.

In an effort to make up for lost time, Brazilian authorities are considering accelerating the use of computers in instruction. To combat the problem of software piracy—an estimated 68 percent of all software in Brazil has been illegally copied—Microsoft has negotiated an arrangement whereby it will provide ten million dollars worth of software to three hundred thousand Brazilian public schools in return for promises that only legal software will be used. This is wishful thinking on the part of Bill Gates and his lawyers, but it reinforces Microsoft's presence in a country where advances in technology use have been dramatic.

THE ENVIRONMENT

Brazil is also attempting to slow if not stop the centuries-old pattern of environmental devastation. After decades of inactivity, the government has taken steps to control the pillage of the Amazon rain forest. Environmentalists have warned of grave consequences if deforestation is not slowed: from 1996 through 1998, more than sixty thousand square kilometers of forest were lost, an area one and a half times the size of

Switzerland. In early 1998, Congress voted to give the federal environmental agency legal authority to enforce environmental protection laws, although major provisions were deleted that would have made penalties tougher and the government did not appropriate adequate funds for enforcement of the law. Faced with what a study labeled "rampant illegal logging," officials sold rights to cut timber in 12,355 acres near the Tapajós River in Pará state as a first step in opening the Amazon to regulated commercial development. "Ninety-nine percent of the Amazon is being exploited without any control or design," the head of the Brazilian branch of Conservation International, a Washington-based environmental group has charged. Others criticized the decision, arguing that opening up the forest for large-scale commercial development would devastate the ecosystem no matter how careful the plans for sustainable development. Twenty-two Asian development companies awarded contracts to cut trees on virgin lands in the state of Amazonas had been responsible for destroying 90 percent of the timberland in Thailand and Vietnam, nearly the entire forested area of Borneo, and half of the trees in Papua–New Guinea. In February 1998, the Cardoso administration enacted a law aimed to protect the Amazon Basin, although the legislation was weakened when the president vetoed a provision that would have permitted government agents to fine farmers who continued to burn down trees without prior approval.

Whether these conservation policies will work remains to be seen. Large portions of the forested Amazon region are burning at any given time. The law that settlers must keep 80 percent of their lands forested has not yet been enforced. Brazil's environmental protection agency has about eighty forest rangers in the whole of the Amazon, a desperately inadequate number in an area spanning thousands of square miles. The courts have ruled that the agency does not have the authority to collect the fines it imposes. Roads are being blasted out of the earth to provide access to markets for the huge soybean plantations located on the sites of ancient rain forests; companies from China, Malaysia, Korea and other nations that use clearcutting techniques have started to log the forest. The roads may make clearcutting profitable, thereby putting additional pressure on the Brazilian government to sell off even more of the Amazon in exchange for hard currency and for private gain.

SOCIAL ISSUES

The Brazilian constitution guarantees the right to strike. The labor code requires all workers and employers to pay a labor union tax but restricts union organization to one per city, the so-called *unicidade* rule. No more than one union per profession is permitted, either. There have been modifications to this system recently, but it is still very difficult to form rival unions or working-class associations. Approximately 20 to 30 percent of the workforce is organized, and strikes are fairly frequent, especially over wages. Teachers, postal workers, police, train and local transit workers, employees of automobile plants, metal workers, electric workers, and dockworkers all went on strike in 1997. Laws prohibit forced labor, debt peonage, and child labor, but in remote areas these practices are reported to persist. Official figures have reported that nearly 3.8 million children under the age of fourteen work, often alongside other family members, in the fields or feeding wood into charcoal ovens or herding domestic animals. Some private associations, including the Toy Manufacturers Federation for Children's Rights (ABRINQ), have successfully pressured employers (including Volkswagen and General Motors) to stop hiring underage factory workers. The ABRINQ also won funding in five states, including Mato Grosso do Sul, to send children to school who had been working.

The United Nations lists Brazil as sixty-third among nations in terms of salaries, health care, and opportunities for education. The official minimum wage in 1998 was twenty reals ($110) a month, insufficient to provide an adequate standard of living for a family. The workweek is supposed to be forty-four hours, but some workers are required to work longer hours without receiving overtime pay. One in four Brazilians in 1998 earned less than a dollar a day. Non-whites earn on average 43 percent as much as whites. Brazil's diverse ethnic and racial groups are underrepresented in government and politics, which remain a preserve for the affluent classes.

Women's issues have entered public debate, but in muted fashion. Women earn fifty-four cents on the dollar compared with men, eleven cents less than in the United States. Women encounter a "glass ceiling": they hold no cabinet ministries or federal judgeships, yet they hold 40 percent of all jobs. Some changes are being legislated; a 1996 law requires that for every five nominees for political office, one must be a woman. Physical abuse of women remains a major problem, although women have received, in recent decades, equal status before the law. As late as the 1960s, an abused woman could not press charges against her partner unless he agreed, and women separated from their husbands had to receive their written permission to open bank accounts or travel out of the country. Only in 1991 did the Supreme Court strike down the age-old claim of "defense of honor" for cases in which husbands kill their wives who they believe are deceiving them.

Progress for women has traditionally depended on social class, and it continues to do so. Elite women now enter professional careers in higher proportions than in the United States or Europe. Affluent women lead modern, comfortable lives. Among members of the working middle class, women often hold jobs as teachers or clerks and then return home to care for their families, although in Brazil many if not all middle-class families employ maids to prepare meals, clean, and watch the children. Among the lower class, and especially the vast numbers of urban and rural poor, women's lives are harsh. Cut off from educational opportunities and forced to work in the informal sector of the economy if they cannot find regular jobs, they are paid less than men. Poor women are often victims of domestic violence and abandonment; the high rates of deaths in childbirth are due in part to lack of proper health care, as well as to the fact that while Brazil bans abortions, hundreds of thousands of women attempt to terminate their pregnancies illegally, some with deadly results to themselves.

ECONOMIC REALITIES

For decades, Brazil aspired to a role in world leadership. One of the likely reasons for the country's declaration of war on the Axis powers in 1942 was to gain recognition from the United States of its authority in the hemisphere, since Argentina refused to grant it. The Dutra government was angered by the failure of Washington to support Brazil as a permanent member of the United Nations Security Council in 1946, and from 1982 until 1988 Brasília opposed the desire of the major industrial powers to reform world trade under GATT without first dealing with existing issues in contention, such as agriculture and textiles. This was probably a negotiating ploy—Brazilian officials knew that bringing these issues to the table would likely doom any GATT agreement—but Brazil pursued the position until 1988, when it agreed with the GATT principles.

The reason for Brazil's position was that its policy makers have traditionally feared the influence of foreign multinational corporations. During the 1970s, one of the loudest voices raised against "internationalization" was that of Fernando Henrique Cardoso, who warned against "imperialist penetration," even against linkages to the international system originating at home, because they too led to domination by outside powers. Thirty years later, as Brazil's president, Cardoso moderated his criticism, calling the process of opening to the outside world a strategic element in domestic modernization. Brazil's new economic policy mirrors those of most of the countries of the developing world, and it brings with it the demise of the developmentalist state—in Brazilian terms, closure for the model of government introduced and developed by Getúlio Vargas between 1930 and 1954.

Since the late 1980s, foreign investors have seen Brazil as an extraordinary opportunity for growth. More than $45 billion entered Brazil in 1997 in direct investment. Multinational investment, from telecommunications to fast food to industrial production to agriculture, has produced a boom economy—and booming profits. It has not, however, increased significantly the number of jobs, since new factories rely increasingly on robotics and computers; agro-industrial production requires far fewer laborers than traditional farms and plantations. Foreign firms have introduced innovative ways to make the land productive. In the Northeast, corporate fruit growers have introduced Israeli drip-irrigation systems and have imported earthworms from Europe that burrow into the soil and make it porous (to the end that the growers hope, the rain will not run off). Many foreign-owned corporations provide housing, schools, and training for workers. On the other hand, many corporations hire mostly women, because women, who are rarely unionized, accept lower wages than men. Those who are employed by the factories are fortunate, because the new industrialization is efficient; however, many men and women are stranded on the peripheries of the new high-tech manufacturing zones.

It has been difficult to overcome the legacy of Brazil's economic and monetary instability. Currency weakness and other problems increased the cost of living from 1930 to 1960 by an enormous amount, and Brazilians lived for years with the anxiety of chronic inflation, although some astute members of the affluent classes, especially during the 1980s, benefited from it, acquiring real estate, houses, and condominiums cheaply by clever maneuvering with mortgages and loans. Most, however, did not benefit. High bank interest and tax charges made Brazilian products uncompetitive on the world market. Indexing policies benefited some and harmed others. Ordinary people suffered: in the first three months of 1964, prices rose at an annual rate of 144 percent. Successive governments issued worthless money, then changed the name of the currency back and forth from *réis* to *mil-réis* to *cruzeiros* to *cruzados* and, in the 1990s, to the *real*—its name a variation on the name of Brazil's currency during the colonial era.

The Asian crisis and stock market volatility in the West revealed Brazil's vulnerability to world economic conditions. Observers pointed out that the country's budget overruns amounted to 8 percent of the gross domestic product and warned President Cardoso to take bold steps to curtail spending. With an economy twice the size of Russia's, Brazil has traditionally balked at cost cutting, with the exception of the early 1980s, when obeying International Monetary Fund prescriptions resulted in a painful recession. The size of Brazil's economy means that it cannot be bailed out by foreign capital: the time has come when Brazil can only do this itself.

The problem was, however, that Cardoso's congressional political allies remained firmly committed to maintaining the old ways of government, characterized by inconstancy, frequent schisms, deal making, and partisan defections. Since the restoration of democracy, no political party has achieved near majority status; Cardoso had to run at the head of a five-party coalition led by the *tucanos* at the political center. His election-campaign pledge of $150 billion for social programs, to be spent over the next four years, appealed to voters and promised to lubricate the vast national patronage machinery but did little to reassure bankers or lending agencies. In mid-October 1998, fresh from his narrow reelection (by a plurality of 1 percent, which permitted him to avoid a runoff), he cautiously reiterated his campaign promise. "I received once again through the ballot boxes the support of the Brazilian people," he stated at a press conference, "which gives me a new mandate." He promised to overhaul the bloated pubic sector but stopped short of taking quick, emergency measures.

The struggle for Brazil to put aside its historical protectionist outlook, then, has been a difficult one and illustrates the dilemma of a country seeking to gain international respect while feeling vulnerably in transition from Third World to First World status. Protectionism has resulted in what consumers wryly call the *custo Brasil*—a situation in which products cost more in Brazil and are of lesser quality. Affluent Brazilians for years have combatted this reality by taking shopping trips to the United States, often paying for their airfare by selling on their return some of the items they purchased. In 1998, the average Brazilian tourist visiting New York City spent $1,350, compared to $355 for British visitors and $639 for Germans. Some 333,000 Brazilians visited New York in 1998, in fourth place after residents of the United Kingdom, Germans, and Japanese.

Reasons for the survival of protectionism are many. Critics once pointed to the traditional expectation in diplomatic negotiations that Brazilian representatives always had to refer back to their government for instructions, despite the high reputation of Brazil's foreign service (Itamaratí) for sending out ambassadors and trade representatives of the highest qualifications. Under the Cardoso administration, diplomats received permission to negotiate on their own, proactively suggesting to Itamaratí how negotiations should proceed. This new attitude yielded positive results in the GATT talks in 1987 under Rubens Ricupero, not by coincidence the first nontechnical diplomat to be named to head the Brazilian mission in Geneva. Flexible and willing to make concessions, and not agreeing with Brasília's suspicion of GATT as a "rich men's club," Ricupero earned the respect of other negotiators and in the end improved Brazil's bargaining position.

On the other hand, it is clear that Brazil's embrace of globalization has harmed innovative local experiments. The shoe industry in southern Brazil, beginning in the late 1970s, shared information on production, quality control, and design through trade associations and in some cases pooled resources to obtain better prices for supplies. When government incentives, including favorable exchange-rate policies, began to shift in the early 1990s, the collective efforts of the shoe manufacturers proved insufficient. The result was that cooperation gave way to fierce competitiveness, smaller firms were wiped out, and the survivors pulled up stakes in the face of labor intransigence and moved their plants to the impoverished Northeast, in an echo of the Rust Belt exodus in the United States.

Brazilian economic policy in recent years has pleased the International Monetary Fund, which holds annual bilateral discussions with all debtor nations. In 1998, the IMF's directors praised the Cardoso administration for taking hard measures to relieve pressures on the currency caused by the Asian economic crisis. The measures included the doubling of interest rates and the enactment of a strong fiscal-reform package. Directors noted that per capita real GDP had grown for the last five years, and they applauded the acceleration of the privatization program. They also, however, expressed worry about the fact that more than half of Brazil's current account deficit was financed by direct foreign investment. At the same time, international reserves fell.

One interesting by-product of the campaign to attract foreign investment, at a time that international reserves were falling, has been the reemergence of Portugal as a major trading and investment partner of its former colony. After independence, the influence of the former mother country nearly vanished, replaced by Great Britain, whose banks financed a century of infrastructure building. By the mid-1990s, Portugal had become Brazil's third-largest investor, after the United States and Germany. Portugal's Telecom's purchase in 1998 of Brazil's public Telebrás gave the company rights to a population of thirty-six million, more than four times the size of Portugal itself. Other Portuguese investors included Electricidade de Portugal, a power utility, and several banks. Banco Boavista, for example, has opened more than 170 branches across Brazil; two other Portuguese banks have obtained more than 1,500 branches throughout Brazil in an aggressive campaign of acquisition.

Another new major investor in the late 1980s was Spain. Its former phone monopoly, Telefonica, bought seven billion dollars' worth of telephone contracts, including rights to service in São Paulo. The move proved risky: buffeted by the crises in Asia and Russia, the company lost one-quarter of its market capitalization, or ten billion dollars in one month, August 1998. Yet Telefonica's $15.7 billion investment in Latin America represented only 15 percent of its earnings, permitting its officers the luxury of waiting out the economic crisis of the late 1990s until sunnier days returned. Another luxury for foreign investors was that they did not have to finance their investments locally in Brazil, where interest rates climbed to 40 percent or higher. This fact, plus their use of highly trained technicians, seemed to give foreign firms a considerable advantage over domestic firms in Brazil.

Brazil's embrace in the 1990s of free market economics has shown how precarious its economic structure has remained. Ninety-five percent of the working population is dependent on the public sector for retirement pensions. This puts great pressure on politicians to prop up the bureaucratic system at any cost. In 1996 the government spent 5 percent of its gross domestic product on social security, yet benefits remained insufficient. Basically the system never goes bankrupt but it is always insolvent, Brazilian experts confess.

With the turn to free market economics, the gap between rich and poor has widened. Child labor has not only persisted in some places but may be more widespread than is known. In 1998, it was disclosed that Brazil's citrus industry—booming as the result of sales to Minute Maid and Tropicana in the United States—was hiring children as young as six years of age to work in groves, carrying bags sometimes double their weight.

Privatization, outsourcing, and other such programs to save costs, given Brazil's strong tradition of trade unionism among skilled workers, require the approval of the Brazilian government. More than $24 billion dollars flowed into the federal treasury in 1997 from privatization of what observers have termed "the overblown state sector." Many of the states, facing revenue shortfalls, also jumped on the privatization bandwagon. The troubled state bank of Rio de Janeiro, for example, was sold to the privately held Banco Itaú. A Dutch financial conglomerate, ABN AMRO, paid $2.1 billion for 40 percent of the voting shares and 100 percent of the nonvoting shares of a new holding company that would control Banco Real, Brazil's fourth-largest private-sector bank. Itaú itself tried to buy Banco Real, but the Dutch offer was considered a better one. The announcement of the deal met with extreme acrimony in Brazil from other bankers, who criticized the government for "a lack of transparency in the approval of the acquisition" and questioned the extent to which foreign participation should be permitted in Brazilian financial institutions. Clearly, the bankers were appealing to economic nationalism, but government approval went forward. Under the 1988 constitution, the conditions under which foreign capital would be allowed to penetrate Brazil was to be regulated by "complementary" laws, but ten years later no laws had been passed, effectively giving decisions to the president and the head of the central bank, on a case-by-case basis. In late 1998, negotiations went forward for the privatization of Banespa, an even bigger bank, with fifty-eight billion dollars in assets and 569 branches in every Brazilian state.

Selling off state cartels and monopolies made excellent sense business-wise, but the question of rates remained uncertain. In the past, many staple items, including basic food products, bus and train fares, and utility charges, had always been subsidized by the state as a means of reducing discontent. The need to pacify stockholders brought nervousness about what might happen if these charges suddenly were raised. Privatization, which started in 1991 but has gathered steam since, raised fears of labor unrest. The Telebrás system, for example, has seventy thousand strongly unionized workers, many of them facing layoffs or firing after downsizing. When the government sold the Vale do Rio Doce power utility, it was forced at the last minute to offer assurances to workers facing job insecurity.

The rapidly changing economic scene has forced many of Brazil's largest enterprises to reform themselves. For the first time since its founding in 1808, the Bank of Brazil, the country's largest bank, with $80 billion in assets, moved to reduce the bank's role as backup to the government so that it can expand into new business areas. Its new goals run the risk of losses, but the policy has also opened the door to trimming its workforce. The Bank of Brazil holds several advantages in its quest for profitability, one of them being that the salaries of more than three million government employees are paid by direct deposit to accounts at the bank. The government, however, put off some unpopular decisions entirely. These include the intention to reduce retirement benefits; many—including "superstar" university professors—receive 100 percent of their salaries after they step down but are permitted to take new jobs, often at other universities.

Questions remain about the ability to discharge the huge public debts incurred by state and local governments. States and cities account for more than a quarter of Brazil's $60 billion budget deficit and a large portion of the $290 billion national debt. Some have acted responsibly—in his first term, São Paulo's governor Mário Covas cut the state's payroll cost from 80 percent of revenues to 61 percent by removing redundant employees—but others, including the state of Rio de Janeiro, flirt with bankruptcy. In 1997, some cities and states issued bonds under fraudulent pretexts, paying $74 million in fees and commissions to banks and brokers and costing taxpayers $211 million. The Central Bank liquidated twenty-three banks and brokerage houses as a result of the scandal. Meanwhile, courts remain reluctant to punish financial crimes, leading observers to worry that "bigger fish" would be permitted to continue acting with impunity. In 1999, the refusal by Minas Gerais governor Itamar Franco to meet his state's debt obligation set off a crisis that forced the Cardoso administration to devaluate the *real*, in turn triggering economic recession and massive losses of jobs across Brazil.

Hoping that it will get beyond its fiscal dilemmas, the Cardoso administration has targeted the year 2010 for the completion of "Brazil in Action," a multibillion-dollar project aimed at integrating the nation's infrastructure. It includes no fewer than fourteen transportation plans. The highway and port modernization programs alone are to cost $9 billion. The plans envision a mix of public and private-sector funds, including heavy foreign investment. They include privatization of railways, highways, and airports. Railroad track will be improved to bypass the current transportation system, which uses trucks. Port facilities will be improved across the country, not only at Santos, Brazil's leading facility, but at Septiba in Rio de Janeiro, Suape in Pernambuco, and Pecém in Ceará. One of the new ports, Itacoatiará, sits on the Amazon River,

2,500 kilometers into the heart of the rain forest. New inland waterways for shipping are planned for the Madeira River in the Amazon Basin, the Araguaia-Tocantins, the São Francisco, and, with highest priority, the Tietê-Paraná in the south.

One of the newest factors in the process of economic development is the creation in the mid-1990s of Brazilian-based multinational firms. These multilatinas are located in at least eight countries, all in South America plus Mexico. The leading Brazilian firms include Gerdau, with steel mills in Canada, Argentina, Uruguay, and Chile; Brahma, the fifth-largest beer and beverage producer in the world, which started out as a German brewery in southern Brazil; and Odebrecht, a construction company with massive projects in eleven countries, including major highway building in south Florida. The banking network Itaú rivals some of the largest American banks in its scope. Brazilian multinationals operate on a completely different basis than most other Brazilian corporations. Some take advantage of "clustering," the grouping of related industries to cut manufacturing costs. One of the most successful examples of clustering in Brazil has been the reorganization of automobile manufacturing in the "ABC" region outside of São Paulo. Here, manufacturers take advantage of cheap outsourcing by buying glass, rubber, steel, and adhesives, products made by nonunion workers in the clustered plants.

The Southern Cone's common market holds the key to at least some portion of the future economic progress of Brazil. The trading bloc came about much more rapidly than was anticipated, and it has encouraged Brazil and Argentina to follow Uruguay's traditional policy of open markets. The economic revolution wrought by free trade with Paraguay, Uruguay, and Argentina has sharply reduced Brazil's traditional isolation from its regional neighbors. One sign of this is the surge in tourism across borders, not only to take advantage of favorable currency exchange rates but to visit tourist sites. Even more far reaching was the decision in late 1998 by the Brazilian senate to make Spanish obligatory within five years for Brazil's six and a half million public school students. "We have become so much a part of MERCOSUL that we are making Spanish an official language in our schools," a legislator has said.[1] Several southern states already are teaching Spanish in their schools, although Brazil will need seventy-five thousand new Spanish teachers to be able to implement bilingualism. The innovation has been reciprocal: in teacher preparatory courses in Argentina, more than 8,200 teachers are enrolled in courses to learn to teach Portuguese.

TOURISM

Because Brazil is farther from the United States or Europe than for example, Mexico or the Caribbean, tourism has been slow to develop. Well-to-do Brazilians, moreover, have historically preferred to travel abroad than to visit other regions in their own country. In recent years, though, this has started to change. The creation of MERCOSUL has also encouraged tourism from neighboring Argentina and Uruguay. Favorite tourist destinations include Manaos, which has a free port where goods are sold tax-free; Salvador in the state of Bahia, the leading center of Afro-Brazilian culture; and beautiful Rio de Janeiro. Tourism declined in Rio during the early 1990s, because of street crime and pollution, but authorities have taken steps to improve conditions, and as a result tourism is slowly returning to pre-1990 levels. International tourists come more frequently during Carnival; visitors from Western Europe come during their winter to the beaches along the coastal *zona da mata*, where the sun seems always to shine and the Brazilian landscape seems a tropical paradise.

Ecotourism has become popular in recent years. In the municipality of Bonito, in Mato Grosso do Sul, 330 kilometers from the State capital, Campo Grande, a group of entrepreneurial ranchers have constructed around a combination of dude ranches, underwater exploration, and river rafting a tourist infrastructure so successful that unemployment in the region has been eradicated. Sensitive to ecotourists, the ranchers use solar panels to provide energy for refrigeration and have mounted cleanup efforts in local rivers and lakes. Guides are vetted by the local government, and the town is one of the few in the Brazilian interior to practice recycling.

In Praia do Forte, 750 miles northeast of Rio de Janeiro, a pioneering marine conservation project called Tamar (from *tartaruga marinha*, or sea turtle) receives more than three hundred thousand visitors each year, all of them attracted by the idea of saving the habitat for the five endangered species of sea turtles who nest on Brazil's Atlantic coast. Over the past eighteen years, Tamar employees have helped release 2.8 million turtle hatchlings into the sea. They run programs to teach fishermen and hunters to stop raiding nests, and through an astute program of public relations and advertising, with corporate financial support, they have made the sea turtle into a popular symbol of the need for environmental protection. The key to Tamar's success is its paying more than four hundred residents along the coast north and south of Praia do Forte as part-time beach monitors. Each monitor is given responsibility during nesting season for two miles of beach, taking vulnerable eggs and hatchlings to hatcheries and protecting them, as much as possible, against human predators. Tamar maintains twenty-one visitors centers up and down the coast and sells turtle-related souvenirs manufactured by local residents. The program is an enormous success. Foreign journalists note that even though the streets of Praia do Forte remain unpaved, fifteen hotels and several restaurants have been built to handle the influx of tourists. The hotels are "turtle friendly," low-rise, dimly lit, and set back from the beach. By offering jobs to the region's perennially poor residents, moreover, Tamar has created the most significant innovation: community incentives for cooperation. Now, in addition to payments as monitors, local residents work for the ecotourism industry and share the benefits of progressive-minded employers, who provide day-care centers and educational opportunities as well as wages.

OUTMIGRATION

The government's enthusiastic endorsement in the 1990s of free market economics, as well as the relative weakness of Brazil's labor unions, have made the country highly attractive for foreign investment. As the number of wealthy Brazilians at the top of the economic ladder has increased dramatically, so too have conditions driven many Brazilians to leave the country. For generations, Brazilians seeking better opportunities opted to migrate to other regions within the country, unlike people in Mexico and most of the countries of the Caribbean Basin. But this has changed—so much that authorities, fearing a brain drain, have initiated a campaign against emigration. *Não mude do Brasil, ajude mudar o Brasil* ("Don't abandon Brazil; help it to change") goes one of the slogans.

The richest families and individuals have always had second and third homes and apartments in Paris, New York, or Miami. Celebrities like car racer Emerson Fittipaldi and entertainer Xuxa and entrepreneur Sílvio Santos find secure foreign residences a way to escape the paparazzi. Others have moved out of Brazil because of the rising incidence of kidnapping for ransom of the most wealthy. A much larger percentage of the tens of thousands of Brazilians who have gone to the United States and Canada, however, either go to opportunities to do business (operating import-export firms and banks, or providing services to the local expatriate Brazilian communities) or to work at menial jobs in order to save enough money to return to Brazil with a nest egg. Women who work off the books as house cleaners earn two thousand dollars per month, ten times more than they ever could earn in Brazil for similar work. Except for the celebrities, who can hire immigration attorneys, the Brazilians working outside of Brazil do so without work permits. Their lives, therefore, are precarious; they have no safety nets, and they are subject to all the dangers of living in a foreign country without protection.

By 1989, two thousand Japanese-Brazilians had already left for Japan, where many were received less than enthusiastically by employers due to their "foreign" traits, their inability to speak Japanese and their exuberant personalities in contrast to the passivity expected of workers in Japan. As many as seven hundred thousand Brazilians lived in the United States, many of them having overstayed their tourist visas in search of jobs to permit them to accumulate enough capital to return to Brazil and start businesses. Some of these emigrants have remained abroad, such as the sad case of an unemployed former conductor of a leading Brazilian symphony orchestra, whose wife supports him by cleaning houses. This brain drain is also accompanied, in the case of affluent Brazilians, by capital flight. Before the 1970s it was common for wealthy Brazilians to have apartments in Paris; since then the trend has been to purchase expensive homes and condominiums in Coral Gables and Miami Beach, aided by the strong, overvalued Brazilian *real*.

Among the thousands of Brazilians who have settled in the United States—sometimes earning green cards, sometimes not—are middle-class Brazilian men and women with professional degrees from Brazil's interior. So many people from the small cities of Minas Gerais, for example, have followed this route that the city of Governador Valladares has become, it is said, the major Brazilian center for falsified documents, including visas and passports. For most of the emigrants, forged papers are not necessary: they simply buy a round-trip ticket to Orlando, Miami, or New York and overstay their tourist visa indefinitely, hoping to be including in the periodic amnesties declared by the U.S. government. Many of the stories of these emigrants are poignant: bright, university-educated journalists or college professors working for a thousand dollars a month handing out advertising fliers on the streets of New York. But most find jobs, often in the businesses of Brazilians who have preceded them. So many Brazilians live in New York City that West 46th Street is the heart of "Little Brazil," supporting an enormous infrastructure of retail shops, caterers, printers, newsstands, shopper's services, and translators to serve visiting Brazilian tourists. The esteemed Rio de Janeiro carnival society, the Escola de Samba Império Serrano, had for its 1999 Carnival theme "A Street Called Brazil"—meaning 46th Street. Between 160,000 and 180,000 Brazilians live and work in south Florida, some of them on expired visas or otherwise as illegal aliens. Tourists from Brazil spend up to a half-billion dollars a year in Florida; these semipermanent residents earn and spend up to $5 billion annually, according to the Miami Beacon Council. They find things easier than in Brazil: free public education, cheap gasoline, inexpensive telephone service, low unemployment. Newcomers, whether relatives or compatriots from the same Brazilian towns and cities, link up with the networks established by the earlier arrivals. Three thousand Brazilians operate retail businesses in Miami, many of them catering to fellow Brazilians.

Brazil will achieve valid First World status when it extends effective citizenship to the poor and abandons differential privilege in favor of a more equitable form of representation. There must be increased public accountability for government officials and equitable enforcement of laws and regulations. Politicians must enact reform even if it means reducing their personal privileges. Some success has been achieved recently, notably the government's emphasis on an intensive elementary school experience aimed at teaching not only academic skills but at improving the health and nutrition of school-age children. The bloated public payroll must be pared. Between 1991 and 1996, the number of federal civil servants fell from 1.94 million to 1.85 million, but the salaries of even the reduced number of bureaucrats rose from twenty-four to 40.7 billion *reais* per year.

Brazil remains one of the most unequal societies in the world. Fernando Henrique Cardoso explained this during his 1994 presidential campaign in a different way: "Brazil is no longer an underdeveloped country, but it is an unjust country." His first term in office showed signs of continued exclusion of much of the population from meaningful economic gain, although the percentage of Brazilians in extreme poverty dropped from 35 to 25 percent. Improving the lives of all Brazilians formed a key portion of his reelection platform, and he has until the year 2002 to accomplish what he had pledged.

The work of politicians is made easier in Brazil by the attitude of the people. Brazilians have showed remarkable patience in the face of hardship. Of them, Roberto DaMatta, a perceptive observer, writes, "These people, the Brazilian people, intrigue me with their generosity, their wisdom, and above all, their unfailing hope."[2]

NOTES

1. Pedro Simon, of the majority Democratic Movement Party, quoted by Andres Oppenheimer, "Embracing Bilingualism," *Miami Herald*, 17 August 1998, 6A.

2. Roberto DaMatta, cited by Marshall Eakin, *Brazil: The Once and Future Country*, 2d ed. (New York: St. Martins Griffin, 1998) vi.

Notable People in the History of Brazil

Abreu, Capistrano de (1853–1927). Distinguished journalist and historian who traveled the length and breadth of Brazil and excelled in historical criticism and broad-based research.

Alvarengo, Manuel Inácio da Silva (1749–1814). A *mulato* writer and poet of the Arcadian school who portrayed Brazil as a bucolic setting filled with shepherdesses and nymphs, and emphasized emotion and beauty. His poems were written to be sung. After 1777 he took up residence in Lisbon, where he became a leading member of the Lusitanian New Arcadia movement.

Amado, Jorge (1912–   ). The son of a cacao planter in Ilhéus, south of the capital of Salvador on the Bahian coast, Amado published his first novel, *Cacau*, when he was nineteen. Passionately socially conscious as a young man in the 1930s, as an older writer he mined the genre of popular regional fiction and peopled his work with colorful characters and humorous plots.

Chalaça (Francisco Gomes da Silva) (1791–1852). The personal secretary to the Emperor Pedro I. Gomes da Silva came to Brazil with the transmigration in 1808 and stayed when his sovereign declared Brazilian independence. He was a member of Pedro's "Secret Cabinet" and also held diplomatic posts in Italy and elsewhere.

Chateaubriand, Assis (Francisco de Assis Chateaubriand Bandeira de Mello) (1892–1968). A northeasterner from the small state of Paraíba, Chateaubriand studied law at Recife and went on to a long career as one of Brazil's major journalists and newspaper publishers. Over time he branched out into radio, magazines, and, in the 1950s, television. He served in Congress and later as ambassador to Great Britain.

Cícero, Padre (Cícero Romão Batista) (1844–1934). A charismatic defrocked Catholic priest who spent his life in his native Ceará, in the early 1900s he attracted thousands of rural people to his backlands town of Juazeiro, where they lived lives of piety and devotion to him. To this day, backlands families have shrines with statues of the priest in his black monk's habit.

Crespo, Antonio Gonçalves (1846–1883). A *mulato* poet who lived most of his life in Portugal. There, he wrote nostalgic poems about his family life in Brazil. He possessed what Edimilson de Almeida Pereira has called "an ambiguous vision of his ethnicity," at times praising blacks, at times linking blacks to vice and defects.

Cruz e Silva, João (1861–1898). A poet born to slave parents in the southern province of Santa Catarina. He was tutored by a senior Brazilian army officer and apprenticed to a printer. He wrote abolitionist articles and became an actor, touring the country. His writings represent the high point of Brazilian Symbolism. He died of tuberculosis in Minas Gerais.

Damião de Bozzano, Frei (1898–1997). An Italian-born Capuchin monk who entered his religious order at age twelve and was sent to Brazil in 1931. He spent sixty-six years in the impoverished Northeast, mostly in the arid interior. He was famous for his apocalyptic sermons. "Who does not accept Jesus Christ," he often said, "will go to Hell head first." He preached against dancing, popular music, and television, but he maintained a large following. More than eighty miracles and faith healings were attributed to him.

Fernandes, Florestan (1920–1995). The son of a poor family who became one of Brazil's leading sociologists. Started working at the age of six as a delivery boy and ultimately studied at the Faculty of Philosophy in São Paulo. A lifetime Marxist and the author of several theoretical works on Brazilian life, he was a stern critic not only of Brazilian capitalism but of the country's record of race relations. He was one of the organizers of the Workers' Party (PT).

Gonçalves Dias, Antonio (1823–1864). The son of an Indian-African slave. His works were self-consciously Indianist, extolling the virtues of Brazil's indigenous culture. His works include *Primeiros Cantos* (1846) and *Os Timbiras* (1857).

Jesus, Carolina Maria de (1914–1977). An illegitimate black woman born in the small city of Sacramento, Minas Gerais, who overcame impoverishment to become the author of the best-selling book in Brazilian publishing history when in 1960 her diary, *Quarto de Despejo*, was published by Francisco Alves. A feisty yet compassionate woman, de Jesus was scorned not only by her fellow *favelados* but by Brazilians of higher social class, who resented her lack of formal manners and felt her unworthy of fame. The last years of her life were spent in isolation and near poverty.

Miranda, Carmen (1909–1955). A Portuguese-born singer and actress raised in Brazil who as a cartoonlike Caucasian *baiana*, dressed in banana-laden tutti-frutti headdresses and platform heels, became one of Hollywood's highest-paid stars during the 1940s. Studio executives forced her to play the same empty role in every movie, and when she returned to Brazil she was booed by audiences. Before her death at forty-six she had become clinically depressed and dependent on sleeping pills.

Nina Rodrigues, Raimundo (1862–1906). A Bahian physician who published careful ethnographic studies of race and Afro-Brazilian culture, and taught forensic medicine at the Bahian Medical Faculty. Like Euclides da Cunha, he worried that racial traits in blacks that he considered "primitive" might some day overcome European culture in Brazil. He also produced pioneering studies of messianic movements and popular religiosity.

Patrocinio, José de (1853–1905). A journalist and abolitionist of *mulato* birth. He opposed capital punishment and in his 1877 novel *Os Retirantes* wrote moving reports of the devastating Northeast droughts. His less-known *Pedro Espanhol* (1884) probes the state of interracial relations in Brazil. Patrocinio idealized blacks but held his black protagonists to European norms of attractiveness and behavior.

Ribeiro, Darcy (1923–1997). An anthropologist, cabinet minister, educator, novelist, and, during the 1940s, official of the federal Indian Protection Agency. Ribeiro was instrumental in convincing the government of the need to protect Brazil's surviving indigenous population in the Amazon Basin and along the country's northern frontier from the incursions of developers and prospectors. In 1964 he was exiled to Uruguay but returned a decade later by special permission when he was diagnosed with lung cancer. He survived for another twenty-three years, devoting himself to the needs of indigenous tribes. He never had children, but two years before he died he hosted a party for fifty women he had known well. The only men at the party were the waiters.

Rondón, Cândido Mariano da Silva (1865–1927). Founder and first director of the Indian Protection Service in 1911, which was organized as an agency of the Brazilian army.

Segall, Lazar (1891–1957). An artist and painter who, though an immigrant from Vilna, Lithuania, had studied in Berlin and Dresden and became one of the most sensitive portraitists of Brazilian life in the twentieth century. He arrived in São Paulo in 1912 to visit relatives and returned to war-torn Europe, where he gained fame as an artist. In 1923, however, he came to Brazil to stay, splitting his time between Brazil and Paris. He joined the modernists.

Souza, Herbert José de (1937–1997). Known as "Betinho," a sociologist who almost single-handedly crusaded during the 1980s and 1990s for assistance to Brazil's fifty million poor, and the hungry. A gaunt man who died of AIDS he contracted from a blood transfusion—de Souza was a hemophiliac—he was at first ridiculed for his cadaverous appearance and persistent scolding, but ultimately he was applauded for his tenacity in speaking out for the needs of the dispossessed.

Teffe, Nair de (1887–1945). The wife of President Hermes da Fonseca (1910–1914), she smoked, frequented bars, and played the guitar, in defiance of upper-class norms. Eschewing the ceremonial duties of a First Lady, she worked as a newspaper caricaturist and became a patron of theatrical and musical groups.

Torelli, Apparício (1895–1971). An irreverent gadfly, journalist, and intellectual, he dubbed himself the "Duke of Itararé," after the name of a battle during the 1930 Revolution, and later promoted himself to baron. Born in São Leopoldo, Rio Grande do Sul, he worked as a reporter and then started his own newspaper in Rio de Janeiro, *A Manhã*, that became the leading voice of the left until it was shut down in the late 1930s. He was jailed several times during the Vargas period, but in 1945 he reopened *A Manhã*.

Verger, Pierre Fatimbi (1906–1995). French-born photographer and ethnographer whose pioneering work on Yoruba culture and the links between West Africa and Bahia kept alive the Afro-Brazilian memory. In his later decades, he was honored by the defenders of Afro-Brazilian culture and given his Yoruba middle name. He took up residence in Vila Americana, one of the poorer neighborhoods in Salvador, and trained to be a *babalão*, a *candomblé*, a master of secrets.

Glossary of Selected Terms

ABERTURA: Political opening during the final years of the dictatorship (1978–1985).

ALVORADO PALACE: Presidential residence in Brasília.

ARENA: Alliance for National Renewal, the pro-military government political party during the post-1964 dictatorship.

BACHAREL: Holder of a B.A. degree or, in nineteenth-century Brazil, a law graduate.

BANDEIRANTES: Colonial-era frontier prospector and hunter for Indians (to be enslaved).

BUMBA MEU BOI: Rural northeastern folkloric pageant.

CABOCLO: Person of mixed African, Indian, and European background.

CABRA: Person of mixed Indian and European ancestry.

CAFÉ COM LEITE: "Coffee with milk" policy of rotating control of government between São Paulo (coffee) and Minas Gerais (dairy production).

CANDOMBLÉ: Afro-Brazilian spiritist religion.

CAPOEIRA: Afro-Brazilian choreographed martial art.

CARIOCA: Inhabitant of city of Rio de Janeiro.

CHIMANGOS: Moderate elite political faction during the Regency. *See also* EXALTADOS

COLONO: Immigrant contract workers hired as agricultural laborers.

CORONEL: Rural strongman, usually also a political boss.

CRENTE: Evangelical Protestant.

CREOLE: Person born in the New World.

CRUZEIRO, CRUZADOS: Units of currency.

DESPACHANTE: Expediter, to cut through red tape or get special treatment for client.

DISTENSÃO: Gradualist policy to restore democracy.

EMPIRE: Brazil's government between 1822 and 1889, headed by a constitutional monarch.

ENGENHO: Sugar plantation with mill driven by oxen or water power.

ESTADO NOVO: Authoritarian regime (1973–1945).

EXALTADOS: Rivals to Chimango faction during Regency.

EXÚ: Impish *condomblé* spirit.

FARINHA: Flour made from dried and roasted MANDIOCA tuber.

FAVELA: Urban shantyown, called MOCAMBO in the Northeast.

FAZENDA: rural agricultural property or ranch.

FAZENDEIRO: Proprietor of a FAZENDA.

FILHOTISMO: Nepotism.

FLUMINENSE: Inhabitant of province (or state) of Rio de Janeiro.

FORRO: Colonial-era designation for free black.

GAÚCHO: Inhabitant of Rio Grande do Sul; cowboy.

INCONFIDENCIA MINEIRA: Unsuccessful plot to separate from Portugal.

INTEGRALIST: Member of 1930s Brazilian fascist political movement.

IPIRANGA: Site of Brazil's declaration of independence in 1822.

JACARANDA: Dense, dark Brazilian wood.

JAGUNÇO: Blacklands ruffian.

LINHA DURA: Hard-line, term used for a faction within the military during the dictatorship of the 1960s and 1970s.

LUSO-PORTUGUESE: Pertaining to Portugal.

MANDIOCA: Cassava root. *See also* FARINHA.

MASCATE: Portuguese merchant, often an immigrant.

MESTIZO: Person of mixed Indian and European origin.

MINEIRO: Inhabitant of Minas Gerais

MOCAMBO: *See* FAVELA.

MORADORES: Landless rural renters.

MST: Landless Workers' Movement.

MULATA: Woman of mixed African and European origin.

MULATO: Man of mixed African and European origin.

MUNICÍPIO: Municipality; county.

NOVELA: Televised prime-time soap opera.

OLD (or FIRST) REPUBLIC. *See* REPUBLIC.

PANELINHA: Network of friends and relatives.

PANTANAL: The largest ecological sanctuary in the world, in central Brazil, covering 140,000 square kilometers.

PARDO: Person of African ancestry; Negro.

PAULISTA: Inhabitant of the city of São Paulo.

PAULISTANO: Inhabitant of the state of São Paulo.

PELEGO: Honcho working for government trade union. Literally, a sheepskin placed between a saddle and the horse.

PODER MODERADOR: The "moderating power," permitting the Emperor to veto legislation and dissolve parliament when he wished.

QUEBRA-KILOS: Backlands movement in 1870s protesting metric weights and measures.

QUILOMBO: Backlands settlement of fugitive slaves.

REAL, REIAS: Colonial-era unit of currency revived in 1990s.

REPUBLIC: Period between 1889 and 1930 characterized by extreme federalism and domination by the strong states. Also known as OLD (or FIRST) REPUBLIC.

RIO GRANDENSE: Pertaining to the state of Rio Grande do Sul. *See also* GAÚCHO.

SENHOR: Mister.

SENHOR DE ENGENHO: Proprietor of a sugar plantation mill.

SERTÃO: Arid backlands of the interior of the Northeast.

SINDICATO: Trade union

SISTEMA: Term for Brazil's political culture.

SUBÚRBIO: Outlying urban working-class district.

TENENTES: Military cadet rebels of 1922 and 1924 who rose to power after 1930 Revolution.

TROPICALISM: Protest-driven popular music movement of 1960s and early 1970s hostile to the military regime.

UMBANDA: Spiritist cult akin to CANDOMBLÉ.

ZONA DE MATA: Formerly forested coastline in Northeast, whose trees were felled to create plantations.

ZUMBÍ: "King" of fugitive slave settlement at Palmares. *See also* QUILOMBO.

Bibliographic Essay

There are many good sources on Brazil, including a growing number of websites and collections of documents on the Internet. Websites constantly change, but some of the best include LANIC (www. lanic.utexas.edu/la/brazil), the Getúlio Vargas Foundation (www. fgvsp.br/), and an on-line Brazilian search engine, RadarUOL (www.uol.com.br/busca). Those with the ability to read Portuguese, of course, will find a wealth of books and articles in that language. This list represents simply a starting point for sources in English, including important works that have been translated from other languages.

For background, see the multivolume *Cambridge History of Latin America* (Cambridge: Cambridge Univ. Press, 1984–1995), one of whose volumes, mostly on modern Brazil, had still not appeared in 1999. E. Bradford Burn's *A History of Brazil*, 3d ed. (New York: Columbia Univ. Press, 1993); Charles Wagley's *Introduction to Brazil*, rev. ed. (New York: Columbia Univ. Press, 1971); T. Lynn Smith's *Brazil: People and Institutions* (Baton Rouge: Louisiana State Univ. Press, 1972); and Ronald M. Schneider's *Brazil: Culture and Politics in a New Industrial Powerhouse* (Boulder, CO: Westview, 1996). See also, Fernando de Azevedo, *Brazilian Culture: An Introduction* (New York: Macmillan, 1950); and Thomas W. Merrick and Douglas H. Graham, *Population and Economic Development*

196 Bibliographic Essay

in Brazil, 1808 to the Present (Baltimore: Johns Hopkins Univ. Press, 1979); Peter Flynn, *Brazil: A Political Analysis* (London: Ernest Benn, 1978); and Joseph A. Page, *The Brazilians* (Reading, PA: Addison-Wesley, 1995). Marshall Eakin's *Brazil: The Once and Future Country*, 2d ed. (New York: St. Martin's Griffin, 1998), offers an excellent interpretive synthesis of Brazil's history.

Brazil's colonial history from the Portuguese point of view is analyzed by Bailey W. Diffie, *A History of Colonial Brazil: 1500–1792*, ed. Edwin J. Perkins (Malabar, FL: Robert E. Krieger, 1987); and N. P. MacDonald, *The Making of Brazil: Portuguese Roots, 1500–1822* (Sussex, U.K.: Book Guild, 1996). Anthony Smith's *Explorers of the Amazon* (Chicago: Univ. of Chicago Press) describes both Spanish and Portuguese expeditions. See also Sanjay Subrahmanyam, *The Portuguese Empire in Asia, 1500–1700* (London: Longman, 1993). For the eighteenth century, see Kenneth Maxwell's handsomely published *Pombal: Paradox of the Enlightenment* (Cambridge: Cambridge Univ. Press, 1995). See also David Birmingham, *A Concise History of Portugal* (Cambridge: Cambridge Univ. Press, 1993); and the classic studies by C. R. Boxer, *The Portuguese Seaborn Empire, 1415–1825* (Oxford: Oxford Univ. Press, 1963), *The Golden Age of Brazil, 1695–1750* (Berkeley: Univ. of California Press, 1962), and *Race Relations in the Portuguese Empire* (Oxford: Oxford Univ. Press, 1963). For an environmental overview, see Warren Dean's monumental *With Broadax and Firebrand: The Destruction of the Brazilian Atlantic Forest* (Berkeley: Univ. of California Press, 1995). Alida C. Metcalf's *Family and Frontier in Colonial Brazil* (Berkeley: Univ. of California Press, 1992) addresses an important topic in colonial family history. For urban family economic history, see Elizabeth Anne Kuznesof, *Household Economy and Urban Development* (Boulder, CO: Westview, 1986).

For the nineteenth century, see Roderick J. Barman, *Brazil The Forging of a Nation, 1798–1852* (Stanford: Stanford Univ. Press, 1988); Leslie Bethell, ed., *Brazil: Empire and Republic 1822–1930* (Cambridge: Cambridge Univ. Press, 1989), and *Colonial Brazil* (Cambridge: Cambridge Univ. Press, 1987). See also Alan K. Manchester, *British Preeminence in Brazil* (Chapel Hill: Univ. of North Carolina Press, 1933); and Dain E. Borges, *The Family in Bahia, Brazil 1870–1945* (Stanford: Stanford Univ. Press, 1992). Emilia Viotti da Costa's *The Brazilian Empire: Myths and Histories* (Chicago: Univ. of Chicago Press, 1985), interprets the history of the period from the vantage point of a historian of the Left. See also Sandra Lauderdale Graham, *House and Street: The Domestic World of Servants and Masters in Nineteenth-Century Rio de Janeiro* (Austin: Univ. of Texas Press,

1992); and Jeffrey D. Needell, *A Tropical Belle Époque Elite Culture and Society in Turn-of-the-Century Rio de Janeiro* (Cambridge: Cambridge Univ. Press, 1987).

Good surveys of the slave system are found in A. J. R. Russell-Wood, *The Black Man in Slavery and Freedom in Colonial Brazil* (London: Macmillan, 1982); Robert Conrad, *The Destruction of Brazilian Slavery 1850–1888* (Berkeley: Univ. of California Press, 1972), and his *World of Sorrow: The African Slave Trade to Brazil* (Baton Rouge: Louisiana State Univ. Press, 1986); and Robin Blackburn, *The Making of New World Slavery: From the Baroque to the Modern, 1492–1800* (London: Verso, 1997). Celia de Azevedo's *Abolitionism in the United States and Brazil* (New York: Garland, 1995) is a useful comparison. For the late nineteenth century, see Euclydes da Cunha, *Rebellion in the Blacklands*, (trans. Samuel Putnam (Chicago: Univ. of Chicago Press, 1944). Theodore Roosevelt expounded his own ideas on race in "Brazil and the Negro," *The Outlook* 106 (21 February 1914).

For the Old Republic, see June E. Hahner, *Poverty and Politics The Urban Poor in Brazil, 1870–1920* (Albuquerque: Univ. of New Mexico Press, 1986); and Steven C. Topik's *Trade and Gunboats: The United States and Brazil in the Age of Empire* (Stanford: Stanford Univ. Press, 1997). The transition to the Vargas era is dealt with by Joseph L. Love, *Rio Grande do Sul and Brazilian Regionalism, 1882–1930* (Stanford: Stanford Univ. Press, 1971), and his *São Paulo in the Brazilian Federation, 1889–1937* (Stanford: Stanford Univ. Press, 1980), as well as by companion volumes by John D. Wirth on Minas Gerais (Stanford: Stanford Univ. Press, 1977) and Robert M. Levine on Pernambuco (Stanford: Stanford Univ. Press, 1978). Also see Eul-Soo Pang, *Bahia in the First Brazilian Republic* (Gainesville: Univ. Presses of Florida, 1979), and Teresa A. Meade's *"Civilizing" Rio: Reform and Resistance in a Brazilian City, 1889–1930* (University Park, PA: Penn State Univ. Press, 1997). Michael Conniff's *Urban Politics in Brazil: The Rise of Populism, 1925–1945* (Pittsburgh: Univ. of Pittsburgh Press, 1981) analyzes populism in Rio de Janeiro. Agricultural issues and benefits to workers are addressed in Thomas H. Holloway, *Immigrants on the Land* (Chapel Hill: Univ. of North Carolina Press, 1981). See also Maxine L. Margolis, *The Moving Frontier* (Gainesville: Univ. Presses of Florida, 1973); and Mauricio A. Font, *Coffee, Contention, and Change in the Making of Modern Brazil* (Cambridge: Basil Blackwell, 1990).

Overviews of the Vargas period are provided by Robert M. Levine, *The Vargas Regime* (New York: Columbia Univ. Press, 1970), and *Father of the Poor?* (Cambridge: Cambridge Univ. Press, 1998); Thomas E. Skidmore, *Politics in Brazil, 1930–1964* (New York: Oxford Univ. Press, 1967); John W. F. Dulles, *Vargas of Brazil: A Political Biography* (Austin: Univ. of Texas Press, 1967); Ronald M. Schneider, *"Order and Progress": A Political History of Brazil* (Boulder, CO: Westview, 1991); and Michael L. Conniff and Frank D. McCann, Jr., eds., *Modern Brazil: Elites and Masses in Historical Perspective* (Lincoln: Univ. of Nebraska Press, 1989).

Vargas's personal legacy is analyzed in Joan L. Bak, "Political Centralization and the Building of the Interventionist State in Brazil," *Luso-Brazilian Review* 22, no. 1 (Summer 1985): 9–25; Carmen Nava, "Lessons in Patriotism and Good Citizenship: National Identity and Nationalism in Public Schools during the Vargas Administration, 1937–1945," *Luso-Brazilian Review*, 35, no. 1 (Summer 1998): 39–64; and John D. Wirth, *The Politics of Brazilian Development, 1930–1954* (Stanford: Stanford Univ. Press, 1970). For opposition to Vargas—a subject infrequently studied—see John W. F. Dulles, *The São Paulo Law School and the Anti-Vargas Resistance* (Austin: Univ. of Texas Press, 1986). Frank D. McCann, Jr., *The Brazilian-American Alliance* (Princeton, NJ: Princeton Univ. Press, 1973), and Stanley E. Hilton, *Brazil and the Great Powers, 1930–39* (Austin: Univ. of Texas Press, 1977) deal with trade policy and Brazil's entry in World War II. McCann's "Brazil and World War II: The Forgotten Ally. What did you do in the war, Zé Carioca?" in *Estudios Interdisciplinarios de America Latina y el Caribe* (Tel Aviv) 6, no. 2 (1995): 35–70, provides an excellent summary of the larger picture. For Brazil's role in the Third International, see Manuel Caballero, *Latin American and the Comintern, 1919–1943* (Cambridge: Cambridge Univ. Press, 1986), as well as Stanley E. Hilton's *Brazil and the Soviet Challenge, 1917–1947* (Austin: Univ. of Texas Press, 1991) and John W. F. Dulles's *Anarchists and Communists in Brazil, 1900–1935* (Austin: Univ. of Texas Press, 1973) and its sequel, *Brazilian Communism, 1935–1945: Repression During World Upheaval* (Austin: Univ. of Texas Press, 1983). Frank D. McCann's *The Brazilian-American Alliance, 1937–1945* (Princeton, NJ: Princeton Univ. Press, 1973), is the best available source on wartime issues.

The period following Vargas's death is covered by John W. F. Dulles's detailed biography, *Carlos Lacerda, Brazilian Crusader*, 2 vols. (Austin: Univ. of Texas Press, 1996). Miguel Arraes, a prominent radical politician, has published *Brazil: The Power and the People* (Harmondsworth, U.K.: Pelican Books, 1972). Political studies include Riordan Roett, *Brazil: Politics in a Patrimonial Society*, 4th ed. (New York: Praeger, 1992) and Wendy Ann Hunter, *Eroding Military Influence in Brazil* (Chapel Hill: Univ. of North Carolina Press, 1997). Cultural issues, including links between intellectuals and social activists, are considered in Augusto Boal's *Theater of the Oppressed*, trans. C. A. McBride (New York: Urizen Books, 1974) as well as Mark Dinneen, *Listening to the People's Voice* (London: Keegan Paul, 1996); Paulo Freire, *The Pedagogy of the Oppressed* (New York: Herder & Herder, 1970); and Anthony Hozier, *Documents on the Theater of the Oppressed* (London: Red Letters, 1985). The excesses of the military dictatorship from 1964 to 1983 are covered in The Archdiocese of São Paulo, *Torture in Brazil* (Austin: Univ. of Texas Press, 1998). See also Alfred C. Stepan, ed., *Authoritarian Brazil: Origins, Policies, and Future* (New Haven, CT: Yale Univ. Press, 1973) and the same author's *The Military in Politics: Changing Patterns in Brazil* (Princeton, NJ: Princeton Univ. Press, 1971). Popular culture in the Northeast is treated by Candace Slater's *Stories on a String* (Berkeley: Univ. California Press, 1982).

The destruction of the Amazonian ecosystem is described in two books by George Monbiot: *Amazon Watershed* (London: M. Joseph, 1991) and *Brazil: The Flight to Amazonia* (Atlantic Highlands, NJ: Zed Books, 1993). See also Shelton H. Davis's *Victims of the Miracle: Development and the Indians of Brazil* (Cambridge: Cambridge Univ. Press) and Robin Hanbury-Tenison, *A Question of Survival for the Indians of Brazil* (London: Survival International, 1973). The role of the police is treated by Martha K. Huggins, *Political Policing: The United States and Latin America* (Durham, NC: Duke Univ. Press, 1998). For the issue of censorship, see Anne-Marie Smith, *A Forced Agreement: Press Acquiescence to Censorship in Brazil* (Pittsburgh: Univ. of Pittsburgh Press, 1997).

Economic issues are treated in Stephen Haber, ed., *How Latin America Fell Behind: Essays on the Economic Histories of Brazil and Mexico* (Stanford: Stanford Univ. Press, 1997); Warren Dean, *The Industrialization of São Paulo* (Austin: Univ. of Texas Press, 1969); Joseph L. Love and Nils Jacobsen, eds., *Guiding the Invisible Hand: Economic Liberalism and the State in Latin American History* (New York: Praeger, 1988), especially Steven C. Topik's essay in that volume, "The Economic Role of the State in Liberal Regimes: Brazil and Mexico Compared"; and Topik's seminal "The State's Contribution to the Development of Brazil's Internal Economy, 1850–1930," in the *Hispanic American Historical Review* 65, no. 2 (1985): 203–28 as well as his *The Political Economy of the Brazilian State, 1889–1930* (Austin: Univ. of Texas Press, 1987). Richard M. Morse, "Manchester Economics and Paulista Sociology," in John D. Wirth and Robert L. Jones, eds., *Manchester and São Paulo: Problems of Rapid Urban Growth*, pp. 7–34 (Stanford: Stanford Univ. Press, 1978); Carlos F. Díaz-Alejandro, "Latin America in the 1930s," in Rosemary Thorp, ed., *Latin America in the 1930s* pp. 17–49 (London: St. Anthony's/Macmillan, 1984); and Joseph L. Love, *Crafting the Third World: Theorizing Underdevelopment in Rumania and Brazil* (Stanford: Stanford Univ. Press, 1996).

Bert J. Barickman's *A Bahian Counterpoint: Sugar, Tobacco, Cassava, and Slavery in the Recôncavo, 1780–1860* explores the growth of local food production and other economic networks in the midst of the export-dominated plantation economy. Wade Davis's *One River* (London: Touchstone, 1998) offers a study of science, ethnobotany, and economic life in the Amazon Basin. Simon Schwartzman's *A Space for Science: The Development of the Scientific Community in Brazil* (University Park: Pennsylvania State Univ. Press, 1991) provides a comprehensive overview.

For labor, see Gay Seidman, *Manufacturing Militance: Workers' Movements in Brazil and South Africa* (Berkeley: Univ. of California Press, 1994); Joel W. Wolfe's *Working Women, Working Men: São Paulo and the Rise of Brazil's Industrial Working Class* (Durham, NC: Duke Univ. Press, 1993); and Barbara Weinstein, *For Social Peace in Brazil* (Chapel Hill: Univ. of North Carolina Press, 1996). See also John D. French, "The Populist Gamble of Getúlio Vargas in 1945," in David, Rock, ed., pp. 141–65, *Latin America in the 1940s* (Berkeley: Univ. of California Press, 1994); Michael L. Conniff, "Voluntary Associations in Rio, 1870–1945: A New Approach to Urban Social Dynamics," *Journal of Interamerican Studies and World Affairs* 17 (1975): 64–81; Hobart A. Spalding, Jr., *Organized Labor in Latin America* (New York: New York Univ. Press, 1977); and Kenneth Paul Erickson, *The Brazilian Corporative State and Working Class Politics* (Berkeley: Univ. of California Press, 1977). Useful also is Marshall C. Eakin's *British Enterprise in Brazil: The St. John d'el Rey Mining Company and the Morro Velho Gold Mine, 1830–1960* (Durham NC: Duke Univ. Press, 1990).

Social dynamics and women's issues are explored in Sonia E. Alvarez, *Engendering Democracy in Brazil: Women's Movements in Transition* (Princeton, NJ: Princeton Univ. Press, 1990); Susan K. Besse's *Restructuring Patriarchy: The Modernization of Gender Inequality in Brazil, 1914–1940* (Chapel Hill: Univ. of North Carolina Press, 1996); and June E. Hahner, *Emancipating the Female Sex: The Struggle for Women's Rights in Brazil* (Durham, NC: Duke Univ. Press, 1990) Elizabeth and K. David Jackson have published a translation of Patrícia Galvão's 1933 proletarian novel, *Industrial Park* (Lincoln: Univ. of Nebraska Press, 1993), with a very useful afterword by David Jackson. Assorted social issues are examined in Edmar L. Bacha and Herbert S. Klein's *Social Change in Brazil, 1945–1985: The Incomplete Transition* (Albuquerque: Univ. of New Mexico Press,

1989) and Robert M. Levine, *Brazilian Legacies* (New York: M. E. Sharpe, 1997).

The family is treated by Dain Borges, *The Family in Bahia, Brazil, 1870–1945* (Stanford: Stanford Univ. Press, 1992); and Linda Lewin, *Politics and Parentela in Paraíba: A Case Study of Family-Based Oligarchy in Brazil* (Princeton, NJ: Princeton Univ. Press, 1987), and her "Some Historical Implications of Kinship Organization for Family-Based Politics in the Brazilian Northeast," *Comparative Studies in Society and History* 21, no. 2 (April 1979): 262–92. On Brazil's twentieth-century conservative tradition, see Jeffrey D. Needell, "History, Race, and the State in the Thought of Oliveira Vianna," *Hispanic American Historical Review* 75, no. 1 (February 1995): 1–30.

Useful recent studies on race include Kim D. Butler's *Afro-Brazilians in Post-Abolition São Paulo and Salvador* (New Brunswick, NJ: Rutgers Univ. Press, 1998) and Anthony Marx's *Making Race and Nation: A Comparison of the United States, South Africa, and Brazil* (Cambridge: Cambridge Univ. Press, 1998). See also George Reid Andrew's *Blacks and Whites in São Paulo, 1888–1998* (Madison: Univ. of Wisconsin Press, 1991); Thomas E. Skidmore, *Black into White* (New York: Oxford Univ. Press, 1974); Michael George Hanchard's *Orpheus and Power* (Princeton NJ: Princeton Univ. Press, 1994); Robert M. Levine and José Carlos Sebe Bom Meihy, *The Life and Death of Carolina Maria de Jesus* (Albuquerque: Univ. of New Mexico Press, 1995); Robert M. Levine, "The First Afro-Brazilian Congress," *Race: A Journal of Race and Group Relations* 15, no. 2 (1973): 185–94; and Dain Borges, "The Recognition of Afro-Brazilian Symbols and Ideas, 1890–1940," *Luso-Brazilian Review* 32, no. 2 (Winter 1995): 59–78.

A poignant analysis of an important urban issue is by Tobias Hecht, *At Home in the Street: Street Children of Northeast Brazil* (Cambridge: Cambridge Univ. Press, 1998).

Index